EYEWITNESS TRAVEL

TOP 10
LONDON

ROGER WILLIAMS

Top 10 London Highlights

The Top 10 of Everything

CONTENTS

London Area by Area

Streetsmart

Within each Top 10 list in this book, no hierarchy of quality or popularity is implied. All 10 are, in the editor's opinion, of roughly equal merit.

Front cover and spine *London's iconic Big Ben*
Back cover *Soldiers Trooping the Colour outside Buckingham Palace*
Title page *Visitors enjoy the view of the Thames from the London Eye*

Welcome to
London

River city. Royal city. City of palaces and pubs, museums and monuments. Hotbed of theatre. Shopping mecca. Financial powerhouse. London is all these things and more... so who could argue when we say that it's the world's most exciting metropolis? With Eyewitness Top 10 London, it's yours to explore.

We love London: the culture, the chaos, the noise. What could be better than strolling along the cobbled streets of **Covent Garden**, sipping a cocktail in a rooftop bar, sailing along the Thames between the **Houses of Parliament** and **Tate Modern**, browsing the cutting-edge boutiques of **Spitalfields** and scouting the stalls for a bargain or time-travelling back to Shakespeare's England, standing rapt among the crowds at the **Globe Theatre**? It's all here, packed into a few square miles of the world's most energetic streetscape.

This city is a cultural colossus, boasting the world's busiest theatre district, a bar or restaurant on every corner, and a packed calendar of eye-catching ceremonies and festivals, from **Trooping the Colour** to the **Notting Hill Carnival**. It does history and pageantry like nowhere else, but we think it's also the most cosmopolitan city on Earth. Home to 300 languages, it's a modern-day Babel, where every neighbourhood has its own vibrancy and verve.

Whether you're coming for a weekend or a week, our Top 10 guide brings together the best of everything the city can offer, from hip **Hoxton** to sophisticated **St James's**. The guide gives you tips throughout, from seeking out what's free to avoiding the crowds, plus 13 easy-to-follow itineraries, designed to help you visit a clutch of sights in a short space of time. Add inspiring photography and detailed maps, and you've got the essential pocket-sized travel companion. **Enjoy the book, and enjoy London.**

Clockwise from top: **British Museum, Big Ben, red telephone boxes, St Paul's and the Millennium Bridge, Westminster Abbey, Tate Britain, Kew Gardens**

Exploring London

For things to see and do, visitors to London are spoiled for choice. Whether here for a short stay or just wanting a flavour of this great city, you need to make the most of your time. Here are some ideas for two and four days of sightseeing in London.

Shakespeare's Globe is a replica of the original Globe Theatre.

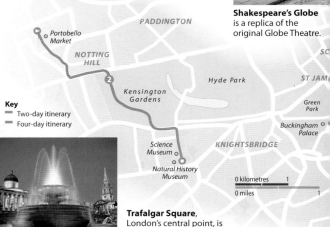

PADDINGTON

Portobello Market

NOTTING HILL

Hyde Park

SO

ST JAM

Kensington Gardens

Green Park

Buckingham Palace

Key
▬ Two-day itinerary
▬ ▬ Four-day itinerary

Science Museum

KNIGHTSBRIDGE

Natural History Museum

0 kilometres   1
0 miles   1

Trafalgar Square, London's central point, is beautifully lit up at night.

Two Days in London

Day ❶
MORNING
Take a Beefeater tour of the **Tower of London** (see pp38–41), then visit **St Paul's Cathedral** (see pp42–5).
AFTERNOON
Cross **Millennium Bridge** (see p64), for a panorama of the River Thames. Explore the **Tate Modern** (see pp28–9) before taking in a play at **Shakespeare's Globe** (see p89).

Day ❷
MORNING
Begin at **Buckingham Palace** (see pp24–5) and, if it's August or September, tour the State Rooms. Afterwards, head to **Westminster Abbey** (see pp34–5) to see the monuments of English monarchs.

AFTERNOON
After lunch, spend 2 hours at the **National Gallery** (see pp16–17) in Trafalgar Square. Then take a "flight" on the **London Eye** (see pp26–7).

Four Days in London

Day ❶
MORNING
Start with a full morning exploring the **Tower of London** (see pp38–41), then cross imposing **Tower Bridge** (see p141) and stroll along the river past **HMS Belfast** (see pp64–5).
AFTERNOON
Take lunch at **Borough Market** (see p91), just around the corner from the towering **Shard** (see p27). Roam the **Tate Modern** (see pp28–9) before catching an evening performance at **Shakespeare's Globe** (see p89).

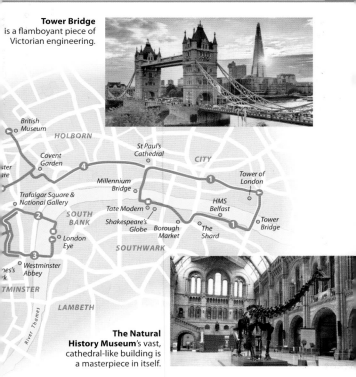

Tower Bridge is a flamboyant piece of Victorian engineering.

The Natural History Museum's vast, cathedral-like building is a masterpiece in itself.

Day ❷
MORNING

Begin in Notting Hill, with a morning turn around **Portobello Road** market (see p126–7). Walk south from there through the stately expanse of **Kensington Gardens** (see p56).

AFTERNOON

Exit the park into South Kensington's museum quarter, for an afternoon exploring the **Science Museum** (see pp22–3) and the **Natural History Museum** (see pp20–21).

Day ❸
MORNING

Choose between the **London Eye** (see pp26–7) or **Westminster Abbey** (see pp34–5). Not far away is **Trafalgar Square** (see p95), where you can admire Nelson's Column before taking in the old masters at the **National Gallery** (see pp16–17).

AFTERNOON

Meander through **St James's Park** (see p119) before enoying afternoon tea at Inn the Park. Peek through the gates at **Buckingham Palace** (see pp24–5), then hit swish **St James's** (see pp118–23) for dinner and cocktails.

Day ❹
MORNING

Start at the **British Museum** (see pp12–15), a two-million-year trove of human civilisation, then head down to **Covent Garden** (see pp104–11) for a leisurely stroll around the Apple Market and to marvel at the performances of the street acrobats.

AFTERNOON

St Paul's Cathedral (see pp42–5) is a short way by Tube. In the evening, return west to **Leicester Square** (see p97), where the bright lights of London's Theatreland await.

Top 10 London Highlights

**The Great Court,
British Museum**

ᴛᴏᴘ10 **London Highlights**

A city of infinite colour and variety, London is both richly historic, tracing its roots back over 2,000 years, and unceasingly modern, at the forefront of fashion, music and the arts. A selection of the best London has to offer is explored in the following chapter.

British Museum (1)
The oldest national public museum in the world contains a rich collection of treasure and artifacts *(see pp12–15)*.

(2) National Gallery and National Portrait Gallery
The nation's most important art collections are held here, including this 1581 miniature of Sir Francis Drake *(see pp16–19)*.

(3) Natural History Museum
The enormous and varied collection here explores the geology of the Earth *(see pp20–21)*.

Science Museum (4)
A huge museum with fascinating interactive exhibits that explain and demonstrate the wonders of science *(see pp22–3)*.

(5) Buckingham Palace
The official home of the Queen, where the changing the guard takes place *(see pp24–5)*.

6 London Eye

The world's tallest cantilevered observation wheel offers great views of the city (see pp26–7).

7 Tate Modern and Tate Britain

London's two Tate galleries house a collection of international art and modern work (see pp28–31).

8 Westminster Abbey and Parliament Square

This royal abbey has, since 1066, been the place where all Britain's monarchs have been crowned (see pp34–7).

9 Tower of London

The Tower has been a royal palace, fortress and prison, and is the home of the Crown Jewels (see pp38–41).

10 St Paul's Cathedral

Sir Christopher Wren's Baroque masterpiece still dominates the City skyline (see pp42–5).

0 kilometres 1
0 miles 1

FINSBURY
OLD STREET
CLERKENWELL RD
ALDERSGATE ST
LONDON
WALL
CITY ROAD
BISHOPSGATE
COMMERCIAL ST
'S INN RD
OLBORN
FLEET STREET
EMBANKMENT
CHEAPSIDE
CANNON ST
EASTCHEAP
10
OUTH BANK
WATERLOO RD
BLACKFRIARS RD
River Thames
SOUTHWARK
BOROUGH HIGH ST
GREAT DOVER ST
LONG LANE
TOWER BRIDGE RD
9
7
ABETH RD
MBETH

British Museum

The world's oldest national public museum has over 8 million items spanning the history of the world's cultures, from the stone tools of early man to 20th-century prints. The collection was started with the bequest of a physician and antiquarian, Sir Hans Sloane, in 1753. In the 18th and 19th centuries travellers and emissaries, such as Captain James Cook, Lord Curzon and Charles Townley, added treasures from around the world. The present building was completed in 1852. The central courtyard is used as a public space (see p15).

Parthenon Sculptures ①

This spectacular 5th-century BC frieze from the Parthenon **(right)** was made under Pericles and shows a procession in honour of the goddess Athena. It was obtained in 1779 by Lord Elgin, Ambassador to Constantinople.

② Mummified Cat

Cats and sacred cows were mummified in Ancient Egypt. This cat comes from Abydos and dates from the 1st century AD **(left)**. Many Egyptian deities took on animal shapes, as seen on wall paintings and other artifacts.

③ Ram in a Thicket

Decorated with shells, gold leaf, copper and lapis lazuli, this priceless ornament comes from Ur in Sumer, one of the world's earliest civilizations. Games and musical instruments are also displayed.

④ Double-Headed Serpent Mosaic

Carved in wood and covered with turquoise mosaic, this Aztec ornament was probably worn on the chest on ceremonial occasions.

⑤ Rosetta Stone

In 196 BC Egyptian priests wrote a decree about Ptolemy V on this granite tablet in Greek, in demotic and in Egyptian hieroglyphics. Found in 1799, it proved crucial in deciphering Egyptian pictorial writing.

⑥ Portland Vase

It is not known where and when this 1st-century blue-and-opaque-glass vase was found. In 1778, it was purchased by Sir William Hamilton, Britain's ambassador to Naples, who sold it to the Duchess of Portland. It had to be reassembled after a visitor smashed it into 200 pieces in 1845.

⑦ Stone Lintel

Originating in China and featuring an early depiction of the historical Buddha, this would have been placed over the doorway of a temple or pagoda.

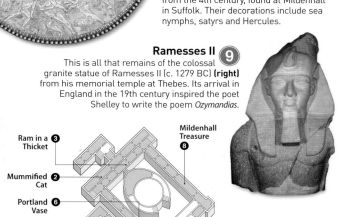

8 Mildenhall Treasure

Some of the greatest early English treasures are these silver plates **(left)** from the 4th century, found at Mildenhall in Suffolk. Their decorations include sea nymphs, satyrs and Hercules.

Ramesses II 9

This is all that remains of the colossal granite statue of Ramesses II (c. 1279 BC) **(right)** from his memorial temple at Thebes. Its arrival in England in the 19th century inspired the poet Shelley to write the poem *Ozymandias*.

Ram in a Thicket ❸

Mummified Cat ❷

Portland Vase ❻

Stone Lintel ❼

Mildenhall Treasure ❽

❹ Double-Headed Serpent Mosaic

❿ Mask of the Nulthamalth

Key to Floorplan
- Lower floor
- Ground floor
- Upper floor

Ramesses II ❾

Parthenon Sculptures ❶

❺ Rosetta Stone

❿ Mask of the Nulthamalth

The *Nulthamalth* (or fool dancer) is an important figure among the Kwakwaka'wakw people who enforces correct behaviour. This indigenous culture originates from the Pacific Northwest coast.

NEED TO KNOW

MAP L1 ■ Great Russell Street WC1 ■ 020 7323 8299
■ www.britishmuseum.org

Open 10am–5:30pm Sat–Thu, 10am–8:30pm Fri. *Great Court:* 10am–6pm Sat–Thu, 9am–8:30pm Fri

Free, except major temporary exhibitions

Free guided tours

■ There are three cafés and one restaurant.

■ Picnics can be eaten in the forecourt by the main entrance.

■ Highlights tours give an introduction to the collection.

■ The British Museum shop sells reproduction artifacts.

Museum Guide
Free maps are available and guides are on sale at the information desks. Otherwise start to the left of the main entrance with the Assyrian, Egyptian, Greek and Roman galleries. The Asian collection provides a change from Classical material, as do the early British, medieval and Renaissance galleries on the east side.

British Museum Collections

1 Middle East
Some 6,000 years of history start with the spectacular carved reliefs depicting a variety of scenes from the Assyrian palace of Nineveh.

2 Ancient Egypt and Sudan
An extraordinary array of mummies and sarcophagi are among thousands of objects in one of the world's greatest collections.

3 Greece and Rome
There are several rooms covering the marvels of the Classical world (c.3000 BC to c.AD 400). The sculptures that once decorated the outside of the Parthenon are a particular highlight.

4 Asia
Buddhist limestone reliefs from India, Chinese antiquities, Islamic pottery and a jaw-droppingly large cache of Japanese relics.

5 Africa
The museum holds 350,000 objects from indigenous peoples around the world. The Africa gallery holds an interesting collection of sculpture, textiles and graphic art.

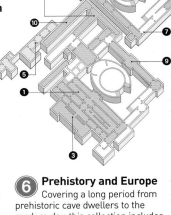

6 Prehistory and Europe
Covering a long period from prehistoric cave dwellers to the modern day, this collection includes Lindow Man, the body found preserved in a peat bog of a man who died some time between 2 BC and AD 119, and fine decorative arts including medieval jewellery and Renaissance clocks.

7 Coins and Medals
A comprehensive collection of more than 750,000 coins and medals dating from the 7th century BC to the present day.

8 Prints and Drawings
Priceless prints and drawings from the Renaissance form one part of this varied and rotating collection.

9 Enlightenment
This exhibition features the museum's 18th-century collections from around the world.

10 The Joseph E. Hotung Great Court Gallery
This small gallery is used for temporary exhibitions.

Ancient Greek vase

THE GREAT COURT

A magnificent glass-roofed addition encloses the heart of the British Museum. Opened in December 2000, the Great Court was designed by architect Sir Norman Foster. In the centre of the Court is the domed Reading Room, built in 1857. Holding one of the world's most important collections of books and manuscripts, the Reading Room has been the workplace of some of London's greatest writers and was used to host major exhibitions between 2007 and 2013. The Great Court is the capital's largest covered square and contains shops, cafés and the British Museum's main ticket and information desk, supplying visitors with everything they need for an informed visit.

The Reading Room was restored to its original design.

The Great Court, at the centre of the museum, has a tesselated roof constructed out of 3,312 unique panes of glass. It surrounds the Reading Room.

TOP 10
LIBRARY READERS

1 Karl Marx
(1818–83), German revolutionary

2 Mahatma Gandhi
(1869–1948), Indian leader

3 Oscar Wilde
(1854–1900), playwright and wit

4 Virginia Woolf
(1882–1941), Bloomsbury novelist

5 W B Yeats
(1865–1939), Irish poet and playwright

6 Thomas Hardy
(1840–1928), English novelist

7 George Bernard Shaw
(1856–1950), Irish playwright

8 E M Forster
(1879–1970), English novelist

9 Rudyard Kipling
(1865–1936), Poet, novelist and chronicler of the British Empire

10 Leon Trotsky
(1879–1940), Russian revolutionary

🔟⭐ National Gallery

The National Gallery has around 2,300 pictures, from the early Renaissance to the Impressionists (1250–1900), forming one of the greatest collections in the world. Containing work by the most influential painters of the main European schools, the collection was acquired by the government from John Julius Angerstein in 1824, and moved to the present building (also home to the National Portrait Gallery, *see pp18–19*) in 1838. The Sainsbury Wing, built in 1991, houses the excellent early Renaissance collection and temporary blockbuster exhibitions.

① The Virgin of the Rocks

This Renaissance masterpiece by Leonardo da Vinci (1452–1519) was originally painted as an altarpiece for a church in Milan. The Virgin and Child, with St John the Baptist and an angel, are depicted within a strange cavernous landscape.

② The Arnolfini Portrait

One of the most famous paintings from the extensive Flemish collection is this unusual portrait of an Italian banker and his wife in Bruges. Jan van Eyck (c.1385–1441) brought oil painting to a new and colourful height.

③ The Ambassadors

Symbols, such as the foreshortened skull foretelling death, abound in this painting by Hans Holbein (1533).

④ The Wilton Diptych

A highlight of Gothic art, this exquisite English royal painting **(right)**, by an unknown artist, shows Richard II being recommended to the Virgin by saints John the Baptist, Edward and Edmund.

⑤ The Rokeby Venus

Painted in Rome to replace a lost Venetian painting, *The Rokeby Venus* **(left)** is the only nude by Diego Velázquez (1599–1660), court painter to Spain's Philip IV. Venus, the godess of Love is depicted here with her son, Cupid, who holds a mirror up for her to see her reflection and that of the viewer.

6 The Sunflowers

Van Gogh (1853–90) painted this work **(left)** in Arles in France during a period of rare optimism while he was awaiting the arrival of his hero, the avant-garde painter Paul Gauguin.

8 Mystic Nativity

Feminine grace has never been depicted better than by the painter Sandro Botticelli (1445–1510). Painted in a centennial year, *Mystic Nativity* reflects his own anxieties, with an inscription from *Revelation*.

7 A Young Woman Standing at a Virginal

Peace and calm rule the works of the Dutch painter Jan Vermeer (1632–75). Many of his interiors were painted in his home in Delft, but it has never been possible to identify his models.

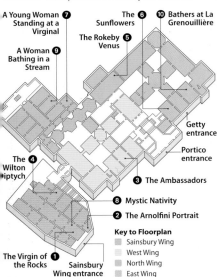

A Young Woman Standing at a Virginal **7**

A Woman Bathing in a Stream **9**

The Sunflowers **6**

The Rokeby Venus **5**

10 Bathers at La Grenouillière

Getty entrance

Portico entrance

The Wilton Diptych **4**

3 The Ambassadors

8 Mystic Nativity

2 The Arnolfini Portrait

The Virgin of the Rocks **1**

Sainsbury Wing entrance

Key to Floorplan
- Sainsbury Wing
- West Wing
- North Wing
- East Wing

9 A Woman Bathing in a Stream

This portrait by Rembrandt (1606–69) was painted when his technical powers were at their height, and shows his striking brushwork and mastery of earthy colours.

10 Bathers at La Grenouillière

Claude Monet (1840–1926), the original Impressionist, explored the effect of light on water at La Grenouillère, a popular bathing spot on the Seine close to Bougival to the west of Paris, where he worked alongside fellow painter Auguste Renoir.

NEED TO KNOW

MAP L4 ■ Trafalgar Square WC2 ■ 020 7747 2885 ■ www.nationalgallery.org.uk

Open 10am–6pm Sat–Thu (10am–9pm Fri)

Free, except major temporary exhibitions

Free guided tours at 11:30am and 2:30pm daily (also 4pm Sat & Sun, 7pm Fri)

■ There is a café, an espresso bar and a good restaurant.

■ The Sainsbury Wing has an excellent art bookshop.

■ Audio tours are available and trails can be downloaded from the museum's website.

■ Short lunchtime talks are held at 1pm Mon and Wed.

Gallery Guide

The gallery is divided into four areas. The Sainsbury Wing contains the Early Renaissance collection. The West Wing displays works from 1500 to 1600, the North Wing 1600–1700, and the East Wing 1700–1900. Although the main entrance is on Trafalgar Square, the Sainsbury Wing makes a more sensible starting point.

🔟⭐ National Portrait Gallery

This is one of the most unexpectedly pleasing galleries in London. Unrelated to the neighbouring National Gallery, it was founded in 1856. Well-known names can be put to some not-so-well-known faces, and there are some fascinating paintings from Tudor times to the present day. Royalty is depicted from Richard II (1367–1400) to Queen Elizabeth II, and the collection also holds a 1554 miniature, the oldest self-portrait in oils in England. The displays are changed regularly so many paintings from the collection are not always on view.

1 Queen Elizabeth I

This anonymous portrait **(right)** is one of several of Elizabeth I, who presided over England's Renaissance (1533–1603). The Tudor rooms are the most satisfying in the gallery, featuring portraits of central figures of the period, from courtiers to dramatists.

2 The Brontës

Found on top of a cupboard in 1914, this portrait of the sisters, Charlotte, Emily and Anne Brontë, from Yorkshire, was painted by their brother, Branwell. He appears as a faint image behind them.

3 William Shakespeare

This is the only portrait of England's famous playwright **(below)** known with certainty to have been painted during his lifetime (1564–1616).

4 The Whitehall Mural

The cartoon of Henry VIII and his father Henry VII by Hans Holbein (1537) was drawn for a large mural in the Palace of Whitehall, lost when the palace burnt down in 1698.

5 George Gordon Byron, 6th Lord Byron

This oil painting of Lord Byron (1788–1824), by Thomas Phillips, depicts the Romantic poet and champion of liberty dressed in Albanian costume. He died while supporting Greek insurgents in their fight against the Ottoman Empire.

Key to Floorplan
■ Ground floor
■ First floor
■ Second floor

6 Horatio Nelson

This 1800 portrait by Friedrich Heinrich Füger depicts Nelson after the Battle of the Nile. It is the only known image of him in civilian dress. Apart from Queen Victoria and the Duke of Wellington, he was painted more than any other British figure in history.

7 Sir Walter Raleigh

The portrait of military and naval commander and writer Sir Walter Raleigh was painted in 1602 when he was at the height of his renewed favour with Queen Elizabeth I. The image, by an unknown artist, depicts Raleigh and his son dressed in fine costumes.

8 Charles II

Produced around 1680 and attributed to English portrait painter Thomas Hawker, this painting (below) depicts King Charles II, who reigned from 1660 to 1685, towards the end of his life, looking rather languid and gloomy. The image may not be particularly aesthetically pleasing, but it is an imposing one.

9 Germaine Greer

The feminist author of *The Female Eunuch* is brilliantly captured (above) by Portuguese artist Paula Rego, the first artist-in-residence at the National Gallery. It is one of the most popular commissions in the gallery.

10 Prince William and Prince Harry

Commissioned in 2009, this first double portrait of the princes was painted from life by Nicola Jane ("Nicky") Philipps. It shows the Princes wearing the dress uniform of the Household Cavalry (Blues and Royals).

NEED TO KNOW

MAP L3 ■ St Martin's Place WC2 ■ 020 7306 0055 ■ www.npg.org.uk

Open 10am–6pm daily (to 9pm Thu–Fri)

Free (separate charge for some exhibitions)

■ **The Portrait Restaurant** has great views across Trafalgar Square, down Whitehall to Parliament.

■ The bookshop stocks a huge range of fashion, costume, history and biography titles.

■ The ground-floor gift shop has good postcards.

■ A range of talks take place at lunchtimes, with regular evening lectures on Thursdays and Fridays.

Gallery Guide
The National Portrait Gallery's three floors are arranged chronologically. Take the escalator to the second floor and start with the Tudor and Stuart galleries (1–8). Men and women of industry, science and art from the 18th and early 19th century are in rooms 9 to 20. The first floor has eminent Victorians and early photographs, taking the collection up to the present. The ground-floor galleries also have 20th- and 21st-century works.

★ Natural History Museum

There are some 70 million specimens in the Natural History Museum's fascinating collections. Originally the repository for items brought home by Charles Darwin and Captain Cook's botanist, Joseph Banks, among others, the museum combines traditional displays with innovative, hands-on exhibits. With kid-pleasers such as the impressive dinosaur collection and the life-sized model of a blue whale, it remains one of London's most popular museums. Still a hot-house of research, it employs more than 300 scientists and librarians.

3 Treasures

Treasures is an apt title for this extraordinary collection, from a rare first edition of Darwin's *On the Origin of Species* to the dinosaur teeth that led to the discovery that giant reptiles once walked the Earth. The 22 objects on display here have been chosen for their scientific and historical importance and are true movers and shakers of natural history.

4 Model Baby

A giant model of an unborn baby in the Human Biology galleries demonstrates sounds heard in the womb. Other hands-on exhibits test abilities and reactions and show how physical characteristics are inherited.

5 Images of Nature Gallery

This spectacular gallery showcases the museum's most beautiful historic artworks and modern images of nature such as this 17th-century Nautilus Shell **(above)**. More than 110 exhibits span 350 years to the present day.

1 Fossils

Marine reptiles that existed at the time of the dinosaurs have survived as some remarkable fossils **(above)**, such as the pregnant female Ichthyosaur, found in a Dorset garden, which lived 187–178 million years ago.

Hintze Hall 2

The museum's cathedral-like hall has for the last 35 years hosted "Dippy", the famous Diplodocus skeleton **(right)** and a 1,300-year-old giant sequoia, and showcases many of the collection's greatest treasures in the Cadogan Gallery.

6 Spirit Collection

Get a fascinating glimpse of some of the 22 million zoological specimens the museum looks after, including those collected by Charles Darwin.

7 Darwin Centre

One of the centre's many attractions is the eight-storey Cocoon, a permanent exhibition where visitors can see insect specimens as well as world-leading scientists at work.

8 Blue Whale

The Mammal gallery houses this fascinating exhibit, where both modern mammals and their fossil relatives are dwarfed in comparison to the astounding life-sized model of a blue whale, the largest mammal on the planet.

Key to Floorplan
- Ground floor
- First floor
- Second floor

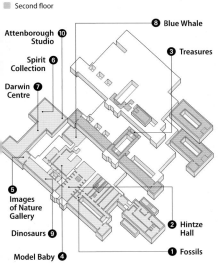

- **8** Blue Whale
- **3** Treasures
- Attenborough Studio **10**
- Spirit Collection **6**
- Darwin Centre **7**
- **5** Images of Nature Gallery
- Dinosaurs **9**
- Model Baby **4**
- **2** Hintze Hall
- **1** Fossils

9 Dinosaurs

T. Rex, one of the museum's life-like animatronic models, lurches and roars in this popular gallery. More traditional exhibits of fossilized skeletons are also on display. Taking pride of place in the Earth Hall is 6-m (19.5-ft) *Sophie*, **(above)** the most intact Stegosaurus fossilized skeleton ever found.

10 Attenborough Studio

On the ground floor of the Darwin Centre, the Attenborough Studio is a state-of-the-art audio-visual facility with 64 seats. The venue hosts events, films and talks covering all aspects of life on earth as well as scientific discovery.

NEED TO KNOW

MAP B5 ■ Cromwell Road SW7 ■ 020 7942 5000 ■ www.nhm.ac.uk

Open 10am–5:50pm daily. Last admission 5:30pm

Closed 24–26 Dec

Free (admission charge for some special exhibitions)

■ Try the restaurant in the green zone, or the other two cafés and snack bars.

■ A number of different tours are available, including a visit to the outdoor Wildlife Garden. Details at the Central Hall information desk.

Museum Guide
The Natural History Museum is divided into four zones: the blue zone, which includes the dinosaur gallery and Images of Nature; the green zone, which has the ecology and creepy-crawlies galleries; the orange zone, which has a wildlife garden; and the red zone, incorporating the geological displays.

The ornately embellished Cromwell Road entrance leads to the Hintze Hall with its grand staircase.

An additional entrance on Exhibition Road leads to the red zone.

🔟 ⭐ Science Museum

Packed with hands-on exhibits, this museum explores the world of science through centuries of scientific and technological development. The collection showcases how Britain led the Industrial Revolution, with looms and steam engines, navigation and early flight. It also has displays on contemporary science, climate change and cutting-edge technologies, with many interactive exhibits in the hi-tech Wellcome Wing. The museum is also home to Media Space, a new photography and art gallery.

5 Apollo 10 Command Module

The Apollo 10 Command Module, which went around the moon in May 1969, is on display, as is a replica of the Apollo 11 Lunar Lander **(left)**. Buzz Aldrin and Neil Armstrong stepped onto the moon from the original in July 1969 and became the first humans to set foot on the lunar surface.

6 Media Space

This new photography and art gallery presents a changing programme of exhibitions drawn from the National Photography Collection and broader Museum collections to examine the relationships between art, photography, science and technology.

1 Exploring Space

Rockets, satellites, space probes and landers can all be explored, and you can learn about Sputnik, the world's first satellite, how we sent spacecrafts to other planets and walked on the moon.

2 Information Age

The Queen opened this fascinating gallery with her first tweet in October 2014. It is divided into six themes and covers 200 years of communication and modern information technology from the earliest telegraph messages to the internet and mobile phones.

3 The Secret Life of the Home

This gallery contains a wacky variety of household gadgets and gizmos, from washing machines and vaccum cleaners to burglar alarms.

4 Puffing Billy

Puffing Billy **(below)** is the world's oldest remaining steam locomotive. It was built in England in 1813 and used to transport coal. George Stephenson's famous 1829 *Rocket*, the first locomotive engine to pull passenger carriages, is also on display.

❼ Who Am I?

The continually updated Who Am I? gallery presents the latest in brain science and genetics through interactive exhibits and object-rich displays.

❾ Flight

This gallery is filled with extraordinary aircraft reflecting both UK and international achievements in aviation. Highlights include Amy Johnson's *Gipsy Moth*.

❿ IMAX 3D Cinema

The cinema **(above)** shows mainly 3D films on a screen taller than four double-decker buses. An impressive six-channel surround sound system will totally immerse you in the action.

Who Am I? ❼
Flight ❾
❺ Apollo 10 Command Module
❿ IMAX 3D Cinema
❻ Media Space
Information Age ❷
❽ Pattern Pod
❹ Puffing Billy
❸ The Secret Life of the Home
❶ Exploring Space

Key to Floorplan
- Basement
- Ground floor
- First floor
- Second floor
- Third floor
- Fourth floor
- Fifth floor
- Wellcome Wing

Pattern Pod ❽

Suitable for children under eight, this multi-sensory gallery **(right)** introduces ideas about patterns in the world. The electronic kaleidoscope and interactive exhibits make science fun.

NEED TO KNOW

MAP B5 ■ Exhibition Road SW7 ■ 020 7942 4000 ■ www.science museum.org.uk

Open 10am–6pm daily (last entry 5:15pm)

Closed 24–26 Dec

Free (separate charge for special exhibitions, simulator rides and IMAX cinema)

■ There is a restaurant, several cafés and a picnic area.

■ Printed What's On guides provide details of exhibits.

■ The museum store is good for innovative gifts.

Museum Guide
The museum is spread over seven floors. Space exploration, steam engines and the IMAX cinema are on the ground floor. Information Age, the Media Space photography gallery and climate science are on the second floor. Flight and the interative games and simulators of Launchpad can be found on the third floor. The fourth and fifth floors are dedicated to medical history. The Secret Life of the Home can be found in the basement.

⭐ Buckingham Palace

London's most famous residence, and one of its best recognized landmarks, Buckingham Palace was built as a town house for the first Duke of Buckingham around 1705. In 1825, George IV commissioned John Nash to extend the house into a substantial palace. The first resident of the palace was Queen Victoria, from 1837. The extensive front of the building was refaced by Sir Aston Webb in 1914. The palace is now home to the present Queen and the State Rooms are open to the public during summer. Many royal parks and gardens in London are also accessible to the public *(see pp54–7)*.

1 The Balcony
On special occasions, the Queen and other members of the Royal Family step on to the palace balcony to wave to the crowds below.

2 Queen's Gallery
The gallery hosts a changing programme of exhibitions of the Royal Collection's master-pieces, including works by artists such as Johannes Vermeer and Leonardo da Vinci.

3 Changing the Guard
The Palace guards, in their familiar red tunics and tall bearskin hats **(below)**, are changed at 11:30am in summer (and alternate days Aug–Mar, weather permitting). The guards march to the palace from the nearby Wellington Barracks.

Buckingham Palace

4 Grand Staircase
The Ambassadors' Entrance leads into the Grand Hall. From here the Grand Staircase, with gilded balustrades, rises to the first floor where the State Rooms are found.

5 Throne Room
This houses the thrones of Queen Elizabeth and Prince Philip used for the coronation. Designed by John Nash, the room has a highly ornamented ceiling and magnificent chandeliers.

6 Picture Gallery
One of the largest rooms in the palace it has a barrel-vaulted glass ceiling and a number of paintings from the Royal Collection, including works by Rembrandt, Rubens and Van Dyck.

7 State Ballroom

Banquets for visiting heads of state are held here **(left)**. The most glittering annual event is the Diplomatic Reception in November, attended by over 1,500 guests from about 130 countries.

8 Brougham

Every day a horse-drawn Brougham carriage sets out to collect and deliver royal packages between Buckingham Palace and St. James's Palace.

PALACE LIFE

The official business of the monarchy takes place in Buckingham Palace, which has a staff of over 800. The Duke of Edinburgh, Duke of York, Prince Edward and the Princess Royal all have offices here. The most senior member of the Royal Household is the Lord Chamberlain. The Master of the Household and the Palace's domestic staff organize many functions every year, including Investitures for recipients of awards which are given by the Queen.

9 Royal Mews

Caring for the horses that pull the royal coach on state occasions, these are the finest working stables in Britain. The collection of coaches, motorcars and carriages includes the magnificent Gold State Coach, used at every coronation since 1821.

10 Palace Garden

The 40-acre Palace garden is an oasis for wildlife and includes a 3-acre lake. It can be visited on tours. There are at least three Royal garden parties in summer each year, which over 30,000 people in total attend **(below)**.

NEED TO KNOW

MAP J6 ■ Buckingham Palace SW1 ■ 020 7766 7300 ■ royalcollection.org.uk

Under 5s free. Combined tickets available

State Rooms: Aug: 9:15am–7:45pm daily (last adm 5:15pm), Sep: 9:15am–6:15pm daily (last adm 4:15pm). Adm: adults £21.50; students & over 60s £19.60; under 17s £12.30; family £55.30

Royal Mews: Apr–Oct: 10am–5pm daily (last adm 4:15pm), Feb, Mar & Nov: 10am–4pm daily (last adm 3:15pm). Adm: adults £9; students and over 60s £8.30; under 17s £5.40; family £23.40

Queen's Gallery: 10am–5:30pm daily (last adm 4:15pm), Aug–Sep: opens 9:30am. Adm: adults £10; students and over 60s £9.20; under 17s £5.20; family £25.20

TOP 10 ⭐ London Eye

An amazing feat of engineering, the world's tallest cantilevered observation wheel offers fascinating views over the whole of London. Towering over the Thames opposite the Houses of Parliament, it was built to celebrate the millennium year, and has proved enormously popular. Its 32 enclosed capsules each hold 25 people and offer total visibility in all directions. A rotation on the London Eye takes 30 minutes and, on a clear day, you can see up to 40 km (25 miles) across the capital and the south of England.

2 Houses of Parliament

The London Eye rises high above the Houses of Parliament *(see p36)* on the far side of the Thames. From here you can look down on Big Ben **(left)** and see the Commons Terrace, where Members of Parliament and the House of Lords drink, dine and discuss policy by the river.

1 BT Tower

Built for the Post Office in 1961–4, this 190-m (620-ft) tower is now a TV, radio and telecommunications tower. It was given Grade II Listed Building status in 2003, meaning its defunct antennas needed special permission to be removed.

3 One Canada Square

With its distinctive pyramid roof, One Canada Square is located in the heart of Docklands which is the East London business and finance centre. It stands in the middle of the Isle of Dogs.

The London Eye, South E

4 Wren Churches

The enormous dome of St Paul's Cathedral **(right)** *(see pp42–5)* stands out as the star of the City churches. Pricking the sky around it are the spires of some of Wren's other churches, including St Bride's, the tallest, on which wedding cakes have been modelled, and Wren's own favourite, St James's on Piccadilly.

5 Alexandra Palace

The world's first high-definition public television broadcasting service was transmitted by the BBC from Alexandra Palace on 2 November 1936. There are exhibition halls and an ice rink here.

6 Crystal Palace

This TV and radio transmission mast to the south of the city is near the site of the 1851 Great Exhibition "Crystal Palace" that was moved here from Hyde Park in 1852 and burned down spectacularly in 1936.

7 The Shard

Designed by Renzo Piano, this 306-m (1,004-ft) glass spire **(left)** rises from the South Bank at London Bridge and gives the city skyline a new defining point. The 95-storey building house offices, restaurants and a hotel. There is an observation deck on the 72nd floor.

MILLENNIUM LEGACY

The London Eye was one of a number of nationwide projects designed for the Millennium. The focus in London was on the enormous Millennium Dome, a spectacular structure built in Greenwich to house a national exhibition. Other projects were Tate Modern (see pp28–9) and the Millennium Bridge, the Waterloo Millennium Pier, the Great Court at the British Museum (see pp12–15) and the opening up of Somerset House (see p105).

8 Heathrow

To the west of the city, London's main airport is one of the busiest international airports in the world. The Thames acts as a kind of runway, as planes line up overhead to begin their descent.

9 Queen Elizabeth II Bridge

On a clear day you can just make out the lowest downstream crossing on the Thames, a huge suspension bridge at Dartford, some 32 km (20 miles) away. Traffic flows in a tunnel under the river, south over the bridge.

10 Windsor Castle

Windsor Castle sits by the Thames to the west of London **(below)**. The largest occupied castle in the world, it is still a favourite residence of the royal family.

NEED TO KNOW

MAP N5 ■ South Bank SE1 ■ 0871 781 3000 ■ www.londoneye.com

Open Sep–Mar: 10am–8.30pm daily; Apr–Jun: 10am–9pm daily (9.30pm Fri & Sat May–Jun); Jul–Aug: 10am–9.30pm (11.30pm Fri); closed 25 Dec and 2 weeks in Jan. Ticket office opens 9.30am

Prices vary. Reductions for children, the disabled and senior citizens

Timed tickets on the hour and half-hour

■ There are cafés in County Hall and on the South Bank.

■ Tickets are available on the day but advanced booking is advisable at weekends and in the school holidays.

■ All capsules are fitted with interactive tablet guides.

TOP 10 ★ Tate Modern

Affiliated with Tate Britain *(see pp30–31)*, one of London's most exciting galleries is housed in the old Bankside power station, on a riverside site opposite the City. In 2016 a new building will be added to this site. Large enough for huge installations, the galleries provide an airy space for the collection of international modern art. This includes works by Dalí, Picasso, Matisse, and Warhol as well as work by many acclaimed contemporary artists. The displays are changed frequently.

2 The Snail
This 1953 cutout is one of Henri Matisse's (1869–1954) final works, completed whilst he was bedridden. The paper spirals represent a snail's shell.

3 Black on Maroon
One of a series of large contemplative abstracts by the artist Mark Rothko (1903–70), the sombre and meditative *Black on Maroon* was painted in 1958 and later donated to the Tate.

1 Three Dancers
Pablo Picasso (1881–1973) was noted for the different painting styles he mastered as he pushed the boundaries of Modern Art. The energetic, unsettling *Three Dancers* (1925) followed the most serene stage of his work, and marked the beginning of a radical phase of distortion and emotional violence in his art **(above)**.

4 Whaam!
Inspired by an image from *All American Men of War*, published by DC Comics in 1962, Roy Lichtenstein (1923–97) created *Whaam!* **(below)** in 1963. He was inspired by comics and advertisements, presenting powerful or emotive scenes in an impersonal and detached style.

5 Coffee
Pierre Bonnard (1867–1947) frequently painted life at the dining table. In this 1915 canvas, the artist portrayed his wife Marthe sipping coffee with her pet dachshund by her side, suggesting an intimate domestic routine.

6 Summertime No. 9A

The American Jackson Pollock (1912–56) was the pioneer of Action Painting. He created his first "drip" artwork in 1947, pouring paint onto huge canvases on the floor. Pollock embraced the element of chance while controlling the rhythm and flow, thickness and layering of the paint in such works. *Summertime No. 9A* dates from 1948.

The Tate Modern

7 Composition with Yellow, Blue and Red

The Dutch painter Piet Mondrian (1872–1944) gradually refined his art to a rigorous and pure abstract language of straight lines and squares of primary colours, painting this between 1937 and 1942.

8 The Reckless Sleeper

René Magritte (1898–1967) painted this work in 1928, exploring Surrealism and Freudian symbolism. A man sleeps in an alcove above a tablet embedded with everyday (but interpreted as Freudian) objects, as if dreamed by the sleeper.

9 Fish

Constantin Brancusi (1876–1957) created *Fish* **(right)** in 1926. Known for his ability to capture the essential qualities of his subjects in elementary, abstract forms, this sculpture presents a bronze "fish" on a polished metal disc balanced on a smooth, carved wooden base.

10 Spatial Concept "Waiting"

The Italian-Argentine artist Lucio Fontana (1899–1968) first began to puncture canvases in the late 1940s, creating a group of works known as the *Tagli* ("cuts") between 1958 and 1968. Although these cuts were carefully premeditated, they were executed in an instant. In this 1960 work, *Spatial Concept "Waiting"*, the cut erupts from the surface, giving the impression of a gesture towards the viewer in a way that is at once energetic and threatening.

NEED TO KNOW

MAP R4 ■ Bankside SE1 ■ 020 7887 8888 ■ www.tate.org.uk

Open 10am–6pm Sun–Thu, 10am–10pm Fri–Sat; closed 24–26 Dec

Free (admission charge for temporary exhibitions)

Tate-to-Tate boat service from Bankside connects with Tate Britain *(see p30)*

■ There is a great view from the restaurant on level 6. The café on level 1 overlooks the gardens. The espresso bar on level 3 has riverside balconies.

■ With more than 10,000 titles, the Turbine Hall bookshop claims to be the largest art bookshop in London.

■ Daily events of cinema, video, talks and gallery tours are advertised in the main hall.

Gallery Guide

The main entrance is on Holland Street, from where a ramp descends into the huge Turbine Hall below ground level, on level 0, where the coat check, information, ticket office, main shop and temporary installations are located. You can also enter the gallery via the café or the entrance on level 1 next to the Millennium Bridge.

The main themed galleries are on level 2 (Poetry and Dream) and level 4 (Structure and Clarity; Energy and Process).

Major exhibitions are on levels 3, and level 6 has a restaurant with river views. The Tate's works of art are sometimes moved temporarily, loaned out, or removed for restoration so works described here may not always be on display.

TOP 10 ⭐ Tate Britain

Opened in 1897 as the National Gallery of British Art, the magnificent collection at London's first Tate gallery ranges from 1500 to the present day. Its founder was Henry Tate (1819–99), who made his fortune from sugar. The collection contains works by all Britain's major painters, and was greatly added to by J M W Turner. Paintings are often moved to Tate's other galleries, loaned out or removed for restoration. The works on these pages, therefore, may not always be on display.

1 Norham Castle, Sunrise
J M W Turner (1775–1851) was the great genius of English land-scape painting. This 1845 work **(above)** typifies his use of abstraction and luminosity of colour.

2 The Deluge
Irish artist Francis Danby (1793–1861) was known for his fantasy landscapes and large-scale biblical subjects. This painting depicts the Old Testament story of the great flood sent by God.

3 Wooded Landscape with a Peasant Resting
Thomas Gainsborough's (1727–88) family groups in landscapes are among the finest "conversation pieces" in English art. An artistic interpretation of his native Suffolk, this is one of his earliest land-scapes, painted in 1747.

4 Elohim Creating Adam
Poet, mystic, illustrator and engraver William Blake (1757–1827) claimed to be guided by visions. *Elohim Creating Adam* is typical of his work. Illustrating the Book of Genesis, it shows Adam growing out of the earth ("Elohim" is the Hebrew name for God).

5 Ophelia
Detailed and accurate observation of nature was a key element of the Victorian Pre-Raphaelite painters, as in this tragic scene from Shakespeare's *Hamlet* **(above)** by John Everett Millais (1829–96) painted in 1852.

6 Flatford Mill
Painted near his home in Dedham Vale, and depicting a mill on the Stour, this is one of the first landscapes by John Constable (1776–1837) that he painted outdoors rather than in his studio **(left)**.

7 Girl with a Kitten

Known for his psychological penetration of his sitters, this 1947 portrait by Lucian Freud (1922–2011) shows the artist's first wife holding a kitten by its neck in a tense grip, seeming to half-strangle it without concern.

9 Carnation, Lily, Lily, Rose

John Singer Sargent (1856–1925) moved to London from Paris in 1885 and adopted Impressionist techniques. The title of this 1886 work **(right)** was taken from a popular song of the time.

10 Three Studies for Figures at the Base of a Crucifixion

Leading light of the Soho arts scene, Francis Bacon (1910–1992) was uncompromising in his view of life. When first shown, this triptych **(below)** caused an immediate sensation, shocking audiences with its savage imagery. It is now among his best-known works.

8 Pink and Green Sleepers

Henry Moore (1898–1986) was an outstanding sculptor whose work is on public display around London. This 1941 drawing by Moore shows two sleeping figures.

NEED TO KNOW

MAP E5 ■ Millbank SW1 ■ 020 7887 8888 ■ www.tate.org.uk

Open 10am–6pm daily; closed 24–26 Dec

Free (admission charge for temporary exhibitions)

Tate-to-Tate boat service between Tate Britain and Tate Modern every 40 minutes from Millbank Pier

■ Basement café; excellent restaurant with good wine list.

■ Free guided tours daily, weekly talks and films shown monthly.

■ Comprehensive art bookshop.

Gallery Guide
The permanent collection occupies most of the main floor. Starting in the north-west corner, it follows a broad chronological sweep from the 16th century to the present. Alongside the permanent collection are a smaller number of regularly changing displays focusing on individual artists, movements or topics. The Turner Bequest – about 300 oil paintings and about 20,000 watercolours by J M W Turner – is displayed in the adjoining Clore Gallery.

Following pages Changing the guard in front of Buckingham Palace

TOP 10 ⭐ Westminster Abbey

A glorious example of Medieval architecture on a truly grand scale, this former Benedictine abbey church stands on the south side of Parliament Square *(see pp36–7)*. Founded in the 11th century by Edward the Confessor, it survived the Reformation and continued as a place of royal ceremonials. Queen Elizabeth II's coronation was held here in 1953 and Princess Diana's funeral in 1997. It was also the venue for the wedding of Prince William to Catherine Middleton in April 2011.

1 St Edward's Chapel

The shrine of Edward the Confessor (1003–66), last of the Anglo-Saxon kings, lies at the heart of Westminster Abbey. He built London's first royal palace at Westminster, and founded the present abbey on the site.

2 Coronation Chair

This chair **(above)** was made in 1301 for Edward I. It is placed in front of the high-altar screen on the 13th-century mosaic pavement when used for coronations.

3 Nave

At 32 m (102 ft), this is the tallest Gothic nave **(right)** in England and took 150 years to build. Designed by the great 14th-century architect Henry Yevele, it is supported externally by flying buttresses.

4 Poets' Corner

This corner of the transept contains memorials to literary giants, including Shakespeare and Dickens.

5 Lady Chapel

The fan vaulting above the nave of this eastern addition to the church is spectacular late Perpendicular **(below)**. Built for Henry VII (1457–1509), it includes two side aisles and five smaller chapels and is the home of the Order of the Bath *(see p38)*.

6 Tomb of Elizabeth I

England's great Protestant queen (1553–1603) is buried in a huge marble tomb complete with recumbent effigy on one side of the Lady Chapel. The tomb of her Catholic rival, Mary Queen of Scots (beheaded in 1587), is on the other side of the chapel. Mary's remains were brought to the abbey by James I in 1612.

7 The Choir

The all-boy Westminster Abbey Choir School, the only school in England devoted entirely to choristers, produces the choir which sings here daily. The present organ was installed in 1937 and first used at the coronation of George VI.

8 Grave of the Unknown Warrior

The body of an unknown soldier from the battlefields of World War I was buried here in 1920. His grave **(above)** represents all those of have lost their lives in war.

9 Chapter House

This octagonal building with a 13th-century tiled floor is one of the largest in England and is where the abbey's monks once gathered. The House of Commons met here between 1257 and 1542. It is now run by the abbey and can also be reached via Dean's Yard.

10 Cloisters

The cloisters were located at the heart of the former Benedictine monastery and would have been the monastery's busiest area. On the east side are the only remaining parts of the Norman church, the Pyx Chamber, where coinage was tested in medieval times, and the Undercroft.

> **ABBEY HISTORY**
>
> A Benedictine monastery was established by St Dunstan (AD 909–988) on what was the marshy Isle of Thorney. King Edward the Confessor re-endowed the monastery, and founded the present church in 1065. William the Conqueror was crowned here in 1066. Henry III's architect Henry of Reyns rebuilt much of the church in 1245. The nave was completed in 1376. The eastern end of the church was extended by Henry VII who had the Lady Chapel built. Finally, in 1734–45, the twin towers on the west front were completed by Nicholas Hawksmoor.

Abbey Floorplan

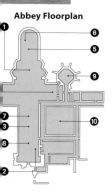

NEED TO KNOW

MAP L6 ■ 20 Dean's Yard SW1 ■ 020 7222 5152 ■ www.westminster-abbey.org

Abbey: 9:30am–3:30pm Mon–Fri (to 6pm Wed), 9:30am–1:30pm Sat. Sun for worship only.
Cellarium Café and Terrace: 8am–6pm Mon–Fri, 9am–5pm Sat, 10am–4pm Sun
Pyx Chamber and Chapter House: 10am–4:30pm Mon–Sat. Adm: adults £20; concessions £17; children 6–16 £9 (5 and under free); for family tickets see website

---

■ Hear the choir sing at 5pm weekdays except Wednesday, 3pm on Saturdays and at Sunday services.

■ Listen to free organ recitals at 5:45pm every Sunday.

■ Guided tours and audio guides are available.

⭐ Parliament Square

The spiritual and political heart of the city, the Palace of Westminster was built here a thousand years ago and has served as a royal household, seat of government and abbey. The square was planned as part of the rebuilding programme after a fire destroyed the palace in 1834. Usually known as the Houses of Parliament, the new Palace of Westminster stands opposite Westminster Abbey. On the north side of the square, Parliament Street leads to Whitehall and No.10 Downing Street.

1 Westminster Abbey
See pp34–5.

2 St Margaret's Church
Winston Churchill was among many eminent figures to marry in this 15th-century church **(below)**. William Caxton (c. 1422–92), who set up the first printing press in England, and the writer and explorer, Sir Walter Raleigh, are both buried here. Charles I is also remembered.

3 Big Ben
The huge Clock Tower of the Palace of Westminster is popularly known as Big Ben **(left)**. The name actually refers to the clock's 13.5-tonne bell, thought to be named after Sir Benjamin Hall, Chief Commissioner of Works when it was installed in 1858.

4 Houses of Parliament
A Gothic revival building by Sir Charles Barry and Augustus Welby Pugin built between 1840 and 1870, the Houses of Parliament **(right)** cover 8 acres and have 1,100 rooms around 11 courtyards. The Commons Chamber is where Members of Parliament sit and debate policy.

5 Westminster Hall
Westminster Hall is about all of the original palace that remained after the 1834 fire. For centuries the courts of law sat beneath its grand 14th-century hammerbeam roof.

6 Central Hall
This large assembly hall, built in Viennese Baroque style, was funded by a collection among the Methodist Church to celebrate the centenary of their founder John Wesley (1703–91).

7 Jewel Tower

Built in 1365 to safeguard the treasure of Edward III, this is an isolated survivor of the 1834 fire. A museum about the history of parliament is housed inside.

8 Winston Churchill Statue

This powerful statue of the UK's wartime leader (1874–1965) is one of several in the square. These include prime minister Benjamin Disraeli (1804–81) and Nelson Mandela (1918–2013).

PARLIAMENT

The 650 publicly elected Members of Parliament sit in the House of Commons, where the Prime Minister and his or her government sits on the right-hand side of the Speaker, who ensures the House's rules are obeyed. The opposing "shadow" government sits on his left. The neighbouring House of Lords is for an unelected upper chamber, which has around 800 members and limited powers. The Prime Minister attends a weekly audience with the Queen, who today has only a symbolic role.

9 Dean's Yard

Buildings around this secluded square were used by monks before the Dissolution of the Monasteries in the 1530s, which closed their school here. A new Westminster School was founded by Elizabeth I in 1560 and it remains one of the country's top public schools.

NEED TO KNOW

MAP M6 ■ Parliament Square SW1
■ www.parliament.uk

The Public Galleries at the Houses of Parliament have limited seating for visitors during debates. Check times online or call 020 7219 4272

Tours can be arranged through MPs at www.parliament.uk

Tickets for tours on Saturdays and during recess are available online or call 020 7219 4114

■ The basement café in Central Hall is a good place for a snack.

■ To avoid long queues for the Public Galleries go after 6pm Mon–Wed.

Plan of the Square

10 Statue of Oliver Cromwell

Oliver Cromwell (1599–1658) presided over England's only republic, which began after the Civil War. He was buried in Westminster Abbey, but after the monarchy was restored in 1660, his corpse was taken to Tyburn and hanged as a criminal.

Tower of London

London's great riverside fortress is usually remembered as a place of imprisonment, but it also has a more glorious past. Originally a moated fort, the White Tower was built for William I (the Conqueror) and begun around 1078. Enlarged by later monarchs – including Henry VIII, who famously sent two of his wives to their deaths on Tower Green – it became home to the city arsenal, the Crown Jewels, a menagerie and the Royal Mint.

3 The White Tower

The heart of the fortress is a sturdy keep, 30 m (90 ft) tall with walls 5 m (15 ft) thick. It was constructed under William I, and completed in 1097, and is the Tower's oldest surviving building. In 1240 it was whitewashed inside and out, hence its name.

4 Imperial State Crown

This is the most dazzling of a dozen crowns in the Jewel House. It has over 2,800 diamonds, and the sapphire at its top is from the reign of Edward the Confessor (r.1042–66). The crown was made for the coronation of George VI in 1937.

1 Yeoman Warders

Some 37 Yeoman Warders **(above)** now include a female Warder. Former non-commissioned military officers with Long Service and Good Conduct Medals, they wear uniforms dating from Tudor times.

The Tower of London

5 Chapel of St John the Evangelist

The finest Norman place of worship in London **(left)**, which remains much as it was when it was built, is on the upper floor of the White Tower. In 1399, in preparation for Henry IV's coronation procession, 40 noble knights held vigil here. They then took a purifying bath in an adjoining room and Henry made them the first Knights of the Order of the Bath. It is still used as a royal chapel today.

2 The Bloody Tower

The displays here explore the dark history of the Bloody Tower where murderous deeds, including the alleged killing of the Little Princes, took place.

6 Ravens

When ravens leave the Tower, the saying goes, the building and the monarchy will fall. There are at least six ravens in residence, looked after by the Ravenmaster.

Plan of the Tower

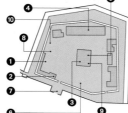

TOWER HISTORY

William I's White Tower was intended to defend London against attacks – and to be a visible sign to the native Anglo-Saxon population of the conquering Normans' power. Henry III (r.1216–72) built the inner wall with its 13 towers and brought the Crown Jewels here. The city arsenal was kept here, and under Henry VIII (r.1509–47) the Royal Armouries were improved. James I (r.1603–25) was the last monarch to stay in residence. All coinage in Great Britain was minted in the Tower's Outer Ward until 1810, when the Royal Mint was established on Tower Hill.

9 The Royal Armouries

This national collection of arms and armour, shared with the Royal Armouries' other museums in Leeds and Portsmouth, was greatly expanded under Henry VIII.

NEED TO KNOW

MAP H4 ■ Tower Hill EC3 ■ 020 3166 6000 ■ www.hrp.org.uk

Open Mar–Oct: 9am–5:30pm Tue–Sat, opens at 10am Sun–Mon; Nov–Feb: 9am–4:30pm Tue–Sat, opens at 10am Sun–Mon (last adm: 30 min before closing); closed 24–26 Dec

Adm: adults £24.50; children 5–15 £11 (under 5s free); family (5 people) £60.70; concessions £18.70

■ Eat at the Tower's café or restaurant.

7 Traitors' Gate

The oak and iron water gate in the outer wall (right) was used to bring many prisoners to the Tower, and became known as Traitors' Gate.

8 Beauchamp Tower

The displays in this tower explore the experiences of real prisoners of the Tower, including Lady Jane Grey and the Kray twins. The tower takes its name from Thomas Beauchamp, Earl of Warwick, who was imprisoned here between 1397–9 by Richard II.

10 Tower Green

The place of execution for nobility, including Lady Jane Grey (1554) and two of Henry VIII's wives – Anne Boleyn (1536) and Katherine Howard (1542).

Tower Prisoners

1 Bishop of Durham
The first political prisoner to be held in the White Tower was Ralph de Flambard, Bishop of Durham. Locked up by Henry I in 1100, he was seen as responsible for the unpopular policies of Henry's predecessor, William II.

2 Henry VI
During the Wars of the Roses, between the rival families of York and Lancaster, Henry VI was kept in Wakefield Tower for five years, until restored to power in 1470.

3 The Little Princes
The alleged murder of Edward, 12, and Richard, 10, in 1483, gave the Bloody Tower its name. It is thought their uncle, Richard III, was responsible.

4 Sir Thomas More
Chancellor Thomas More's refusal to approve Henry VIII's marriage to Anne Boleyn led to his imprisonment in the lower Bell Tower. He was beheaded in 1535.

Sir Thomas More

5 Henry VIII's Wives
Some of the Tower's most famous victims, such as the

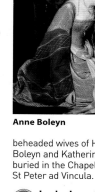
Anne Boleyn

beheaded wives of Henry VIII, Anne Boleyn and Katherine Howard, are buried in the Chapel Royal of St Peter ad Vincula.

6 Lady Jane Grey
In 1554 Lady Jane Grey was queen for just nine days. Aged 16, she was held in the gaoler's house on Tower Green and later executed by order of Queen Mary I.

7 Catholic Martyrs
Under the reign of Elizabeth I (1558–1603), many Catholics were executed. Most, including Jesuits, were held in the Salt Tower.

8 Guy Fawkes
The most famous of the Catholic conspirators, Guy Fawkes tried to blow up King James I and Parliament in 1605. He is burned in effigy each year on 5 November.

9 John Gerard
He escaped from the Cradle Tower with a fellow prisoner in 1597, using a rope strung over the moat by an accomplice in a boat.

10 Rudolf Hess
The Tower's last prisoner was Hitler's deputy. He was held in the Queen's House in 1941, after flying to the UK to ask for peace.

Sites of imprisonment

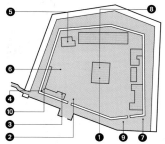

THE CROWN JEWELS

The lavish, bejewelled items that make up the sovereign's ceremonial regalia are all in the care of the Tower of London. The collection dates from 1661 when a new set was made to replace those destroyed by Cromwell following the execution of Charles I in 1649. St Edward's Crown was the first subsequent crown to be made of pure gold, and is the oldest of the 12 crowns here. Other coronation jewels on display include a gold, jewel-studded orb, made in 1661, and a sceptre containing the 530-carat Star of Africa, the biggest cut diamond in the world. The Sovereign's Ring, made for William IV, is sometimes called "the wedding ring of England".

TOP 10 JEWELS

1 Imperial State Crown

2 St Edward's Crown

3 Imperial Crown of India

4 Queen Victoria's Crown

5 Royal Sceptre

6 Jewelled State Sword

7 George V's Crown

8 The Sovereign's Ring

9 The Sovereign's Orb

10 The Sovereign's Sceptre

The Imperial State Crown is heavily encrusted with 2,868 diamonds, 17 sapphires, 11 emeralds, 5 rubies and 273 pearls. It was designed for the coronation of George VI in 1937.

Queen Elizabeth II wore the Imperial State Crown at her coronation, 2 June 1953.

TOP 10 ⭐ St Paul's Cathedral

This is the great masterpiece of Christopher Wren, who rebuilt the City's churches after the Great Fire of 1666. Completed in 1711, it was England's first purpose-built Protestant cathedral, and has many similarities with St Peter's in Rome, notably in its ornate dome. One of its bells, Great Paul, was the largest in Europe until the bell cast for the 2012 Olympics. The hour bell, Great Tom, strikes the hour and marks the death of royalty and senior church officials. The cathedral has a reputation for music, and draws its choristers from St Paul's Cathedral School.

③ Dome
One of the largest domes in the world **(left)**, it is 111 m (365 ft) high and weighs 65,000 tonnes. The Golden Gallery at the top, and the larger Stone Gallery, both have great views.

④ Whispering Gallery
Inside the dome is the famous Whispering Gallery **(right)**. Words whispered against the wall can be heard on the gallery's opposite side.

① Quire
The beautiful stalls and organ case in the Quire are by Grinling Gibbons. Handel and Mendelssohn both played the organ, which dates from 1695.

⑤ St Paul's Watch Memorial
Set in the nave, this honours those who saved St Paul's from destruction during the Blitz by fighting fires started by bombs dropped on and near it.

② The Light of the World
This painting by the Pre-Raphaelite artist William Holman Hunt shows Christ knocking on an overgrown door that opens from inside, meaning that God can enter our lives only if we invite Him in.

⑥ West Front and Towers
The imposing West Front **(right)** is dominated by two huge towers. The pineapples at their tops are symbols of peace and prosperity. The Great West Door is 9 m (29 ft) high and is used only for ceremonial occasions.

7 High Altar
The magnificent High Altar **(right)** is made from Italian marble, and the canopy, constructed in the 1950s after the cathedral was bombed during World War II, is based on one of Wren's sketches.

8 Tijou Gates
The French master metal worker Jean Tijou designed these ornate wrought-iron gates in the South and North Quire, along with the Whispering Gallery balcony and other cathedral metalwork.

9 Mosaics
Colourful mosaic ceilings were installed in the Ambulatory and Quire in the 19th century. They are made with glass tesserae, angled so that they sparkle.

10 Moore's Mother and Child
This piece is one of a growing number of works of art that have been introduced into St Paul's since the 1960s. The sculptor, Henry Moore, is commemorated in the crypt.

ST PAUL'S HISTORY

The first known church dedicated to St Paul was built on this site in AD 604. Made of wood, it burned down in 675 and a subsequent church was destroyed by Viking invaders in 962. The third church was built in stone. Following another fire in 1087, it was rebuilt under the Normans as a much larger cathedral, with stone walls and a wooden roof. This was completed in 1300. In 1666 Sir Christopher Wren's plans to restore the building had just been accepted when the Great Fire of London burned the old cathedral beyond repair.

Cathedral Floorplan

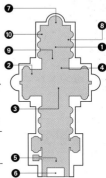

NEED TO KNOW

MAP R2 ▪ Ludgate Hill EC4 ▪ 020 7236 4128 ▪ www.stpauls.co.uk

Open cathedral (sightseeing): 8:30am–4pm Mon–Sat; galleries: 9:30am–4:15pm Mon–Sat

Adm: adults £18; children 6–17 £8 (under 6s enter free); seniors and students 18 and over £16; family £44; for groups, check website. All services are free of charge.

Guided tours usually take place at 10am, 11am, 1pm, 2pm and are included in the admission. Reserve a place at the guiding desk.

▪ Food and drink in the Crypt Café.

▪ You can hear the choir during the very popular choral evensong service (usually at 5pm daily).

▪ Multimedia guides are also available and included in the price of admission.

St Paul's Monuments

Crypt Floorplan

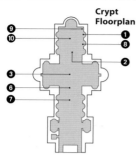

Detail, American Roll of Honour

Memorial Chapel's roll of honour lists the US servicemen killed while stationed in the UK during World War II.

1 Tomb of Christopher Wren

St Paul's architect, Christopher Wren (1632–1723), has a plain tomb in the OBE chapel. Its inscription reads, *"Lector, si monumentum requiris, circumspice"* – "Reader, if you seek a monument, look around you".

2 Wellington's Tomb

The UK's great military leader and prime minister, Arthur Wellesley, 1st Duke of Wellington (1769–1852), lies in the crypt. He also has a monument in the nave.

3 Nelson's Tomb

Preserved in brandy and brought home from Trafalgar, sea hero Admiral Lord Nelson (1758–1805) is in the centre of the crypt.

4 American Memorial

Behind the High Altar on the cathedral floor, the American

5 John Donne's Memorial

The metaphysical poet John Donne (1572–1631) was made Dean of St Paul's in 1621. His memorial is in the Dean's Aisle in the Ambulatory on the cathedral floor.

6 Gallipoli Memorial

This memorial is dedicated to those who died in the 1915 Gallipoli campaign of World War I.

7 Churchill Memorial Gates

These gates commemorate Sir Winston Churchill (1874–1965) who during the 1940–41 Blitz said "at all costs, St Paul's must be saved".

8 The Worshipful Company of Masons Memorial

This City guild's plaque near Wren's tomb reads, "Remember the men who made shapely the stones of Saint Paul's Cathedral".

9 Turner's Tomb

The great landscape painter JMW Turner (1775–1851) is buried in the OBE chapel.

10 OBE Chapel

At the eastern end of the crypt is a chapel devoted to those appointed to the Order of the British Empire, an honour established in 1917, and the first to include women.

Nelson's Tomb, St Paul's Cathedral

ST PAUL'S ROLE IN HISTORY

St Paul's, as the Cathedral for the Diocese of London, belongs to the parishes all across London, as well as to the nation. It is run by a Dean and Chapter of priests. One of the cathedral's main functions is as a place of national mourning and celebration. In the 19th century, 13,000 people filled the cathedral for the funeral of the Duke of Wellington. Queen Victoria's Jubilee was a spectacular occasion held on the steps of the cathedral. The Prince of Wales and Lady Diana Spencer chose to be married at St Paul's rather than the royal Westminster Abbey. The decision helped to portray the couple as the people's prince and princess.

TOP 10
MOMENTS IN ST PAUL'S HISTORY

1 Elizabeth II's Diamond Jubilee (2012)

2 Prince Charles' and Lady Diana's wedding (1981)

3 Winston Churchill's funeral (1965)

4 Martin Luther King Jr preaches (1964)

5 Cathedral bombed (1940)

6 Queen Victoria's Diamond Jubilee (1897)

7 Duke of Wellington's funeral (1852)

8 Nelson's funeral (1806)

9 First service (1697)

10 Gunpowder Plotters executed in the churchyard (1606)

The wedding of Prince Charles and Lady Diana Spencer, 1981

The Duke of Wellington's funeral at St Paul's Cathedral

The Top 10 of Everything

The Lady Chapel,
Westminster Cathedral

TOP 10 Moments in London's History

The Great Fire of London in 1666 devastated one third of the city

1 AD 43: Roman Invasion
The Romans built a bridge across the Thames from Southwark and encircled Londinium with a wall, part of which is still visible in the City *(see pp140–45)*. Their forum was near Cornhill and their amphitheatre lies beneath the Guildhall.

2 1066: Norman Conquest
The next successful invasion of England came from northern France. It was led by William the Conqueror, Duke of Normandy, who was crowned King of England in the newly completed Westminster Abbey *(see pp34–5)* on Christmas Day 1066.

3 1240: First Parliament
The first parliament sat in Westminster and became a seat of government separate from the mercantile City, which continued to expand on the former Roman site.

4 1534: The Reformation
A quarrel between Henry VIII and Pope Clement VII over the king's divorce led to Henry breaking with Rome and declaring himself head of the church in England. Today, the sovereign remains the head of the Church of England.

5 1649: Charles I Executed
Charles I's belief in the divine right of kings led to civil war. The royalist cause was lost and the king was beheaded in 1649. After 11 years of the Commonwealth, his son Charles II returned to the throne to preside over the Restoration.

6 1666: Great Fire of London
Much of the city, including the medieval St Paul's Cathedral and 87 parish churches, were destroyed in the fire, which raged for nearly five days. Afterwards, Sir Christopher Wren replanned the entire city, including the cathedral *(see pp42–5)*.

7 1863: First Underground
Originally designed to link the main London railway termini, the Metropolitan Line was the world's

Interior of Baker Street station

rst underground railway, operating
etween Paddington and Farringdon
treet. Carriages were pulled by
team locomotives until the start of
he 20th century.

 1874: Embankments Built

Built on either side of the river, the
Embankments were among the
great engineering works of the
Victorians. They were designed by Sir
Joseph Bazalgette to contain a vast
new sewage system to take waste to
pumping stations outside London.

 1940–41: The Blitz

Between September 1940 and
May 1941, German air raids left
30,000 Londoners dead. The bombers
destroyed much of the docks, the
East End and the City. The House of
Commons, Westminster Abbey and
the Tower of London were all hit.
Many Londoners sought shelter in
Underground stations at night.

An air warden watching for bombers

 2012: Olympic Games

In 2012, the Olympic and
Paralympic Games were held in
London, with many of the city's iconic
landmarks including Horse Guards
Parade playing host to sporting events.
Part of Stratford was transformed
into a world-class Olympic Park,
with a magnificent stadium and
velodrome, and a spectacular aquatic
centre with a wave-shaped roof.

TOP 10 CULTURAL HIGHLIGHTS

The Great Exhibition of 1851

1 Shakespeare Arrives
The first mention of William
Shakespeare (1564–1616) as a London
dramatist was recorded in 1595.

2 Van Dyck Knighted
The Flemish artist Anthony Van Dyck
was knighted by Charles I in 1632 for
his service as the king's principal royal
portrait painter.

3 Purcell's Appointment
The greatest English composer of his
time, Henry Purcell was appointed
organist at Westminster Abbey in 1679.

4 Handel's Water Music
George Friedrich Handel's *Water Music*
was composed for a performance on
King George I's royal barge in 1717.

5 Great Exhibition
In 1851, the expanding Empire was
celebrated in an exhibition held in a
massive glass structure in Hyde Park.

6 J M W Turner Bequest
Turner's paintings were left to the nation
on condition that they be displayed
together *(see pp30–31)*.

7 Royal Opera Highlight
In 1892 Gustav Mahler conducted the
first UK performance of Wagner's *Ring*
at the Royal Opera House.

8 First Radio Broadcast
The BBC made its first broadcast on
New Year's Day in 1922.

9 Festival of Britain
In 1951, the Festival of Britain was held
at the South Bank to mark the
centenary of the Great Exhibition.

10 Royal National Theatre
The National Theatre company was
founded in 1963 and temporarily
housed at the Old Vic in Waterloo under
Laurence Olivier (later Lord Olivier).

⏱10 Famous Residents

1 Sherlock Holmes
The famous but fictitious detective created by Sir Arthur Conan Doyle first appeared in 1887. He still gets regular fan mail sent to 221b Baker Street, which houses the Sherlock Holmes Museum *(see p136)*.

2 Charles Dickens
The great Victorian novelist and social campaigner (1812–70) lived in Doughty Street for two years from 1837. The house is his only surviving London home, and he thought it "a frightfully first-class family mansion, involving awful responsibilities" *(see p114)*.

3 Dr Johnson
MAP P2 ■ Dr Johnson's House, 17 Gough Square EC4 ■ Open 11am– 5pm Mon–Sat (5:30pm May–Sep) ■ Adm ■ www.drjohnsonshouse.org
"When a man is tired of London, he is tired of life," said Dr Samuel Johnson (1709–84). He lived in this house from around 1748 to 1759 and much of his famous dictionary was compiled here. His companion James Boswell reported on the social comings and goings in the house.

Sherlock Holmes theatre poster

4 John Keats
The London-born Romantic poet (1795–1821) lived in Hampstead from 1818 to 1820 before leaving for Italy to try to cure his fatal tuberculosis. After falling in love with his neighbour's daughter, Fanny Brawne, he is said to have written his famous and beautiful *Ode to a Nightingale* in the garden *(see p147)*.

5 Sigmund Freud
The Viennese founder of psychoanalysis (1856–1939) spent the last year of his life in a north London house. A Jew, he had fled the Nazis before the onset of World War II, bringing his celebrated couch with him *(see p147)*.

6 Lord Leighton
Yorkshire-born Frederic Leighton (1830– 96) was one of the most successful artists in Victorian London and president of the Royal Academy. He had exotic Leighton House built for him between 1865 and 1895 *(see p127)*.

Charles Dickens

7 Thomas Carlyle

MAP C6 ■ Carlyle's House, 24 Cheyne Row SW3 ■ Open Mar–Oct: 11am–4:30pm Wed–Sun ■ Adm ■ www.nationaltrust.org.uk/carlyles-house

The Scottish historian and essayist Thomas Carlyle, famous for his history of the French Revolution, lived in London from 1831 and in this house from 1834.

8 The Duke of Wellington

Arthur Wellesley, 1st Duke of Wellington (1769–1852), lived at Apsley House, popularly known as No. 1 London (the actual address is 149 Piccadilly), following his victories in the Napoleonic Wars (see p120).

9 Georg Friedrich Handel

MAP D3 ■ Handel House Museum, 25 Brook Street W1 ■ Open 10am–6pm Tue–Sat (10am–8pm Thu), noon–6pm Sun ■ Adm ■ www.handelhouse.org

The great German-born composer first visited London in 1710 and settled here in 1712.

William Hogarth

10 William Hogarth

Hogarth's House, Hogarth Lane W4 ■ Open noon–5pm Tue–Sun ■ Closed 1 Jan, Good Fri, Easter Sun, 24–26 Dec ■ www.hounslow.info

The great painter of London life (1697–1764, see pp30–31) was used to the gritty life of the city and called his house near Chiswick "a little country box by the Thames".

TOP 10 BLUE PLAQUES

Circular blue plaques on the walls of some London buildings recall famous residents.

GREATER LONDON COUNCIL

Virginia Stephen (VIRGINIA WOOLF) 1882 – 1941 Novelist and Critic lived here 1907–1911

Virginia Woolf's blue plaque

1 Wolfgang Amadeus Mozart
The German composer (1756–91) wrote his first symphony, aged eight, while at No. 180 Ebury Street.

2 Benjamin Franklin
The US statesman and scientist (1706–90) lived for a time at No. 36 Craven Street.

3 Charlie Chaplin
The much-loved movie actor (1889–1977) was born at No. 287 Kennington Road.

4 Charles de Gaulle
The exiled general (1890–1970) organized the Free French Forces from No. 4 Carlton Gardens during World War II.

5 Mary Seacole
Jamaican nurse and heroine of the Crimean War (1805–81) lived at No. 14 Soho Square.

6 Virginia Woolf
The great English novelist (1882–1941) lived in three different houses in Bloomsbury between 1905 and 1912.

7 Mahatma Gandhi
The "father" of India's independence movement (1869–1948) lived as a law student at No. 20 Baron's Court Road.

8 Jimi Hendrix
The American guitarist (1942–70) stayed in central London at No. 23 Brook Street.

9 Henry James
The American writer (1843–1916) lived in Bolton Street, De Vere Gardens, and in Cheyne Walk, where he died.

10 Giuseppe Mazzini
From 1837 to 1849 the Italian revolutionary and patriot (1805–72) lived at No. 183 Gower Street.

🔟 Literary London

Writer and poet Oscar Wilde

classic piece of English literature, and follows a group of pilgrims travelling from Southwark to Canterbury. In 17,000 lines the characters tell their rollicking tales.

1 Samuel Pepys
The extraordinary *Diary* of Samuel Pepys (1633–1703) begins on New Year's Day, 1660, and ends on May 31, 1669. He vividly describes contemporary life, the Plague and the Great Fire, and a naval attack on England by the Dutch. The work was written in shorthand and only deciphered and first published in 1825.

2 Dr Johnson
Samuel Johnson (1709–84) was a towering literary figure who presided over gatherings in pubs, coffee houses and literary clubs, as well as in his own home *(see p50)*, and had opinions on everything. His satirical poem, *London* (1738), attacked poverty in the city and his parliamentary sketches and dictionary made him famous.

3 Geoffrey Chaucer
Chaucer (c.1343–1400) was a diplomat and son of a London vintner. His *Canterbury Tales* is a

4 Oscar Wilde
Dublin-born Wilde (1854–1900) dazzled London audiences with his plays, and society with his wit. He fell from grace when he was convicted of homosexual activity. His plays, such as *Lady Windermere's Fan* (1892) and *The Importance of Being Earnest* (1895), are frequently revived.

5 Virginia Woolf
Woolf (1882–1941) and her sister Vanessa Bell lived in Gordon Square, where the influential pre-war Bloomsbury Group grew from social gatherings. She developed an impressionistic stream of consciousness in novels such as *Mrs Dalloway* (1925) and *To The Lighthouse* (1927).

6 John Betjeman
A devoted Londoner, with a fine disdain for bureaucracy, mediocrity and hideous architecture, Betjeman (1906–84) was made Poet Laureate of the United Kingdom in 1972. His poems are full of gentle wit and humour and he remains one of the country's favourite poets.

Playwright and author Alan Bennett

Novelist and essayist Zadie Smith

 Colin MacInnes

MacInnes (1914–76) documented the teenage and black immigrant culture in Notting Hill in the 1950s. *City of Spades* (1957) and *Absolute Beginners* (1959) are set among the coffee bars, jazz clubs, drink and drugs scene at a time of great unrest.

8 Martin Amis

Darling of the London literary scene in the 1970s and 1980s, Amis (b.1949) had a famous literary father, Kingsley, and a precocious talent, with his first novel, *The Rachel Papers* (1973), winning a prestigious award for young writers. London has infused novels such as *Money* (1984) and *London Fields* (1989).

9 Zadie Smith

Her first novel, *White Teeth*, a complex tale of immigrant families in north London, made Smith (b.1975) an overnight sensation in 2000. Wickedly funny, it has remarkably well-drawn portraits of London life.

10 Alan Bennett

The Yorkshire-born playwright has lived in Camden for many years. *The Lady in the Van* is his touching and amusing account of an eccentric elderly woman who spent 15 years living in an old yellow van parked in the author's driveway.

TOP 10 LONDON SONGS

1 London's Burning
Commemorating the Great Fire of 1666, this is sung in a round, a device popular since Elizabethan days.

2 London Bridge is Falling Down
A traditional song about old London Bridge, which fell into disrepair.

3 Oranges and Lemons
"…*say the bells of St Clement's*". This children's song rhymes City churches, and is sung as part of a game.

4 Maybe it's Because I'm a Londoner
The theme song of music-hall duo, Flanagan and Allen, it became a patriotic comfort in post-war London.

5 The Lambeth Walk
A song from the 1930s musical *Me and My Girl*, this has been a Cockney favourite ever since.

6 London Pride
An uncharacteristically sentimental Noël Coward song that celebrates the city.

7 England Swings
This hit US song came out in 1965, during the "Swinging London" era, although it's not very progressive.

8 Waterloo Sunset
Pop groups don't usually celebrate London but this 1967 record by The Kinks was an exception.

9 A Nightingale Sang in Berkeley Square
A standard sung by Frank Sinatra and others, it is actually very unusual to hear nightingales in central London.

10 Burlington Bertie
A music-hall song about the life of an aristocratic young Mayfair gentleman in Edwardian London.

Lambeth Walk, Victoria Theatre

⏱10 Royal London

Formal garden, Kensington Palace

1 Buckingham Palace
(see pp24–5).

2 Hampton Court
The finest piece of Tudor architecture in Britain, Hampton Court was given to Henry VIII by the king's ally Cardinal Wolsey. It was enlarged by Henry and then later rebuilt by William and Mary, who employed Christopher Wren as architect. Its many rooms include a huge kitchen, the Cumberland Art Gallery, the Chapel Royal and royal apartments. The stunning gardens, with their famous maze, are as much an attraction as the palace (see p153).

3 Kensington Palace
An intimate royal palace in Kensington Gardens, famous as the home of Princess Diana, its first sovereign residents were William

Hampton Court

and Mary in 1689, and Queen Victoria was born here in 1819. The interior has displays of regal fashion and focuses on the lives of past residents including William and Mary, Victoria and Diana. The Orangery is delightful for coffee (see p125).

4 St James's Palace
Although closed to the public, St James's has a key role in royal London. Its classic Tudor style sets it in the reign of Henry VIII, and while it has had many royal residents, every monarch since Victoria has lived at Buckingham Palace (see p119).

5 Kew Palace and Queen Charlotte's Cottage
Kew, Surrey TW9 ■ Palace: open Apr–Sep: 10am–5:30pm daily; Cottage: open Apr–Sep: 11am–4pm Sat, Sun & public hols ■ Adm ■ www.hrp.org.uk
The smallest royal palace, Kew was built in 1631 and was a residence of George III and Queen Charlotte. Queen Charlotte's Cottage was used for picnics and housing pets. The palace is in Kew Gardens (see p153).

6 Banqueting House
MAP L4 ■ Whitehall SW1
■ Open 10am–5pm daily ■ Adm
■ www.hrp.org.uk
Built by Inigo Jones, this magnificent building is particularly noted for its

Rubens ceiling. It was commissioned by Charles I, who stepped from this room on to the scaffold for his execution in 1649.

7 Queen's House
Romney Road SE10 ■ Train to Greenwich; DLR Cutty Sark, Greenwich ■ Open 10am–5pm daily ■ www.rmg.co.uk

This delightful home in the midst of Greenwich Park was the first Palladian building by Inigo Jones, and once home to the wife of Charles I. Restored to its 17th-century glory, it houses the National Maritime Museum's art collection *(see p60)*.

Queen's House, Greenwich

8 Royal Mews
(see p25).

9 Queen's Chapel
MAP K5 ■ Marlborough Road SW1

This royal chapel is open only to its congregation (visitors welcome as worshippers). Built by Inigo Jones and operational from 1626, its furnishings include a beautiful altarpiece by Annibale Carracci.

10 Clarence House
MAP K5 ■ St James's Palace SW1 ■ Tours: Aug 10am–3:30pm Mon–Fri, 10am–4:30pm Sat & Sun ■ Adm ■ www.royalcollection.org.uk

William, Duke of Clarence lived here after becoming king in 1830. It was home to the Queen Mother until her death in 2002, and since to the Prince of Wales and Duchess of Cornwall.

TOP 10 ROYALS IN EVERYDAY LONDON LIFE

Albert Memorial

1 King Charles Spaniel
These were the favourite dogs of King Charles II. Today, the Queen prefers corgis.

2 Queen Anne's Gate
A delightful small Westminster street with a statue of the queen who gave her name to a style of furniture.

3 Regent's Park
The Prince Regent, later George IV, used John Nash for this ambitious urban plan *(see p135)*.

4 Duke of York Steps
A statue of the "Grand Old Duke of York", subject of the nursery rhyme, is elevated above these steps off Pall Mall.

5 Victoria Station
All the main London railway termini were built in Victoria's reign. This one serves southern England.

6 Albert Memorial
Prince Albert, beloved consort of Queen Victoria, has a splendid memorial in Kensington Gardens *(see p125)*.

7 George Cross
Instituted in 1940 under George VI, this medal is awarded for acts of heroism by civilians.

8 Princess of Wales Pubs
Several pubs have changed their name to remember Diana, Princess of Wales, "the people's princess".

9 Windsor Knot
The stylish Duke of Windsor, who abdicated the throne in 1936, gave the world a wide tie knot.

10 King Edward Potato
This variety of traditional English potato, grown in the UK since 1902, was supposedly named after King Edward VII.

TOP 10 Royal Parks and Gardens

Tazza Fountain in the Italian Gardens, Kensington Gardens

1 Hyde Park
MAP C4 ▪ W2 ▪ Open 5am–midnight daily ▪ www.royalparks.org.uk

One of the most popular features of this huge London park is its lake, the Serpentine, with boats for hire and a swimming area. Horses can be rented and ridden in the park. On Sunday mornings at Speakers' Corner, near Marble Arch, you can get up on a soapbox and address the crowds who gather there.

2 St James's Park
London's oldest and most elegant park was redesigned by John Nash in 1828. Its lake is home to some 15 varieties of water-fowl. It has an attractive restaurant and, in summer, lunchtime concerts are given at a bandstand (see p119).

3 Kensington Gardens
MAP B4 ▪ W8 ▪ Open 6am–dusk daily ▪ www.royalparks.org.uk

A succession of queens living in Kensington Palace between 1689 and 1837 appropriated parts of Hyde Park for their palace gardens. Since opening in 2000, the Diana, Princess of Wales Memorial Playground has proved a great hit with children. The park is also home to the Serpentine Galleries (see p63).

4 Regent's Park
Home to London Zoo, an open-air theatre and a boating lake, Regent's Park is surrounded by John Nash's Classical terraces. The fragrant Queen Mary's Garden is a delight (see p135).

5 Green Park
MAP D4 ▪ SW1 ▪ Open all day, year-round ▪ www.royalparks.org.uk

Originally called Upper St James's Park, it was enclosed by Charles II in 1668 to create a link between Hyde Park and St James's Park. There are deckchairs for hire in summer.

The bandstand at Regent's Park

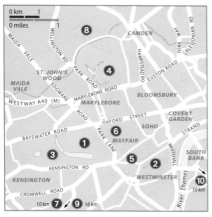

8 Primrose Hill
MAP C1 ■ NW1
■ Open 5am–dusk daily
■ www.royalparks.org.uk
North of Regent's Park, Primrose Hill offers spectacular views of the city skyline from its 63-m (207-ft) summit. Once a popular venue for duels, this small park was purchased by the Crown in 1841 to provide outdoor space for the poor of North London.

9 Bushy Park
MAP X9 ■ Hampton Court Road, Hampton TW11 ■ Hours vary
■ www.royalparks.org.uk
Chestnut Sunday in May, when the trees' blossoms are out, is one of the best times to come to Bushy Park, near Hampton Court. Highlights include the bronze Diana Fountain and the Upper Lodge Water Gardens. Deer also roam this park.

6 Grosvenor Square
MAP D3 ■ W1 ■ Open 7.30am–dusk, daily ■ www.royalparks.org.uk
The hub of high society from the early 18th century until World War II, Grosvenor Square is the only London square that is owned by the Crown. Long home to the imposing American Embassy, the square features a statue of F D Roosevelt.

7 Richmond Park
Kingston Vale TW10 ■ Open 7am–dusk daily (7.30am in winter)
■ www.royalparks.org.uk
Covering an area of 10 sq km (4 sq miles), this is by far the largest Royal Park. Herds of red and fallow deer roam freely across the heath. In late spring, the Isabella Plantation is a blaze of colourful azaleas, camellias and rhododendrons, plus many rare shrubs. The Royal Ballet School has a base in the Palladian White Lodge.

Greenwich Park

10 Greenwich Park
SE10 ■ Open 6am–dusk daily
■ www.royalparks.org.uk
The 0° longitude meridian passes through the Royal Observatory Greenwich, located on a hill in this leafy family park. There are great views of the Old Royal Naval College, and over London (see p153).

Fallow deer, Richmond Park

TOP 10 Churches

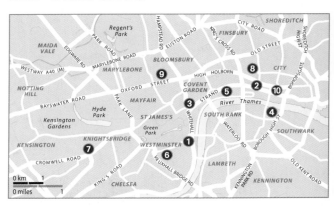

1 Westminster Abbey
See pp34–5.

2 St Paul's Cathedral
See pp42–5.

3 St Martin-in-the-Fields
MAP L4 ■ Trafalgar Square WC2 ■ Open 8:30am–6pm Mon–Fri (to 5pm Wed), 9:30am–6pm Sat, 3:30–5pm Sun, closed 1–2pm Mon–Fri except for services and concerts ■ www.smitf.org

This parish church of Buckingham Palace is famous for its music. There's been a church on the site since the 13th century, and the present building was designed by James Gibbs in 1726. The crypt café is award-winning.

St Martin-in-the-Fields

4 Southwark Cathedral
MAP G4 ■ London Bridge SE1 ■ Open 8am–6pm daily (from 8:30am Sat & Sun) ■ cathedral.southwark.anglican.org

This priory church became a cathedral in 1905. It has many connections with local Elizabethan theatres, and with Shakespeare, who is commemorated in a memorial and a stained-glass window. US college founder John Harvard was baptised here and is remembered in the Harvard Chapel.

5 Temple Church
MAP P2 ■ Inner Temple Lane EC4 ■ Check www.templechurch.com for opening times ■ Adm

This circular church was built in the 12th century for the Knights Templar. Effigies of the knights are embedded in the floor. A chancel was added in the 13th century. The church has been maintained by the Inns of Court since 1608, and was rebuilt after wartime bomb damage in 1958.

6 Westminster Cathedral
■ MAP E5 ■ 42 Francis St SW1 ■ Open 7am–7pm Mon–Fri, 8am–7pm Sat & Sun ■ www.westminster cathedral.org.uk

The main Roman Catholic church in England, Westminster Cathedral was designed in Byzantine Revival style by John Francis Bentley and completed in 1903. Intricate mosaics and over 100 varieties of marble decorate the interior, while the exterior features horizontal bands of white stone across red brickwork.

St Bartholomew-the-Great

8 St Bartholomew-the-Great

A survivor of the Great Fire, this is London's only Norman church apart from St John's Chapel in the Tower of London. It was founded in 1123 by the monk Rahere, a courtier of Henry I, and its solid pillars and Norman choir have remained unaltered since. The 14th-century Lady Chapel, restored by Sir Aston Webb in 1890, once housed a printing press where US statesman Benjamin Franklin worked. The church *(see p144)* has also featured in films, including *Four Weddings and a Funeral* and *Shakespeare in Love*.

7 Brompton Oratory

MAP C5 ■ Brompton Road SW7
■ Open 6:30am–8pm daily
■ www.bromptonoratory.com

Renowned for its rich musical tradition, this Italianate church was established by a Catholic convert, Henry Newman (1801–90). He introduced to England St Philip's Oratory, a community of Catholic priests and lay brothers founded in 16th-century Rome. The building, by Herbert Gribble, opened in 1884, and houses many Italian treasures.

9 All Saints Margaret Street

MAP J1 ■ 7 Margaret Street W1
■ Open 7am–7pm daily ■ www.allsaintsmargaretstreet.org.uk

Designed by William Butterfield and completed in 1859, this is one of the finest examples of High Victorian Gothic architecture, with a patterned brick exterior and a richly decorated interior of inlaid marble, brightly coloured mosaics and stained glass.

Reredos detail, All Saints Margaret Street

10 St Stephen Walbrook

MAP G3 ■ 39 Walbrook EC4
■ Open 10am–4pm Mon–Fri
■ www.ststephenwalbrook.net

Unspectacular on the outside, the interior of St Stephen Walbrook is the best-preserved and most beautiful of all Wren's churches – it was his own parish church. Designed at the same time as St Paul's Cathedral, the space is dominated by its deep, coffered dome with ornate plasterwork, which is raised above a set of twelve Corinthian columns. A simple, white modern altar by Henry Moore sits in the centre of the church.

Rich interior of Brompton Oratory

TOP10 Museums

Main entrance of the British Museum

1 British Museum

The oldest national public museum in the world, and one of the most fascinating in London, contains treasures and artifacts from far and wide *(see pp12–15)*.

2 Natural History Museum

Life on Earth and the Earth itself are vividly explained here using hundreds of traditional and interactive exhibits *(see pp20–1)*.

3 Science Museum

This exciting museum traces centuries of scientific and techno-logical development, with impressive and educational displays throughout *(see pp22–3)*.

4 Victoria and Albert Museum

One of London's great pleasures, this museum of art and design contains 145 astonishingly eclectic galleries covering many periods and styles. Highlights include the Medieval and Renaissance Galleries, with their remarkable collections, and the rooms full of

Chalice, V&A

Indian and Far Eastern treasures. There are also displays of ornate jewellery, fashion, textiles, metalwork, glass, paintings, prints and sculpture *(see p125)*.

5 Museum of London

This comprehensive museum provides a detailed account of London life from prehistoric times to the present day. It is particularly strong on Roman Londinium, but also has a model of Shakespeare's Rose Theatre, an original 18th-century prison cell with graffiti by its prisoners and a reconstruction of a Victorian street *(see p142)*.

6 National Maritime Museum

Greenwich SE10 ■ **Open 10am– 5pm daily (last adm 4:30pm)** ■ **www.rmg.co.uk**

The world's largest maritime museum, part of the Maritime Greenwich World Heritage Site *(see p153)*, details stories from Britain's seafaring past and the continuing effects of the oceans today. The naval coat worn by Nelson at the Battle of Trafalgar is on display, with a bullet hole on the left shoulder. The tragic polar expeditions of explorers are recalled and a simulator shows what it is like to steer a ship into port.

Spitfire, Imperial War Museum

7 Imperial War Museum

Housed in part of the former Bethlehem ("Bedlam") Hospital for the Insane, some of the larger highlights in the new four-level atrium of this museum include aircraft suspended from the ceiling, armoured vehicles, submarines and missiles, along with hundreds of smaller items across four themed exhibits. The 1,300 objects on display range from weapons, uniforms and equipment to diaries and letters, photographs and art. A highlight is the walk through a "trench" with a Sopwith Camel fighter plane swooping low overhead (see p89).

8 Design Museum

MAP A5 ■ Commonwealth Institute Building, Kensington High Street W8 ■ Check website for opening times ■ Adm ■ www.designmuseum.org

Located in a 1960s architectural landmark, this museum is the only one in Britain devoted solely to 20th- and 21st-century British and international design. The regularly changing exhibitions feature the very best of modern design, including both product and graphic design, fashion, furniture and engineering.

9 London Transport Museum

In this former flower-market building, the history of London's transport system is illustrated with posters, photographs, films and examples of early buses, Tube carriages and horse-drawn vehicles. There is also a Family Station, with activities available for children of all ages (see p106).

Interior of a 1960s Tube carriage, London Transport Museum

10 Sir John Soane's Museum

The former home of Neo-Classical architect John Soane is filled with his collection of paintings, sculptures and ancient artifacts. An Act of Parliament negotiated by Soane preserves the house and collection as he left it, for the benefit of students (see p113).

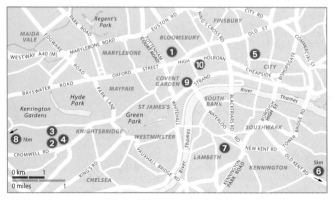

TOP 10 Art Galleries

Tiger in a Tropical Storm (Surprised!) by Rousseau, National Gallery

① The National Gallery and National Portrait Gallery

Located adjacent to each other at the top of Trafalgar Square, these comprehensive galleries make up the core of the UK's art collection (see pp16–19).

② Tate Modern

Housed in a huge converted power station on the south bank of the Thames, this exciting gallery covers modern art from 1900 to the present day (see pp28–9).

③ Tate Britain

The other Tate gallery in London, focusing on work from 1500 to the present, has the best collection of British art in the world (see pp30–1).

④ Dulwich Picture Gallery

If you have time, this suburban gallery is well worth a short train journey. England's oldest public art gallery, it was opened in 1817. The important collection includes Murillo's *Flower Girl*, Poussin's *The Triumph of David* and Rembrandt's *Girl at a Window* (see p154).

⑤ Wallace Collection

This wonderful Victorian mansion belonged to Sir Richard Wallace (1818–90). In 1897, his widow bequeathed the house and their amazing art collection to the nation. Covering two floors, the 25 public rooms are beautifully furnished with one of the best collections of French 18th-century pictures, porcelain and furniture in the world. The paintings are rich and voluptuous – notable works include Nicolas Poussin's *A Dance to the Music of Time* and Frans Hals' *The Laughing Cavalier*. There are English portraits by Gainsborough and Reynolds (see p135).

⑥ Courtauld Gallery

From Fra Angelico to Van Gogh, this is a complete art course in one gallery. The core of the collection is the country's finest Impressionist and Post-Impressionist works, amassed by textile magnate Samuel Courtauld (1876–1947) and other collectors. Many of them are instantly recognisable: Manet's *A Bar at the Folies-Bergère* and *Déjeuner sur l'Herbe*, Van Gogh's *Self-Portrait with Bandaged Ear* and Gauguin's *Te Rerioa*. Visit the Courtauld café or

Van Gogh's Self-Portrait with Bandaged Ear, **Courtauld Gallery**

one of Somerset House's *(see p105)* cafés for a drink afterwards. Tom's Kitchen Terrace is open in spring and summer.

7 Serpentine Galleries

MAP B4 ■ Kensington Gardens W2 ■ Open 10am–6pm Tue–Sun ■ www.serpentine gallery.org

Major contemporary artists tend to be shown in the Serpentine Gallery and the Serpentine Sackler Gallery across the bridge. The former is one of London's most exciting galleries, often transforming its space to suit the work. Installations have been known to spill into the park – even to become an outside tearoom. Busy on warm weekends.

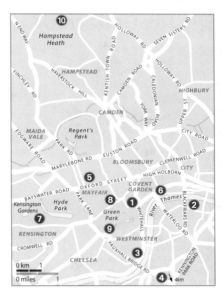

Serpentine Gallery

8 Royal Academy of Arts

The Royal Academy's continual big-name temporary exhibitions draw the crowds, and it is often necessary to reserve a ticket in advance. The traditional Summer Exhibition, which both established and unknown artists can apply to enter, is also extremely popular *(see p119)*.

9 Queen's Gallery, Buckingham Palace

Established in 1962 to display works from the Royal Collection, this fascinating gallery shows paintings and other pieces from the royal collection *(see p24)*.

10 Kenwood House

This majestic mansion with a library designed by Robert Adam has a small but important collection comprising 17th-century Dutch and Flemish works, 18th-century English portraits, and examples of French Rococo. There are statues by Henry Moore and Barbara Hepworth in the landscaped grounds *(see p148)*, which border Hampstead Heath.

Henry Moore piece, Kenwood House

TOP 10 River Sights

Lambeth Palace

Wilde objected to the new-fangled built-in plumbing: he wanted to ring for his hot water like a gentleman. The hotel reopened in 2010 after a multi-million-pound restoration *(see p176)*.

1 Lambeth Palace
MAP F5 ■ Lambeth Palace Road SE1 ■ Open only for occasional tours
The Archbishop of Canterbury's official London residence is a famous riverside landmark. Part of the palace dates from the 13th century, but it is the red-brick Morton's Tower or Gatehouse (1490) that gives the palace a distinctive appearance.

2 Houses of Parliament
See pp36–7.

3 Savoy Hotel
London's first luxury hotel opened in 1889, on the site of the medieval Savoy Palace. Its Chinese lacquered "ascending rooms" were some of the first lifts in Europe. Oscar

4 Millennium Bridge
MAP R3
This stunning, blade-like, steel pedestrian-only suspension bridge links Tate Modern on Bankside with St Paul's Cathedral and the City opposite. It is the first central London river crossing to be built in over 100 years, and makes a delightful and apt approach to Tate Modern.

5 Shakespeare's Globe
This modern reconstruction in oak, thatch and 36,000 handmade bricks is near the site of the original Globe Theatre, which burned down in 1613. The centre of the theatre is uncovered, so performances only happen during part of the year, but an interesting exhibition is open all year round, and there is a café, restaurant and bar with river views *(see p89)*.

6 HMS Belfast
MAP H4 ■ The Queen's Walk SE1 ■ Open Mar–Oct: 10am–6pm daily; Nov–Feb: 10am–5pm daily; closed 24–26 Dec ■ Adm ■ www.iwm.org.uk
The last of the big-gun armoured ships, the nine-deck HMS *Belfast*

Millennium Bridge and St Paul's Cathedral at dusk

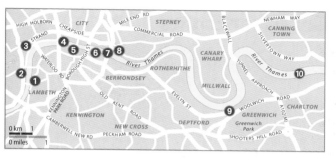

was launched in 1938 and saw active service in World War II and Korea. Retired in 1963, she was opened as a floating naval museum in 1971. Visitors can tour the bridge, the huge engine rooms, the galley and the messdecks, where it is easy to get an idea of what life must have been like on board the ship.

The hull of the *Cutty Sark*

(7) Tower Bridge
London's enduring landmark is a Neo-Gothic wonder. A masterly piece of civil engineering, the bridge was built in 1894 with steam pumps to raise its two halves. Tours of the tower include views from the top and the engine room (*see p141*).

(8) St Katharine Docks
The first piece of modern Docklands development was this handsome dock beside Tower Bridge. Designed by Thomas Telford in 1824, it suffered severe bomb damage during World War II and was refurbished between the 1970s and 1990s. The area is now home to luxury apartments, shops and cafés (*see p142*).

(9) Cutty Sark
King William Walk SE10 ▪ Train to Greenwich; DLR Cutty Sark ▪ Open 10am–5pm daily ▪ Adm ▪ www.rmg.co.uk
Launched in 1869, this is the last of the record-breaking tea-clippers that brought the leaves to thirsty London. The ship was reopened in 2012 by the Queen after a serious fire in 2007. A walk underneath its hull gives a feeling of its might, while its history and life onboard can be explored inside.

(10) Thames Barrier
This huge barrier spanning 520 m (1,700 ft) across the lower reaches of the Thames, just past Greenwich, was built between 1974 and 1982 to prevent dangerous tidal surges from flooding central London. The Information Centre details historical flooding in London. The barrier has been raised over 175 times since it opened (*see p160*).

🔟 Off the Beaten Track

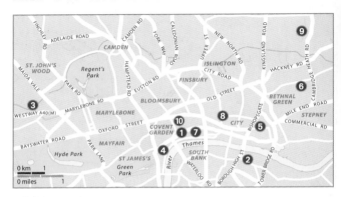

1 St Clement Danes
MAP N3 ■ Strand WC2
■ 020 7242 8282 ■ Open 9am–4pm daily ■ www.raf.mod.uk/stclementdanes

Dating from 1681, this Wren church was bombed in the Blitz of 1941 and rebuilt by the Royal Air Force. Four times daily the bells peal out the tune of "Oranges and Lemons" (see p53). The church sits on an island in the middle of the busy Strand.

2 Old Operating Theatre
MAP K1 ■ 9a St Thomas Street SE1 ■ 020 7188 2679 ■ Open 10:30am–5pm daily ■ Adm ■ www.thegarret.org.uk

This restored operating theatre is a chilling window on 19th-century London. Accessed by a tightly spiralling staircase, it is stocked with intriguing potions and ancient

Old Operating Theatre

remedies. Book ahead for the bloodcurdling Saturday afternoon demonstrations of Victorian surgery.

3 Puppet Theatre Barge
MAP P3 ■ Little Venice W2 ■ 020 7249 6876 ■ www.puppetbarge.com

From late October to July the narrowboats in the canal quarter of Little Venice include the Puppet Theatre Barge, putting on shows for children. It moves to the Thames at Richmond in August and September.

4 Benjamin Franklin House
MAP R2 ■ 36 Craven Street WC2 ■ 020 7925 1405 ■ Historical show noon, 1pm, 2pm, 3:15pm & 4:15pm Wed–Sun; Architectural tour same times Mon ■ Adm ■ www.benjaminfranklinhouse.org

This seemingly modest townhouse was once a hotbed of invention – the great American statesman-scientist lived here from 1759 to 1775, dreaming up the lightning rod and measuring the Gulf Stream. A light and sound show explores his story.

5 Leadenhall Market
MAP J2 ■ Gracechurch Street EC3 ■ Open 10am–6pm Mon–Fri

Leadenhall was once the site of the Roman forum. It still dazzles today, a

Leadenhall Market

warren of cobbled arcades encased in fancy ironwork. Gourmet butchers and cheesemongers vie with slick brasseries and bars for patrons.

6 E Pellici
MAP P1 ■ 332 Bethnal Green Road E2 ■ 020 7739 4873 ■ Open 7am–4pm Mon–Sat

Lauded as the grandest of all the East End's traditional "greasy spoon" cafés, E Pellici has been run by the same Italian family for a century. The breakfasts are legendary.

7 Temple
MAP P3

This legal district, named after the Knights Templar, is near bustling Covent Garden, but feels a world away: a riverside "village" of alley-ways and churches. It's a beguiling spot to escape the West End crowds.

8 Postman's Park
MAP R2 ■ St Martin's Le-Grand EC1 ■ Open 8am–7pm (or dusk if earlier)

The name of this picnic-friendly spot derives from its use by workers from the Post Office nearby. It houses the George Frederic Watts Memorial, honouring people who sacrificed their lives saving others'. Each is remembered on a hand-painted tile.

9 London Fields
MAP R1 ■ London Fields Westside E8 ■ 020 8356 3000 ■ Opening times vary ■ hackney.gov. uk/cp-londonfields.htm

Near Hackney Town Hall lies London Fields Lido, an Olympic-size heated outdoor pool. The park offers tennis courts, a summertime wildflower meadow and a paddling pool. Nearby Hackney Museum explores the area's rich cultural influences.

10 Hunterian Museum
MAP Q2 ■ 35–43 Lincoln's Inn Fields WC2 ■ 020 7869 6560 ■ Open 10am–5pm Tue–Sat ■ www. hunterianmuseum.org

Supplied by bodysnatchers who raided London's graveyards, John Hunter (1728–93) was a pioneer of modern surgery. This free museum is surprisingly beautiful, its cut-glass receptacles floating with botanical and biological samples.

The picnic-friendly Postman's Park

ᴛᴏᴘ10 Children's London

Sumatran tiger, Tiger Territory, London Zoo

① Science Museum
See pp22–3.

② Natural History Museum
See pp20–1.

③ Madame Tussauds
One of London's most popular attractions, this is where you can see everyone from Posh and Becks **(below)** to the Queen. A Spirit of London ride takes you on a whistle-stop tour of the

city's history. The famous Chamber of Horrors puts you face-to-face with London's most infamous criminals and has the very guillotine that beheaded Queen Marie Antoinette in the French Revolution. The Star Wars Experience presents heroes and villains, such as Darth Vader, Princess Leia and Yoda. Book online in advance to avoid the long queues *(see p135).*

④ London Zoo
There's a full day out to be had in this 15-ha (36-acre) zoo. Home of the Zoological Society of London, the zoo emphasizes its important international role in conservation and research work. Kids will enjoy coming face to face with free-roaming monkeys in the Rainforest Life enclosure, crawling into an aardvark's burrow and meeting the birds on Penguin Beach. *[See p135].*

⑤ London Sea Life Aquarium
Located on London's South Bank, the aquarium is home to thousands of marine creatures. A journey through 14 different zones shows them in all their glory. Crocodiles, green turtles and zebra sharks are among the sea life to be seen here. For some interactive fun, visit the rock pools to touch crabs and starfish, with marine experts on hand *(see p90).*

Shark tank, London Sea Life Aquarium

6 Diana Memorial Playground

MAP A4 ▪ Kensington Gardens W2
▪ Open 10am–dusk daily
▪ www.royalparks.org.uk

With its pirate galleon inspired by Peter Pan, the Diana Memorial Playground is the perfect place for imaginations to run wild.

7 V&A Museum of Childhood

This East End museum has one of the world's largest toy collections, including dolls, teddies, games and children's clothes (see p160).

8 Coram's Fields

MAP F2 ▪ 93 Guilford Street WC1 ▪ Open daily ▪ www. coramsfields.org

No adults admitted without a child, says the sign on the gate to this large park for children and teenagers. There's a paddling pool, play areas and a city farm with a pets corner and grazing farm animals.

9 Battersea Park

MAP D6 ▪ Albert Bridge Road SW11 ▪ Zoo: Open 10am–5:30pm Easter–Oct, until 4:30pm (or dusk) in winter, Adm, www.batterseaparkzoo. co.uk ▪ www.batterseapark.org

This large south London park (see p156) is ideal for children, with an adventure playground, a boating lake and recumbent bikes available to rent on summer weekends. It is also home to a children's zoo, with meerkats, chinchillas, pigs and emus, amongst others. At weekends children are allowed to help feed some of the animals.

Torture chamber, London Dungeon

10 London Dungeon

MAP N6 ▪ County Hall, Westminster Bridge Road SE1
▪ Opening times vary; check the website for details ▪ Adm
▪ www.thedungeons.com

The scariest experience in town combines history and horror to celebrate an "orgy of grisly entertainment", with death, violence and gore at every turn. Follow in the bloody footsteps of the Victorian serial killer Jack the Ripper, bear witness to the Guy Fawkes Conspirators show or be condemned by Henry VIII on the fast-flowing Tyrant Boat Ride. Be warned that it's not for the very young or faint-hearted.

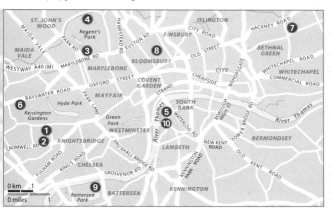

🔟 Performing Arts Venues

Performer at the Royal Opera House

1 Royal Opera House

One of the greatest opera houses in the world, this theatre is home to the Royal Ballet company, and hosts international opera productions. Apart from the sumptuous main auditorium, there are the smaller Linbury and Clore studios, which have music and dance. There are regular backstage tours and occasional big-screen live outdoor simulcasts of productions *(see p105)*.

2 National Theatre

MAP N4 ■ South Bank SE1
■ 020 7452 3000 ■ www.
nationaltheatre.org.uk

Seeing a play here takes you to the heart of London's cultural life. Within the concrete blocks of this innovative building, designed by Denys Lasdun and opened in 1976, you can see a musical, a classic or a new play in one of its three theatres: the Olivier, the Lyttelton or the Cottesloe. Check for free shows and exhibitions in the foyer. Reduced price tickets are sold from 9:30am on the day of the performance.

3 Barbican Centre

Home of one of the best music companies in the world – the London Symphony Orchestra – the Barbican is the City's most important arts complex. Theatre, cinema, concerts, dance and exhibitions can all be seen here, and there are plenty of restaurants, cafés and bars to be enjoyed. The centre also contains a library and convention hall. The Guildhall School of Music and Drama is located nearby *(see p141)*.

4 London Coliseum

MAP L3 ■ St Martin's Lane WC2
■ 020 7845 9300 ■ www.eno.org

London's other principal opera house stages innovative productions sung in English by the English National Opera. Opened in 1904, it was restored to its Edwardian decor in 2004.

London Coliseum

5 Southbank Centre

MAP N4 ■ South Bank SE1
■ 020 7960 4200 ■ www.south
bankcentre.co.uk

The centre contains three concert venues – the Royal Festival Hall, Queen Elizabeth Hall and the Purcell Room – and the Hayward Gallery, Poetry Library, shops and restaurants. It hosts a range of events *(see p88)*.

Exterior of the National Theatre

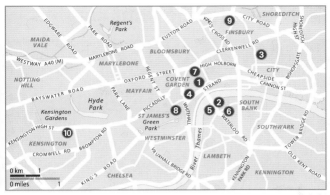

Dancer at Sadler's Wells

6 Old Vic
MAP P5 ▪ The Cut SE1 ▪ 0844 871 7628 ▪ www.oldvictheatre.com

Famed for its associations with Laurence Olivier and other great British actors, this historic theatre gained new verve under Hollywood actor Kevin Spacey, who was artistic director between 2004 and 2015. The adventurous productions include revivals of neglected classics.

7 Donmar Warehouse
MAP P5 ▪ 41 Earlham Street WC2 ▪ 0844 871 7624 ▪ www.donmarwarehouse.com

A little powerhouse, the intimate Donmar has created some of the most dynamic productions in London in recent years, which have gone on to play in larger theatres and be acclaimed worldwide. Such is its reputation that productions often feature star actors such as Tom Hiddleston and Sinéad Cusack.

8 ICA
MAP K5 ▪ The Mall SW1 ▪ 020 7930 3647 ▪ www.ica.org.uk

A stately, colonnaded terrace by John Nash houses London's hippest gallery, the Institute of Contemporary Arts. The ICA's cutting-edge policy on the visual arts includes developing challenging new digital works. Their arts and culture programme also includes exhibitions, films, events, talks and debates.

9 Sadler's Wells

After winning a reputation as the best dance theatre in London in the 1950s, Sadler's Wells now also hosts music and opera. The stunning building prides itself on its community events as well as its international dance shows *(see p150)*.

10 Royal Albert Hall

This distinctive, circular building, designed to resemble a Roman amphitheatre, has a delicate terracotta frieze around the exterior. The electric atmosphere inside make it a premier venue for every kind of concert, including the eight-week "Proms" season *(see p126)*.

Live Music Venues

KOKO venue in Camden

1 Ronnie Scott's
MAP K2

This legendary London jazz club was opened by saxophonist Ronnie Scott (1929–96) in Gerrard Street in 1959. It moved to this location in Soho in 1965. Intimate lamplit tables surround a tiny stage that has hosted such stars as Ella Fitzgerald and Dizzy Gillespie, and continues to attract top names *(see p99)*.

2 100 Club
MAP K2 ■ 100 Oxford Street W1 ■ 020 7636 0933 ■ www.the100 club.co.uk

Atmospheric jazz, blues, rock and pop dive, open till 2am. Its heritage is legendary – the Rolling Stones played here, as did the Sex Pistols and other punk bands of the '70s. Today it also hosts indie groups.

3 The Jazz Café
MAP D1 ■ 5 Parkway NW1 ■ 020 7485 6834 ■ www.thejazzcafe london.com

Top jazz and soul performers, as well as great food, make this a popular venue. The best views are to be had from the balcony tables.

4 O2 Forum
9–17 Highgate Road NW5 ■ Tube Kentish Town ■ 0844 847 2405 ■ www.o2forumkentishtown.co.uk

Originally an Art Deco cinema, this 2,300-capacity music venue in the heart of Kentish Town plays host to big-name acts, with past performers including the Velvet Underground.

5 O2 Academy, Brixton
211 Stockwell Road SW9 ■ Tube Brixton ■ 0844 477 2000 ■ www.academymusicgroup.com/ o2academybrixton

This is a great place to see acts from across the music spectrum. It holds nearly 5,000 but the hall manages to retain an intimate atmosphere with good views of the performers from across the auditorium.

6 KOKO
MAP D1 ■ 1a Camden High Street NW1 ■ 020 7388 3222 ■ www.koko.uk.com

Hosting mainly indie gigs as well as big names such as Prince and Madonna, KOKO is also home to well-known club nights such as the famous "pop" fest, Guilty Pleasures.

7 Eventim Apollo, Hammersmith

5 Queen Caroline Street W6 ■ Tube Hammersmith ■ 020 8563 3800 ■ www.eventimapollo.com

This giant former cinema remains ever-popular and has hosted many of the city's most memorable gigs.

8 The Borderline

MAP L2 ■ Orange Yard, off Manette Street W1 ■ 020 7734 5547 ■ www.theborderlinelondon.com

One of London's best small clubs, Borderline has hosted many international bands. There's at least one band, ranging from country to metal music, every weekday evening.

9 The O2

Peninsula Square, North Greenwich SE10 ■ Tube North Greenwich ■ 0844 856 0202 ■ www.theo2.co.uk

The ill-fated Millennium Dome has been transformed into the O2 arena, hosting the biggest names around. The 2,350-capacity indigo at The O2 is more intimate. Arriving via the Thames Clipper or Emirates Air Line is all part of the fun.

The O2 arena in Greenwich

10 Troubadour Coffee House

MAP A6 ■ 263–7 Old Brompton Road SW5 ■ 020 7341 6333 ■ www.troubadourlondon.com

A coffee house club devoted to live music. All the great 1960s folk singers played here, and today there is a relaxed feel to the evenings of singing, poetry and comedy.

TOP 10 NIGHTCLUBS

Revellers at Heaven nightclub

1 Fabric
MAP Q1 ■ 77a Charterhouse Street EC1
London's best dance venue has three rooms and a 24-hour music licence.

2 333 Mother Bar
MAP H2 ■ 333 Old Street, Hoxton EC1
This three-storey club heaves to drum 'n' bass, hip hop and soul, with live music in the basement.

3 Volupté
7–9 Norwich Street EC4 ■ Tube Chancery Lane
This burlesque club has top cabaret.

4 93 Feet East
MAP H2 ■ 150 Brick Lane E1
Live music and club nights.

5 Cargo
MAP H2 ■ 83 Rivington Street EC2
One of the best places in the capital to hear cutting-edge music.

6 XOYO
MAP H2 ■ 32–37 Cowper St EC2
Two floors with sounds ranging from hip hop to techno and disco with popular weekend residencies.

7 Brixton Jamm
261 Brixton Road SW9 ■ Tube Brixton
The South London venue for indie rock, plus electronic, trance and beats.

8 Ministry of Sound
MAP K3 ■ 103 Gaunt Street SE1
Founded in 1991, this is still one of the best nightclubs in the city.

9 Heaven
MAP M4 ■ Villiers Street WC2
London's best-known gay venue has several bars and dance floors beneath Charing Cross station.

10 Egg London
MAP E1 ■ 200 York Way N7
Hip, multi-level club with three different themed house and techno rooms and cutting-edge DJs.

🔟 Best Places to Eat

1 Anchor & Hope
MAP Q5 ■ 36 The Cut SE1
■ 020 7928 9898 ■ ££

No reservations are taken during the week at this always-bustling gastropub, next to the Young Vic theatre, but it's worth the wait for the superior English fare, such as hare ragout and gourmet sausages. Sunday lunch is hugely popular, so book well in advance.

2 Clarke's
A steady favourite since it opened in 1984, this restaurant serves wonderfully fresh Mediterranean food, with roast and baked dishes to the fore. Sally's Set no-choice menus are the focal point, but there is also a daily changing selection of à la carte dishes. There's a well chosen wine list *(see p131)*.

3 Rasa W1
MAP Q5 ■ 6 Dering Street W1
■ 020 7629 1346 ■ ££

Indian curries are almost a national dish in Britain, but this is quite different from the norm. Exquisite dishes from the Kerala region of southern India, including delicious fish and vegetarian curries. A cookbook on display helps explain dishes you have never heard of.

4 Rules
London's oldest restaurant (open since 1798) is like a Victorian time capsule. The walls above the velvet seats are covered in hunting trophies and portraits of forgotten figures. Game is a speciality, and this is also the place to go for classic English roast beef *(see p111)*.

5 L'Atelier de Joël Robuchon
Michelin-starred Robuchon brings his unbeatable gourmet dining experience to London. Black truffles, lobster and quail are among the ingredients you can expect to find here. Extravagant 5- and 8-course tasting menus are also available for vegetarians. The bar and roof terrace are chic places for a drink *(see p111)*.

6 Hakkasan
Alan Yau, the man behind the highly successful Wagamama chain, founded this seriously stylish dining experience. Michelin-starred Cantonese-style food, such as sautéed sweet ginger and pineapple roasted duck, with dim sum specialities, is served in the luxurious surroundings designed by Christian Liaigre. The cocktails are also sublime *(see p117)*.

Rules, London's oldest restaurant

7 The Ledbury

Australian chef Brett Graham is brilliant – in only a short time his Notting Hill restaurant has won two Michelin stars. Set menus are good value and there's also an outstanding 8-course tasting menu *(see p131)*.

8 The Wolseley

Although it only opened in 2003, the Wolseley has the feel of a 19th-century grand café-brasserie, and Londoners have taken to it as if it has been there forever. It's open from breakfast to dinner, serving finely prepared classic European dishes, and its giant windows offer a great view of Piccadilly *(see p123)*.

The elegant interior of The Wolseley

9 Barrafina

One of the coolest tapas bars around, using top-quality ingredients to excellent effect. Sit at the bar with a small Cruzcampo and watch the experts at work *(see p101)*. There's also a Covent Garden branch.

10 St John

A great restaurant near Smithfield meat market, in a converted smokehouse, the focus is on nose-to-tail eating. It serves a delicious range of high-quality British cooking, as well as having its own bakery. Try the amazing Eccles cakes with Lancashire cheese. The bar-menu snacks are not expensive *(see p145)*.

TOP 10 PLACES TO EAT WITH A VIEW

Galvin at Windows

1 Oxo Tower
Terrific river views from this South Bank landmark *(see p93)*.

2 Hutong
MAP H3 ▪ The Shard, 31 St Thomas Street SE1 ▪ 020 3011 1257
On level 33 of the Shard, with great views of the skyline. The speciality is Sichuan and northern Chinese food.

3 Le Pont de la Tour
MAP H4 ▪ 36D Shad Thames SE1 ▪ 020 7403 8403
Modern French cuisine with a view over iconic Tower Bridge.

4 Tate Modern Restaurant
MAP R4 ▪ Bankside SE1 ▪ 020 7887 8888
Panoramic river views and great food.

5 Portrait Restaurant
MAP L4 ▪ National Portrait Gallery, St Martin's Place WC2 ▪ 020 7312 2490
Views over Trafalgar Square and Whitehall from this rooftop restaurant.

6 Blueprint Café
MAP H4 ▪ 27 Shad Thames SE1 ▪ 020 7378 7031
A spectacular view of London Bridge.

7 Skylon
MAP N4 ▪ Royal Festival Hall SE1 ▪ 020 7654 7800
One of the finest river views in town.

8 Swan at the Globe
MAP G4 ▪ New Globe Walk SE1 ▪ 020 7928 9444
Look over to the City through mullioned windows.

9 Galvin at Windows
MAP D4 ▪ 22 Park Lane W1 ▪ 020 7208 4021
Sumptuous cuisine, views of Hyde Park.

10 Coq d'Argent
MAP G3 ▪ 1 Poultry EC2 ▪ 020 7395 5000
Unparalleled views from this rooftop garden bar and French restaurant.

For a key to restaurant price ranges see p93

🔟 Pubs

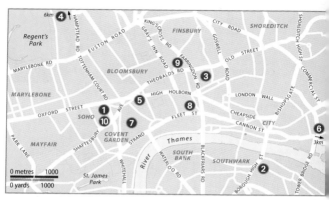

1 The Dog and Duck
MAP L2 ▪ 18 Bateman St W1

This tiled Victorian pub is like a cosy front room in Soho. It has a tiny bar, where you might bump into art students and designers, and a blackboard with the latest selection of beers from all corners of England.

2 George Inn
Dating back to 1676 in parts, this is the only galleried coaching inn left in London, and was given to the National Trust in the 1930s. You can enjoy excellent beers in its myriad old rooms, with lattice windows and wooden beams, or in the large courtyard *(see p92)*.

The galleries of the George Inn

3 Jerusalem Tavern
MAP G2 ▪ 55 Britton Street EC1

A delightful little pub with booths, a small bar and little more than the 18th-century coffee shop it once was. It serves the full range of St Peter's in Suffolk. Light meals are also served at lunchtime, but note that the pub is closed at the weekend.

4 Spaniards Inn
This lovely 16th-century pub on the northern edge of Hampstead Heath, with a large, attractive beer garden, is steeped in history and romance: the notorious 18th-century highwayman Dick Turpin is said to have drank here, along with literary luminaries Keats, Shelley and Byron and artist Sir Joshua Reynolds. Although the bar downstairs has been altered frequently over the decades, the small upstairs Turpin Bar is original *(see p151)*.

5 Princess Louise
MAP M1 ▪ 208 High Holborn WC1

The Princess Louise is a beautiful 19th-century pub with stained-glass windows, nooks and alcoves. An unexpected bonus is the reasonably priced Sam Smiths beer, as well as the hearty and delicious pies and puddings that are served here.

The Lamb and Flag, Covent Garden

7 The Lamb and Flag

This old-world pub tucked up an alley looks much as it did in Charles Dickens' day. In the heart of Covent Garden, it can get crowded – during the summer drinkers spill outside into the quiet alley. The 17th-century poet John Dryden was severely beaten up outside this pub, which was known as The Bucket of Blood because of the bareknuckle fights held here (see p110).

8 Ye Olde Cheshire Cheese

MAP Q2 ■ 145 Fleet Street EC4

In an alley off Fleet Street, this warren of rooms still seems as if it should have sawdust scattered on the floors. Rebuilt in 1667, after the Great Fire of London, it was a favourite of Dr Johnson (see p52) and other writers. Never too crowded, its intimate corners make a good meeting place, made cosier with fires in winter.

Pub sign

6 The Grapes

76 Narrow Street E14

■ DLR Westferry

This classic East End pub has stood here since 1583 – although much of the current building dates from the 1720s – and it features in Charles Dickens' *Our Mutual Friend*. It is now owned by a group that includes actor Sir Ian McKellen, which seeks to maintain all its traditional charm, but which has added a very comfortable, high-quality restaurant on the first floor.

Entrance to The Grapes pub

9 The Eagle

159 Farringdon Road EC1

■ Tube Farringdon ■ No bookings

This bustling Victorian pub is often credited with inventing the "gastropub" concept of serving quality modern cooking in a pub setting. Some gastropubs have become increasingly refined, but the Eagle retains its battered tables and easy-going style.

10 French House

MAP L3 ■ 49 Dean Street W1

This was once a meeting place for the French Resistance during World War II – hence the name. Gaining a reputation as a bohemian bolthole, it was also frequented by artists and poets such as Francis Bacon, Brendan Behan and Dylan Thomas. It is now well known for its refreshing Breton cider and fine wines.

TOP 10 Shops and Markets

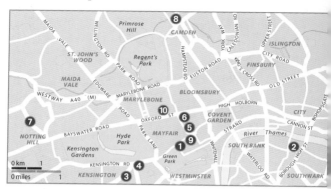

1 Fortnum & Mason

London's most elegant store has hardly noticed the arrival of the 21st century. The ground-floor food hall is famous for its traditional English produce, and lavish picnic hampers can be found, along with a selection of fine wines, in the basement. The upper floors are good for designer men's and women's fashion and stylish gifts (see p122).

2 Borough Market

Nestled alongside Southwark Cathedral, London's oldest food market is also one of its most atmospheric. It currently boasts over a hundred stalls selling high-quality produce from all across the country, as well as exceptional international specialities and snacks (see p91).

Artisan bread, Borough Market

3 Harrods

London's most famous and exclusive department store is more of an event than a shop. Covering seven floors, it is full of extraordinary things to buy – from pianos to children's racing cars – all with equally extraordinary prices. The children's toy department is excellent, and the store's food hall is rightly famous, with bars selling upmarket ice cream, pizzas and countless other treats (see p129).

4 Harvey Nichols

Almost a parody of itself, "Harvey Nicks" is where the glamorous shop. There are wall-to-wall designer labels, an extravagant perfume and beauty department and stylish homeware. The fifth floor is for consuming, with a food hall, sushi bar and the to-be-seen-in Fifth Floor restaurant (see p129).

5 Hamleys

The seven storeys of London's largest toyshop contain just about anything a child might want, from traditional puppets and games to giant stuffed toys, models, arts and crafts supplies and all the latest

Hamleys toyshop on Regent Street

7 Portobello Road

West London's liveliest street sells a mixture of antiques and bric-à-brac. As it heads north, there are food stalls, crafts, clothes and music. Shops and some stalls open daily but the main antiques market is held every Saturday (see p126).

8 Camden Market

A great place to spend a Saturday, this rambling market around Camden Lock takes in several streets and buildings. Street fashion, world crafts... it's as if the 1960s never ended. Do note that Sundays are a crush (see p147).

9 Waterstones Piccadilly

MAP K4 ■ 203–206 Piccadilly

In a magnificent Art Deco listed building, this enormous bookshop has six floors and over 13 km (8 miles) of shelving stocked with books. There are also cafés and even a cocktail bar on the fifth floor.

10 John Lewis

This store has a large and loyal clientele, with departments ranging from kitchenware and haberdashery through furniture, fashion and fabrics to electrical goods and toys. Staff are informed, prices are excellent and the quality is guaranteed (see p138).

electronic gadgets. Of course, there are also many delights here for adults who haven't let go of their childhood (see p98).

6 Liberty

This handsome, half-timbered building dates from 1925 and its fine wood-floored and panelled interior is part of the shopping experience. Long associated with the Arts and Crafts movement, it employed designers such as William Morris to create its fabrics. Great for its own Liberty floral fabrics, home furnishings, men's and women's fashions (see p98).

The handsome interior of Liberty department store

TOP 10 London for Free

1 Changing the Guard
MAP L4 ■ Horse Guards Parade, Whitehall SW1A

The Changing the Guard is world-famous, but it can be tricky to get a good view at Buckingham Palace. Things are more civilized at Horse Guards Parade, where guardsmen arrive on horseback at 11am (10am on Sundays) for the mounted changeover ceremony.

2 Museums and Art Galleries
Many of London's art galleries and museums are free, and it's easy to while away a whole day at Tate Modern (see pp28–9), the British Museum (see pp12–15) or the Natural History Museum (see pp20–21). Less well known is the Royal Institution (see p121), whose Faraday Museum covers the history of scientific endeavour since 1799, ranging from an 1850s magnetic laboratory to a modern nanotechnology one.

3 Walking Tours
07889 259312 ■
www.freelondonwalkingtours.com

Free London Walking Tours offers daily 2-hour strolls around the city. There are several to choose from: Royal London (timed to include the Changing the Guard), Secret London and "Ghostly Haunts". There is no upfront charge, but guides are only paid by tip, so do leave one.

Pageantry at Horse Guards Parade

4 Opera Recitals
Emerging stars of the Royal Opera House perform for free most Monday lunchtimes, when there is a recital in the Crush Room, but it's important to book. Tickets are released nine days ahead, and on the day, from 10am (see p105).

5 Roman London
Not much remains of Roman London, but one surprising remnant can be visited for free at the Guildhall Art Gallery, where the ruins of the city's 2,000-year-old colosseum lurk in a dark basement. Built in c.74 AD and capable of holding more than 6,000 spectators, the amphitheatre would have featured animal hunts, executions and gladitorial combat. Spotlights and sound effects bring the arena to life (see p142).

6 View from Oxo Tower Wharf
Views from the London Eye and the Shard are rightly celebrated, but both are expensive. Instead, take the lift to the top of the Oxo Tower Wharf. The viewing platform over the city skyline is free and the views up and down the river are magnificent (see p90).

Faraday Museum

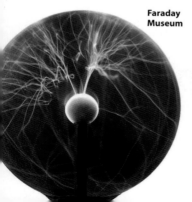

7 Nature Watch at St James's Park

www.royalparks.org.uk
Like all the royal parks, St James's is full of free entertainment, but the show-stealers are its pelicans. In 1664, the first pelicans arrived as a gift from the Russian ambassador. The birds are fed daily at 2:30pm near Duck Island *(see p119)*.

8 Parliamentary Debates

MAP M6 ▪ Palace of Westminster, St Margaret Street SW1A ▪ 020 7219 4272 ▪ www.parliament.uk
You can view debates for free by queuing on Cromwell Green – see the website for times. There are free guided tours of the Palace of Westminster for UK citizens who book ahead by applying to their MP.

Westminster Abbey

9 Divine Music

Westminster Abbey *(see pp34–5)* and St Paul's Cathedral *(see pp42–5)* are must-visits for many, but the admission fees are steep. Visit for free by attending evensong, and experience London's greatest churches the way they were intended – as places for worship and reflection.

10 Stand-up Comedy

MAP M1 ▪ Camden Head, 2 Camden Walk, Islington N1 ▪ 020 7359 0851 ▪ www.angelcomedy.co.uk
Check out the stars of tomorrow at one of London's free comedy clubs. Angel Comedy at the Camden Head pub runs nightly, with a mix of open-mic sessions and established acts.

TOP 10 MONEY-SAVING TIPS

Music at the Southbank Centre

1 For cheap rooms in London, investigate universities (which rent rooms from June to September) and youth hostels. www.lhalondon.com

2 Even if visiting just for a few days, it's worth getting an Oyster card, making bus and underground travel cheaper. oyster.tfl.gov.uk

3 Chinese and Indian restaurants are an affordable dining option, even in central London. Set menus and buffets often offer good value too.

4 Some museums are free and others have free late-afternoon or evening opening. The London Pass gives access to more than 60 major sights. www.londonpass.com

5 There is street entertainment all day at Covent Garden. Leicester Square and the South Bank are also good spots.

6 Look out for free concerts in churches *(see pp58–9)*, and at various locations in the Southbank Centre.

7 Cheap theatre tickets (for the same day only) are available at TKTS, a booth on the south side of Leicester Square.

8 You can get standby tickets for knock-down prices at the Royal Opera House, the National Theatre and the Royal Albert Hall.

9 Santander Cycles is a cheap way to get around the city. Bikes can be hired from as little as £2 – just bring your bank card go to any docking station. www.tfl.gov.uk

10 London's parks offer lots of free entertainment, from exhibitions to bandstand concerts. www.royalparks.org.uk

Festivals and Events

① Notting Hill Carnival
MAP A3 ■ **Notting Hill W11**
■ **Last Sat–Mon in Aug**

This three-day Caribbean festival is Europe's largest carnival, with steel bands and DJs playing everything from calypso to house music, street food, brilliant costumes and lively dancers. Children's parade on Sunday, main parade on Monday.

② RHS Chelsea Flower Show
MAP C6 ■ **Chelsea Royal Hospital SW1** ■ **May** ■ **Adm**

As much a society outing as a horticultural event, this is the Royal Horticultural Society's prestigious annual show. Beautiful and imaginative gardens are created especially for the five-day event.

③ Trooping the Colour
MAP L5 ■ **Horse Guards Parade SW1** ■ **Sat in Jun**

The Queen celebrates her official birthday on Horse Guards Parade where troops of the Household Division, in their famous red tunics and bearskin hats, put on an

Vibrant costume, Notting Hill Carnival

immaculate display of marching and drilling before escorting her to Buckingham Palace.

④ BBC Proms
MAP B5 ■ **Royal Albert Hall SW1** ■ **Mid-Jul–mid-Sep**

This is the most extensive concert series in the world. The famous last concert is relayed live to adjacent Hyde Park, when *Land of Hope and Glory* rocks the Royal Albert Hall *(see p126)* to its foundations.

⑤ Royal Academy Summer Exhibition
MAP J4 ■ **Piccadilly W1** ■ **Jun–Aug** ■ **Adm**

Around 1,100 works are selected from the public as well as Academicians for the art world's most eclectic summer show. Works sell for as little as £100.

⑥ Lord Mayor's Show
MAP R2 (Guildhall) ■ **City of London** ■ **2nd Sat in Nov**

Every year, the City of London elects a Lord Mayor who processes through the Square Mile in a gilded coach. Military bands, floats and city guildsmen in traditional costume go from Guildhall to the Law Courts. There are fireworks in the evening.

Royal Academy Summer Exhibition

7 Guy Fawkes Night
5 Nov

Effigies of Guy Fawkes, who attempted to blow up Parliament in 1605, are burned on bonfires across the country, with accompanying firework extravaganzas. Traditionally children made dummy Guys and asked passers-by for pennies to pay for their little arsenals.

8 Chinese New Year
MAP L3 ■ Soho W1
■ Late Jan–early Feb

Chinatown (see p95) is taken over by dancing dragons breathing fire during this colourful festival. Food and craft stalls are authentically oriental.

Fish Figurine, Chinese New Year

9 BFI London Film Festival
West End ■ Oct–Nov
■ www.bfi.org.uk

Hundreds of international films are shown across cinemas, including the National Film Theatre, during this two-week festival. A booth is set up in Leicester Square to take bookings and distribute festival programmes.

10 Meltdown Festival
Southbank Centre, Belvedere Road SE1 ■ Jun ■ Adm for events

The special attraction of this festival of the arts is that each year it is curated by a different guest director. Past curators include David Bowie, Patti Smith, Yoko Ono and David Byrne.

TOP 10 SPORTS EVENTS

Test match at the Kia Oval

1 The Wimbledon Championships
All England Lawn Tennis and Croquet Club, Wimbledon ■ Jun/Jul
The world's top grass-court tennis championships.

2 The London Marathon
Apr
42-km (26.2-mile) road race from Greenwich Park to The Mall.

3 The Derby
Epsom Downs ■ Jun
This is the historic highlight of the English flat horse racing season.

4 Oxford and Cambridge Boat Race
Putney to Mortlake ■ Mar or Apr
The two universities' annual race covers some 6.5 km (4 miles).

5 The London International Horse Show
Olympia W8 ■ Dec
Family fun at this Christmas show.

6 Rugby League Challenge Cup
Wembley Stadium ■ Aug
The north of England comes to London for this bone-crunching final.

7 FA Cup Final
Wembley Stadium ■ May
The last match of the Football Association Cup.

8 The Six Nations
Twickenham Stadium ■ Feb/Mar/Apr
Rugby contest with England, France, Ireland, Italy, Scotland and Wales.

9 Royal Ascot
Ascot, Berkshire ■ Jun
All London Society goes to the races in stylish hats and glamorous clothes.

10 Test Matches
Lord's and the Kia Oval cricket grounds ■ May–Sep
Top-flight international cricket matches, with games lasting up to five days.

London
Area by Area

The City at dusk

🔟 Westminster, the South Bank and Southwark

Big Ben

Here there is a rich mix of things to do. Sights range from Westminster Abbey and the Houses of Parliament to the Tate's stunning art institutions, the Southbank Centre and Shakespeare's Globe. In between there's the *Golden Hinde II*, the fascinating Imperial War Museum, the spectacular London Eye and other entertainments around County Hall, former headquarters of the Greater London Council. Two footbridges – one at Hungerford Bridge, the other at Tate Modern – help to bring the two sides of the river together.

AREA MAP OF WESTMINSTER, THE SOUTH BANK AND SOUTHWARK

1 Westminster Abbey
London's most venerable and most beautiful church is the scene of coronations and royal weddings and the final resting place of monarchs (see pp34–5).

2 Tate Modern
One of the world's great contemporary art galleries. A boat service connects Tate Britain and Tate Modern, leaving from Bankside Pier outside Tate Modern every 40 minutes (see pp28–9).

3 London Eye
The world's tallest cantilevered observational wheel offers amazing views of the city. Close by, and worth a visit, are the attractions in County Hall – the Sea Life London Aquarium, London Dungeon and Shrek's Adventure (see pp26–7 and p90).

South façade of Westminster Abbey

4 Houses of Parliament
The ancient Palace of Westminster is the seat of the two Houses of Parliament – the Lords and the Commons. A Union flag flies on the Victoria Tower, replaced by the royal standard when the Queen is present. Night sittings are indicated by a light on the Elizabeth Tower – the tower that houses Big Ben, the 14-tonne bell whose hourly chimes are recognized the world over (see pp36–7).

5 Tate Britain
The best of British art is held at the Tate, with works ranging from 1500 to the present (see pp30–31). Look downstream to see the home of UK Foreign Intelligence (MI6). This white and green tiered building overlooking the Thames is built inside a bug-proof "Faraday cage".

Tate Britain

6 Downing Street
MAP L5 ■ Downing Street
SW1 ■ Closed to public

The official home and office of the UK's Prime Minister is one of four surviving houses built in the 1680s for Sir George Downing (1623–84) who went to America as a boy and returned to fight for the Parliamentarians in the English Civil War. The building contains a State Dining Room and the Cabinet Room, where a group of senior government ministers meets regularly to formulate policy. Next door, No. 11, is the traditional residence of the Chancellor of the Exchequer and at No. 12 is the Whips' Office. Downing Street has been closed to the public for security reasons since 1989.

WHITEHALL AND HORSE GUARDS

The wide street connecting Parliament Square and Trafalgar Square is named after the Palace of Whitehall, the main residence of the Tudor monarchs. The palace was guarded on the north side at what is now Horse Guards, where the guard (**below**) is still mounted daily at 11am (10am on Sundays), with a dismounting inspection at 4pm.

7 Churchill War Rooms
MAP L6 ■ Clive Steps, King
Charles Street SW1 ■ Open
9:30am–6pm daily ■ Adm
■ www.iwm.org.uk

During World War II, Winston Churchill and his War Cabinet met in these War Rooms beneath the Government Treasury Chambers. They remain just as they were left in 1945, with spartan rooms and colour-coded phones. Take a guided audio tour through the rooms where ministers plotted the course of the war, or visit the Churchill Museum which records Churchill's life and career.

8 Southbank Centre
MAP N4 ■ South Bank SE1
■ www.southbankcentre.co.uk

The most accessible arts centre in London still has the air of friendly, egalitarian optimism that brought it into life in the 1950s and 60s. The Royal Festival Hall and the Queen Elizabeth Hall have diverse programmes, while the Hayward Gallery is a major venue for both classical and contemporary art exhibitions. The BFI Southbank, run by the British Film Institute, has a varied programme of films. The

Map Room at the Churchill War Rooms

Shakespeare's Globe

National Theatre's three stages (Olivier, Dorfman and Lyttelton) are to the east along the river (see p70).

9 Shakespeare's Globe
MAP R4 ▪ 21 New Globe Walk, Bankside SE1 ▪ Bookings (plays Apr–Oct only): 020 7401 9919 ▪ Exhibition: 9am–5:30pm daily; theatre tour: 9:30am–5pm daily ▪ Adm ▪ www.shakespearesglobe.com

To see a Shakespeare play at the reconstructed Globe is a magical experience. The theatre is open to the skies, with seating in three tiers around the sides and standing in the central courtyard. A second, adjacent indoor venue, the candlelit Sam Wanamaker Playhouse, based on designs of early 17th-century indoor playhouses, has performances year-round – separate tour and exhibition ticket to main Globe. (See p64.)

10 Imperial War Museum
MAP F5 ▪ Lambeth Road SE1 ▪ 020 7416 5000 ▪ Open 10am–6pm daily ▪ www.iwm.org.uk

With some galleries redeveloped in 2014 to commemorate the centenary of the start of World War I, this fascinating museum documents the social effects of war as much as the technology. Concerned with conflicts in the 20th and 21st centuries, its exhibitions will appeal to anyone interested in wartime London.

A DAY BY THE RIVER

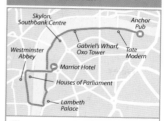

▶ MORNING

Start with breakfast at the **Marriott Hotel**, based in the splendid former headquarters of the Greater London Council. Cross Westminster Bridge to visit **Westminster Abbey** (see pp34–5) and nearby St Margaret's Church.

Continue along Abingdon Street to Lambeth Bridge and re-cross the river. Have a coffee at the delightful little café at Lambeth Pier, passing **Lambeth Palace** (see p64) on your way. Walk along the Albert Embankment for a stunning view of the **Houses of Parliament** (see pp 36–7) across the river.

For lunch, try Skylon (see p93) within the Royal Festival Hall at the **Southbank Centre**.

AFTERNOON

Walk along the Embankment and browse the second-hand book-stalls outside the BFI Southbank. Continue past the craft shops of **Gabriel's Wharf** (see p91) to the **Oxo Tower's** (see p91) designer galleries and take the lift to the tower's viewing platform.

Afterwards, head along the Embankment to **Tate Modern** (see pp28–9) – a wonderful place to spend the rest of the afternoon. Have a drink with more views in the Espresso Bar on level 3. Further downriver, the **Anchor** pub (see p92) is a good place for dinner.

Oxo Tower

The Best of the Rest

1 Clink Prison Museum
MAP G4 ■ 1 Clink Street SE1
■ Open 10am–6pm daily (to 7:30pm Sat & Sun; to 9pm Jul–Sep) ■ Adm
■ www.clink.co.uk

London's notorious medieval prison now houses a small exhibition devoted to crime and punishment.

2 London Sea Life Aquarium
MAP N6 ■ County Hall SE1 ■ Open 10am–7pm daily ■ Adm ■ www2.visitsealife.com/London

See thousands of marine creatures at one of Europe's largest aquariums (see p68) located on the South Bank.

3 Duck Tours
MAP N5 ■ 55 York Road SE1
■ 020 7928 3132 ■ Adm
■ www.londonducktours.co.uk

Amphibious tours that take in several sights by road before the "Duck" plunges into the Thames.

4 BFI IMAX
MAP N4 ■ South Bank SE1
■ Open daily (screening times vary) ■ Adm ■ www.bfi.org.uk

Giant-screen cinema that shows the latest blockbusters plus wildlife and other documentaries.

5 London Dungeon
MAP N6 ■ County Hall SE1
■ Open hours vary ■ Adm
■ www.thedungeons.com

This perennial favourite illuminates the capital's gory history (see p69).

BFI IMAX

6 Florence Nightingale Museum
MAP N6 ■ 2 Lambeth Palace Road SE1 ■ Open 10am–5pm daily ■ Adm
■ www.florence-nightingale.co.uk

Fascinating museum devoted to the life and work of 19th-century nurse Florence Nightingale.

Medical case, Florence Nightingale Museum

7 Golden Hinde II
MAP G4 ■ St Mary Overie Dock, Cathedral Street SE1 ■ Open 10am–5:30pm daily ■ Adm ■ www.goldenhinde.com

A full-size replica of the ship in which Sir Francis Drake circumnavigated the world from 1577 to 1580.

8 Fashion and Textile Museum
MAP H4 ■ 83 Bermondsey Street SE1
■ Open 11am–6pm Tue–Sat (to 8pm Thu), 11am–5pm Sun ■ Adm
■ www.ftmlondon.org

Founded by Zandra Rhodes, the museum showcases the latest in fashion, textiles and jewellery. There are also regular exhibitions.

9 Young Vic Theatre
MAP Q6 ■ 66 The Cut SE1
■ www.youngvic.org

This independent theatre company nurtures young thespian talent and attracts diverse audiences with its critically acclaimed productions.

10 Oxo Tower Wharf
MAP P4 ■ Bargehouse Street SE1
■ Open daily ■ www.oxotower.co.uk

For great city views, take a lift to the public viewing gallery next to the restaurant (see p93). Check out the boutiques and galleries below.

Shopping

(1) Houses of Parliament Shop
MAP L6 ▪ 12 Bridge Street SW1
Buy the day's political reading, plus parliamentary-related prints.

(2) Lower Marsh
MAP P6 ▪ Lower Marsh SE1 ▪ Open 10:30–5pm Mon–Fri, 10am–3pm Sat
This market sells inexpensive music, clothes, hardware and food.

(3) BFI Shop
MAP N4 ▪ South Bank SE1 ▪ Open 11am–8:30pm daily
This film shop selling DVDs, books and gifts is a must for movie buffs.

(4) Southbank Centre
MAP N4 ▪ South Bank SE1
As well as its concert halls and art gallery (see p70), the Southbank Centre contains some excellent shops. The Festival Terrace shop has original design and jewellery, while outside there are second-hand book stalls.

Gabriel's Wharf

(5) Gabriel's Wharf
MAP P4 ▪ Gabriel's Wharf SE1
Shops in riverside Gabriel's Wharf sell glassware, jewellery and ceramics.

(6) Bermondsey Fayre
MAP H5 ▪ 212 Bermondsey St SE1 ▪ Open hours vary ▪ www.bermondseyfayre.com
Appealing clothes and accessories all made by local and independent designers. Small yoga studio, too.

Borough Market

(7) Borough Market
MAP R4 ▪ 8 Southwark Street SE1 ▪ Open 10am–5pm Wed–Thu, 10am–6pm Fri, 8am–5pm Sat ▪ www.boroughmarket.org.uk
Good quality food and drink from all over the country comes to this traditional covered market near Southwark Cathedral.

(8) Contemporary Applied Arts
MAP R4 ▪ 89 Southwark Street SE1 ▪ Open 10am–6pm Mon–Sat ▪ www.caa.org.uk
CAA promotes British art and crafts, and you can find glass, ceramics, textiles, metalwork, furniture and jewellery within. The shop also offers a large selection of books on applied arts as well as arts magazines.

(9) Oxo Tower Wharf
MAP P4 ▪ Bargehouse Street SE1 ▪ Open Tue–Sun
Three floors are given over to designers of fashion, jewellery and interiors and gallery@oxo showcases cutting-edge photography, art, design and architecture.

(10) Konditor & Cook
MAP P5 ▪ 22 Cornwall Road SE1 ▪ Open 7:30am–7pm Mon–Fri, 8:30am–6pm Sat, 11am–5pm Sun
This urban village bakery has a cult following amongst the cake connoisseurs. Its funky iced Magic Cakes are legendary.

See map on pp86–7 →

Pubs and Cafés

1 The Southwark Tavern
MAP G4 ■ 22 Southwark Street SE1

A popular pub with a wide range of drink and food. Upstairs is bright and airy, while the downstairs bar has exposed brick-walled booths.

2 Caffè Vergnano 1882
MAP N4 ■ 10 Festival Terrace SE1

This restaurant serves classic Italian cuisine, and great espresso, in a sleek space on the South Bank.

3 Anchor & Hope
MAP Q5 ■ 36 The Cut SE1

Don't be put off by the queues. The food is some of the best around. Great English ingredients make this a wonderful gastropub experience *(see p74)*.

4 Monmouth Coffee Company
MAP G4 ■ 2 Park Street SE1

Serving arguably the best coffee in London, this atmospheric café in the heart of Borough Market also has delicious pastries and snacks.

5 The Anchor at Bankside
MAP Q4 ■ 34 Park Street SE1

Snug, old English pub with tables outside in summer **(below)**. The dining room upstairs serves traditional English food.

6 Wheatsheaf
MAP G4 ■ 6 Stoney Street SE1

Eclectic selection of British beers and street-food-inspired menu make this a great choice when exploring Borough Market.

7 Tate Modern Café 2
MAP R4 ■ Level 2, Tate Modern SE1

A great place to take a break after exploring the art galleries, with enticing food, good coffee and river views from its floor-to-ceiling windows.

8 Market Porter
MAP G4 ■ 9 Stoney Street SE1

A popular, historic market pub. Open for traders and all-night ravers from 6–8:30am as well as the usual hours.

9 Rake
MAP G4 ■ 14a Winchester Walk SE1

A fine selection of beers is on offer at this pub near Borough Market. The outdoor decking area is great for summer drinks.

10 George Inn
MAP G4 ■ 77 Borough High Street SE1

London's only surviving galleried coaching inn is a maze of plain, wood-panelled rooms and upstairs bars. Food is served from 11am to 11pm daily. Courtyard tables are pleasant in the summer.

Restaurants

PRICE CATEGORIES
For a three-course meal for one with half
a bottle of wine (or equivalent meal),
taxes and extra charges.

£ under £25   **££** £25–50   **£££** over £50

1 The Cinnamon Club
MAP E5 ▪ Old Westminster
Library, 30–32 Great Smith Street
SW1 ▪ 020 7222 2555 ▪ £££
Innovative Indian cuisine using fine
ingredients and rare spicing, served
in a historic Grade II-listed fomer
library in the heart of Westminster.

2 Skylon
MAP N4 ▪ Royal Festival Hall,
Belvedere Road, Southbank SE1
▪ 020 7654 7800 ▪ £££
Named after the symbol of the 1950s
Festival of Britain, the Southbank
Centre's restaurant is a classy affair.
Guests have a fine river view, along
with classic British dining.

The Cinnamon Club

3 Rex Whistler Restaurant
MAP E5 ▪ Tate Britain, Millbank
SW1 ▪ 020 7887 8825 ▪ ££
Named after the artist who painted
the glorious restaurant murals, this
is the place to visit if your looking for
old-fashioned English food and a
great wine list. Lunch only.

4 Roast
MAP G4 ▪ The Floral Hall,
Stoney Street SE1 ▪ 020 3006 6111
▪ £££
In the middle of Borough Market *(see
p91)* is this handsome restaurant with
views of St Paul's. Serves excellent
and well-sourced British cooking.

Oxo Tower Restaurant

5 The Archduke
MAP N5 ▪ 153 Concert Hall
Approach SE1 ▪ 020 7928 9370 ▪ ££
Set in beautifully converted railway
arches, this restaurant serves
steaks, burgers and cocktails. Open
daily with live jazz Mon–Sat.

**6 Smith Square Café
& Restaurant**
MAP E5 ▪ St John's, Smith
Square SW1 ▪ 020 7222 2779 ▪ ££
Tasty, modern food is served in the
hall's crypt at lunch on weekdays
and on regular concert evenings.

7 Gourmet Pizza Company
MAP P4 ▪ 56 Upper Ground,
Southbank SE1 ▪ 020 7928 3188 ▪ £
A range of pizza toppings is offered
at this wonderful riverside shack.

**8 Oxo Tower Restaurant,
Bar and Brasserie**
MAP G4 ▪ Oxo Tower Wharf SE1
▪ 020 7803 3888 ▪ Restaurant: £££
▪ Brasserie: £££
Delicious modern dishes in the
restaurant; live jazz in the bar.

9 Swan at the Globe
MAP R4 ▪ 21 New Globe Walk
SE1 ▪ 020 7928 9444 ▪ £££
Next door to the Globe, with a splendid
view of St Paul's and a creative menu.

10 fish!
MAP G4 ▪ Cathedral Street,
Borough Market SE1 ▪ 020 7407
3803 ▪ ££
Innovative fish dishes are served in
this modern, stylish restaurant.

See map on pp86–7 →

TOP 10 Soho and the West End

London's west end is where everyone heads for a night out. Clubbers from outside London catch the last trains into the capital and head for its many bars and music venues, knowing they won't leave till the break of dawn. Here are the great theatres of Shaftesbury Avenue and Charing Cross Road, the star-struck cinemas of Leicester Square and, at its heart, Soho, abuzz with activity as the night wears on. But it's not all just for the night owl – Trafalgar Square has the National Gallery, the National Portrait Gallery and free lunchtime concerts at St Martin-in-the-Fields.

Eros

AREA MAP OF SOHO AND THE WEST END

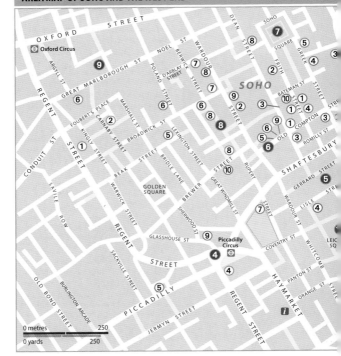

1 National Gallery
See pp16–17.

2 National Portrait Gallery
See pp18–19.

3 Trafalgar Square
MAP L4 ■ WC2

Trafalgar Square – once the royal mews – is a hub of the West End and a venue for public rallies and events. From the top of a 50-m (165-ft) column, Admiral Lord Nelson, who famously defeated Napoleon's fleet at the Battle of Trafalgar in 1805, looks down Whitehall towards the Houses of Parliament. The column is guarded at its base by four huge lions – the work of Edwin Landseer. At the northwest corner of the square, the Fourth Plinth features temporary artworks by leading

National Gallery, Trafalgar Square

national and international artists. On the north side of the square is the National Gallery (see pp16–17) and St Martin-in-the-Fields church (see p58); to the south-west, Admiralty Arch leads to Buckingham Palace.

4 Piccadilly Circus
MAP K3 ■ W1

Designed by the architect John Nash as a junction in Regent Street, Piccadilly Circus is the endpoint of the street called Piccadilly. Its Eros statue – topping a memorial fountain to the Earl of Shaftesbury – is a familiar London landmark and a popular meeting place. The Circus is renowned for its neon advertising displays and the constant hubbub at this busy junction. To the south is the Criterion Theatre, next to Lillywhites – a leading sporting-goods store.

5 Chinatown
MAP L3 ■ Streets around Gerrard Street, W1 ■ www. chinatownlondon.org

Ornate oriental archways in Gerrard Street mark the entrance to Chinatown, an area of London that has, since the 1950s, been the focus of the capital's Chinese residents. Here you can shop at Chinese supermarkets, street stalls and gift shops. The Chinese New Year, celebrated in late January or early February, is one of the biggest in the world outside of Asia. Chinatown abounds with excellent-value restaurants.

6 Old Compton Street
MAP L2

The main street in Soho is a lively thoroughfare both day and night. It is also the centre of London's LGBT scene, and now the site of the popular gay pubs Comptons of Soho and the Admiral Duncan. Soho's vibrant streetlife spills into Frith, Greek and Wardour streets, where pubs, clubs, restaurants and cafés have pavement tables, often warmed by gas heaters in winter. Some, like Bar Italia on Frith Street and Balans Café on Old Compton Street, are open until the early hours. Everywhere fills up when the evening's performance at the Prince Edward Theatre ends. A delicious breakfast is to be had at Patisserie Valerie at No. 44 Old Compton Street, and such long-standing shops as the Italian delicatessen I Camisa, and the Vintage House (over 1,350 malt whiskeys in stock), give the area its village feel. Body tattooists work in this area, and fetish shops show that the sex industry is still flourishing.

7 Soho Square
MAP K2

This pleasant square, crossed by footpaths lined with flowerbeds, is popular at lunchtime, after work and at weekends, especially in summer. Many of the buildings in the square

NELSON'S COLUMN

The centrepiece of Trafalgar Square, this huge column **(below)** is topped by a statue of Horatio, Viscount Nelson (1758–1805). Britain's great naval hero was fatally shot at his hour of greatest triumph, the drubbing of the French and Spanish fleets off Cape Trafalgar, southern Spain. His lasting affair with the vivacious Emma Hamilton enhanced his romantic image.

have long been occupied by film, TV production and other media companies. On the north side is a church built in 1893 for French Protestants under a charter granted by Edward VI in 1550. The redbrick St Patrick's, on the east side, sometimes has music recitals. On the corner of Greek Street is the House of St Barnabas, a charitable foundation for the homeless in an 18th-century building, which is occasionally open for cultural events.

Mock-Tudor cottage, Soho Square

Berwick Street Market

⑧ Berwick Street Market
MAP K2

There has been a market on this street since the 18th century, and the daily fruit and vegetable stalls remain cheap, cheerful and thoroughly Cockney, though becoming increasingly foodie. Some traders still talk in old money ("ten bob" is 50p) and round things up to a "nicker" or a "quid" (£1). It opens around 9am six days a week (closed Sundays).

⑨ The Photographers' Gallery
MAP D3 ■ 16–18 Ramilies St W1 ■ 10am–6pm Mon–Sat, 10am–8pm Thu, 11am–6pm Sun

Displayed across three floors of exhibition space are works from both emerging global talent and established artists, as well as pieces from the gallery's historical archives. There are also talks, workshops, courses, a bookshop and a café.

⑩ Leicester Square
MAP L3 ■ Leicester Square W1

When this square was originally laid out in the 1670s it was a grand and fashionable place to live. Celebrities of the 17th and 18th centuries to live here include Sir Isaac Newton and the painters Joshua Reynolds and William Hogarth. Today the square forms the heart of London's West End entertainment district and houses the Empire and Art Deco Odeon cinemas. There is also a booth called "TKTS" on the south side of the square where cut-price theatre tickets can be bought.

A WALK AROUND THE WEST END

▶ **MORNING**

Start the day in **Trafalgar Square** *(see p95)* at 8:30am when the fountains are switched on and view the latest art on the Fourth Plinth. You could spend a day at the **National Gallery** *(see pp16–17)*, but limit yourself to an hour or two, perhaps just visiting the Sainsbury Wing.

☕ For coffee, head next door to the Portrait Restaurant at the **National Portrait Gallery** *(see pp18–19)*. It has fine views over Trafalgar Square. Head up Charing Cross Road to Leicester Square. Note the statues of Shakespeare and Charlie Chaplin in the middle of the square. Continue towards the bright lights of **Piccadilly Circus** *(see p95)* and the famous statue of Eros, and then walk up Shaftesbury Avenue, centre of the city's theatre district. Turn off here into bustling **Chinatown** *(see p95)*, with its colourful shops and great-value restaurants.

🍽 Lunch in Chinatown is obligatory. Enjoy the bustle of the Golden Dragon on Gerrard Street, or the calm of the excellent Joy King Lau on Leicester Street, just off Lisle Street *(see p101)*.

AFTERNOON

Give the afternoon over to colourful and lively **Soho**. Eat a peach fresh from the stall in **Berwick Street Market**, then stroll up Wardour Street, home of the movie industry. Reward yourself with tea and a slice of cake at the delightful **Maison Bertaux** *(see p100)* in **Greek Street**.

See map on pp94–5 ←

Shopping

1 Hamleys
MAP J2 ■ 188–196 Regent Street W1

London's largest toyshop is worth a visit just to see their fabulous window displays (see pp78–9).

2 The Kooples
MAP J3 ■ 22 Carnaby Street W1

A fashion label inspired by rock 'n' roll, founded by three French brothers but with a very British edge.

3 Foyles
MAP L2 ■ 107 Charing Cross Road WC2

In a street of bookshops, this grandmother of all bookshops is something of an institution.

4 Lillywhites
MAP K3 ■ 24–36 Regent Street SW1Y

There are plenty of bargains to be found at Lillywhites. The famous sporting goods store is spread over six enormous floors.

5 Milroy's of Soho
MAP L2 ■ 3 Greek Street W1

A West End whisky specialist, Milroy's of Soho has a small bar where malts can be sampled.

6 Liberty
MAP J2 ■ 210–220 Regent Street W1

One of London's most appealing department stores. Opened in 1875, the shop remains famous for its "Liberty Print" fabrics (see p79).

7 Agent Provocateur
MAP E3 ■ 6 Broadwick Street W

Sexy high-quality lingerie and swimwear retailer co-founded by Joseph Corré, Vivienne Westwood's son, and his wife Serena Rees. Give in to temptation and treat yourself!

8 Lina Stores
MAP K3 ■ 18 Brewer Street W1

Taking its name from the Genovese woman who originally established it, this family-run Italian deli has been operating at this address since 1944 Excellent-quality Italian produce is imported and fresh pasta is made on the premises every day.

9 Algerian Coffee Stores
MAP K3 ■ 52 Old Compton Street W1

Opened in 1887, this is one of the oldest shops in Soho. It exudes the wonderful aroma of the more than 80 kinds of coffee it sells. Over 120 types of speciality teas and herbal infusions can also be bought here.

10 David Drummond
MAP L3 ■ 11 Cecil Court WC2

The most charming of the antiquarian bookshops in Cecil Cour is crammed with theatrical memorabilia, plays and posters.

Liberty department store

Late Night Venues

1 Ronnie Scott's
MAP L2 ■ 47 Frith Street W1
■ 020 7439 0747
London's premier jazz venue is buzzing every night of the week *(see p72)*.

2 100 Wardour Street
MAP K3
■ 100 Wardour Street W1
All-day restaurant serving modern European dishes with a twist. Live music and DJs in the evening. There is also a lounge and bar.

3 Café Boheme
MAP L2 ■ 13 Old Compton Street W1
A French-style bistro where sandwiches, salads and light meat and fish dishes are served until 3am Monday to Saturday.

4 Jazz After Dark
MAP L2 ■ 9 Greek Street W1
Things don't get going here much before 9pm, and then the jazz and blues go on until 2am Tuesday to Thursday and 3am Friday to Saturday. BBQ mixed grill and tapas are on the menu.

5 Balans Café
MAP L2 ■ 34 Old Compton Street W1
This lively bar is open 24 hours a day. Hot dishes and sandwiches accompany the wines and cocktails. Their eggs benedict is to die for!

6 Milk and Honey
MAP K2 ■ 61 Poland Street W1
■ 020 7065 6800 ■ www.mlkhny.com
One of Soho's best-loved bars for cocktail enthusiasts, with three floors in which to sip, sup and be seen. Reservations are a must.

7 Bar Rumba
MAP K3 ■ 36 Shaftesbury Avenue W1
Promising "every kind of dance music except rumba", this basement is open until 3am every night.

Ronnie Scott's jazz club

8 PizzaExpress Jazz Club
MAP K2 ■ 10 Dean Street W1
This Soho branch of the PizzaExpress chain (more than 50 outlets in London) stays open until midnight, with its regular jazz nights proving an attractive draw.

9 Jewel Piccadilly
MAP K3 ■ 4–6 Glasshouse Street W1
A chic bar and club attract the young, the beautiful and occasionally the famous. Great cocktails and a decent list of bar food and snacks is served. Open until 1am Monday to Saturday, 12:30am on Sunday.

10 El Camión Mexicano
MAP K3
■ 25–27 Brewer Street W1
As the pubs close, night owls head for El Camión, which serves a late-night Mexican menu from 11pm to 2am. The Pink Chihuahua cocktail bar downstairs stays open until 3am Monday to Saturday.

El Camión Mexicano restaurant

See map on pp94–5

Pubs and Cafés

① Patisserie Valerie
MAP L3 ▪ 44 Old Compton Street W1

A classic Soho café with a wide range of delicious cakes and pastries: the fresh croissants make it a good place for breakfast. Its Frenchness extends to the Toulouse-Lautrec-style cartoons by Terroni.

② Maison Bertaux
MAP L3 ▪ 28 Greek Street W1

This little corner of Paris in the heart of Soho attracts a faithful clientele, who love its delicious coffee and heavenly cakes.

③ French House
MAP L3 ▪ 49 Dean Street W1

A small, one-bar establishment where conversation flows freely among strangers, this Soho pub was once the haunt of the artist Francis Bacon (1909–92).

④ Bar Italia
MAP L2 ▪ 22 Frith Street W1

Sit at the bar or out on the pavement and enjoy the best Italian coffee in London. A huge screen at the back of the bar shows Italian football matches. Only closed 5–7am daily.

⑤ Fernandez and Wells
MAP K3 ▪ 73 Beak Street W1

This lovely coffee shop serves excellent coffee along with delicious croissants, pastries, sandwiches and

A taste of Paris at Maison Bertaux

cakes. It is also open for breakfast, when you can order grilled pancetta or black pudding with egg mayonnaise in a bun.

⑥ The Admiral Duncan
MAP L3 ▪ 54 Old Compton Street W1

A small, lively bar in Old Compton Street – one of dozens in the area with a gay clientele.

⑦ The Breakfast Club
MAP K2 ▪ 33 D'Arblay Street W1 ▪ 020 7434 2571

Excellent all-day breakfast spot with six locations across London. Go for the chorizo hash browns.

⑧ Beatroot
MAP K2 ▪ 92 Berwick Street W1

A small, bright vegetarian restaurant serving delicious salads and hot dishes, packed in boxes.

⑨ The Cork and Bottle
MAP L3 ▪ 44–6 Cranbourn Street WC2

This basement wine bar is a favourite with connoisseurs due to its exceptional wine list and the eclectic menu designed to accompany it.

⑩ The Coach and Horses
MAP L3 ▪ 29 Greek Street W1

Long associated with writers and journalists, since 2012 this Soho institution has had the unusual distinction of being the only vegetarian and vegan pub in London.

Delicious cakes at Patisserie Valerie

Restaurants

PRICE CATEGORIES
For a three-course meal for one with half a bottle of wine (or equivalent meal), taxes and extra charges.

£ under £25   ££ £25–50   £££ over £50

1 Ceviche
MAP L3 ▪ 17 Frith Street W1 ▪ 020 7292 2040 ▪ ££

Opened in 2012, this Peruvian restaurant has been a big hit. Named after its signature dish of citrus-cured fish, it has a laid-back atmosphere and the food is delicious.

2 Arbutus
MAP L2 ▪ 63–4 Frith Street W1 ▪ 020 7734 4545 ▪ ££

Black leather banquette seating and wood flooring at this Michelin-starred restaurant, with typical dishes including squid and mackerel "burgers" and bavette of beef.

3 Burger and Lobster Soho
MAP K2 ▪ 36–8 Dean Street W1 ▪ 020 7432 4800 ▪ ££

Offering perfectly cooked, meaty burgers, juicy steamed or char-grilled lobster and buttery lobster rolls with wasabi mayo. Service is quick, amiable and polished.

4 Joy King Lau
MAP L3 ▪ 3 Leicester Street WC2 ▪ 020 7437 1132 ▪ £

A diverse selection of Cantonese dishes. At lunchtime there is an enormous choice of delicious dim sum, served from trolleys.

5 Restaurant Yoshino
MAP K3 ▪ 3 Piccadilly W1 ▪ 020 7287 6622 ▪ ££

Traditional favourites such as sushi and tempura are served here. Try the Japanese barbecue (each table has a smokeless grill) and cook pieces of meat, fish and tofu just the way you like it. Yoshino has a deli on Shaftesbury Avenue.

6 Yauatcha
MAP K2 ▪ 15–17 Broadwick Street W1 ▪ 020 7494 8888 ▪ ££

Book ahead to enjoy steamed scallop *shu mai* or venison in puff pastry at this Michelin-starred dim sum spot.

7 J Sheekey
MAP L3 ▪ 28–35 St Martin's Court WC2 ▪ 020 7240 2565 ▪ £££

The best fish restaurant in London in a charming setting, with dishes including shellfish and fishcakes.

8 Imli Street
MAP K2 ▪ 167–9 Wardour Street W1 ▪ 020 7287 4243 ▪ ££

Authentic vibrant, spicy Indian street food, served tapas-style.

9 Busaba Eathai
MAP K2 ▪ 106–110 Wardour Street W1 ▪ 020 7255 8686 ▪ ££

Trendy Thai restaurant with a minimal interior.

10 Barrafina
MAP L2 ▪ 54 Frith Street W1 ▪ 020 7440 1456 ▪ ££

Enjoy quality tapas at the counter in this stylish restaurant. However, you should expect to queue.

The sleek interior of J Sheekey

See map on pp94–5

🔟 Covent Garden

One of London's liveliest areas, Covent Garden is a popular destination for Londoners and tourists alike. At its heart is the capital's first planned square, laid out in the 17th century by Inigo Jones and completed by the addition of the Royal Opera House. Whilst the Piazza is renowned for its luxury stores, nearby Neal Street and Neal's Yard are home to independent boutiques. To the south of Covent Garden is Somerset House, which contains the Courtauld Gallery and is the setting for outdoor concerts in summer and a superb ice skating rink in winter. To get the full impact of the imposing riverside setting, enter from the Embankment side.

Seven Dials

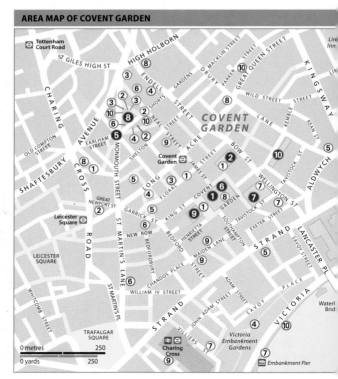

AREA MAP OF COVENT GARDEN

Previous pages Ballet at the Royal Opera House

1 The Piazza and Central Market

MAP M3 ▪ WC2

For 300 years, Covent Garden was a fruit, vegetable and flower market – immortalized by Lerner and Loewe's hit musical *My Fair Lady*. By 1980 the central Victorian halls, with their lovely iron and glass roofs, had been transformed into a vibrant, modern-day marketplace, surrounded by cafés and bars and enlivened by regular street entertainment.

2 Royal Opera House

MAP M2 ▪ Bow Street WC2
▪ **Exhibitions 10am–3:30pm Mon–Fri** ▪ **020 7304 4000** ▪ **www.roh.org.uk**

London's impressive premier music venue is home to both the Royal Opera and Royal Ballet companies (see p70). The present Neo-Classical theatre was designed in 1858 by E M Barry and incorporates a portico frieze recovered from the previous building, which was destroyed by fire. The Opera House has expanded into the lovely glass and wrought-iron floral hall, once part of Covent Garden market and now housing a restaurant and champagne bar.

3 Courtauld Gallery

MAP N3 ▪ Strand WC2
▪ **Open 10am–6pm daily (last adm 5:30pm)** ▪ **Guided tours Tue, Thu & Sat** ▪ **Adm** ▪ **www.courtauld.ac.uk**

Founded in 1932 for the study of the history of art, the Courtauld Institute is part of the University of London. Located in the North Wing of Somerset House, its gallery is particularly strong on Impressionist paintings. A range of events is held here including Sunday talks and Monday and Friday lunchtime talks.

4 Somerset House

MAP N3 ▪ Strand WC2
▪ **Open 10am–6pm daily** ▪ **Adm** ▪ **www.somersethouse.org.uk**

Once a riverside palace, and later home to the Navy Board and Inland Revenue, Somerset House's upper floors are now occupied by over 100 organizations. Much of the building, though, is open to the public. Aside from housing the Courtauld Gallery, there are the Embankment Galleries, whose exhibitions span design, fashion, architecture and photography.

Apple Market, Covent Garden

5 Seven Dials
MAP E3 ■ WC2

"Covent Garden's hidden village", this unusual street layout was created by Thomas Neale (1641–99), MP as a way to increase rents, which were then charged by frontage size rather than interior space. The sundial at the central monument has only six faces. The seven streets leading off it contain a mix of shops, offices, restaurants and theatres.

6 Benjamin Pollock's Toyshop
MAP M3 ■ 44 The Market, Covent Garden WC2 ■ Open 10:30am–6pm Mon–Wed, 10:30am–6:30pm Thu–Sat, 11am–6pm Sun ■ www.pollocks-coventgarden.co.uk

Established in the 1880s by Benjamin Pollock, a toy theatre producer, this shop is a treasure trove of theatrical gifts and traditional toys, including theatres, for both children and adult collectors. The range includes marionettes and puppets, musical boxes and paper dolls.

7 London Transport Museum
MAP M3 ■ Covent Garden Piazza WC2 ■ Open 10am–6pm Mon–Thu, Sat & Sun; 11am–6pm Fri ■ Adm ■ www.ltmuseum.co.uk

This museum explores London's transport, and its society and culture

COVENT GARDEN ARCHITECT

Inigo Jones (1573–1652) designed Covent Garden (below) as London's first planned square. The low roofs and classical portico of St Paul's Church were influenced by the Italian architect Andrea Palladio (1518–80). As set designer for royal masques, Jones was responsible for introducing the proscenium arch and moveable scenery to the London stage.

along the way, through some 450,000 objects. See vehicles that have served the city for over two centuries. The shop sells souvenir model buses, taxis and goods with the distinctive London Underground symbol (see p61).

8 Neal's Yard
MAP M2 ■ Neal Street WC2

This delightful enclave is full of colour, with painted shop fronts, flower-filled window boxes and oil drums, and cascades of plants tumbling down the walls. This is

Buses on show at the London Transport Museum

Neal's Yard Remedies

▶ MORNING

Take the Tube to Leicester Square and head up nearby Monmouth Street, where the delicious smell of coffee roasting will lead you to the **Monmouth Coffee Company** *(see p110)* for coffee and a pastry. Continue up Monmouth Street until you reach the small entrance to **Neal's Yard** and buy some natural soap at Neal's Yard Remedies. Check out the cheese in Neal's Yard Dairy round the corner in Short's Gardens, before exploring the shops in Earlham Street. Visit **Covent Garden Piazza** *(see p105)* for the street entertainers outside Inigo Jones's elegant **St Paul's Church**. Take a look inside before eating lunch in the charming French **Brasserie Blanc** *(see p111)*.

AFTERNOON

Before leaving the Piazza, pop into **Benjamin Pollock's Toyshop**, then turn down Russell Street and Wellington Street to the Strand. Cross the road and turn left to **Somerset House**, home of the **Courtauld Gallery** *(see p105)*. Start with their collection of Impressionist and Post-Impressionist art. Pause to relax by the courtyard fountains or in one of the gallery's cafés before checking out the Embankment Galleries at riverside level, with exhibitions dedicated to a programme of contemporary arts, including design, fashion, architecture and photography. For more contemporary art, exit Somerset House and walk along the Strand to the Strand Gallery at 32 John Adam Street.

alternative London, with wholefood cafés and such alternative therapies as Chinese medicines and acupuncture. Visit the now global Neal's Yard Remedies for natural cures and beauty products. Try a variety of British cheeses at Neal's Yard Dairy round the corner in Shorts Gardens.

9 St Paul's Church
MAP M3 ■ Bedford Street WC2 ■ Open 8:30am–5pm Mon–Fri, 9am–1pm Sun ■ www.actorschurch.org

Inigo Jones built this church (known as "the actors' church") with the main portico facing east, onto the Piazza, and the altar at the west end. Clerics objected to this unorthodox arrangement, so the altar was moved. The entrance is through the garden while the grand east door is essentially a fake.

10 Theatre Royal, Drury Lane
MAP M2 ■ Catherine Street WC2 ■ Guided tours

Drury Lane is synonymous with the London stage. The theatre has a splendid entrance, with magnificent stairways leading to the circle seats. The auditorium is large enough to put on the biggest musical extravaganzas, including *South Pacific*, *My Fair Lady*, *The Producers*, *Hello, Dolly!* and *Miss Saigon*. The first theatre on this site was built in 1663 for Charles II, whose mistress Nell Gwynne trod the boards.

See map on pp104–5 ⬅

The Best of the Rest

1 Free Entertainment
MAP M3 ▪ WC1

Every day from 10am to 10pm there are street entertainers in the Piazza, while opera singers and classical musicians perform in the courtyard of the Central Market building.

2 Donmar Warehouse

This 251-seater venue produces some of the most exciting theatre in London. There's plenty of new writing on offer but it also stages at least one classic per season *(see p71)*.

3 The Tintin Shop
MAP M3 ▪ 34 Floral Street WC2

Everything from keyrings and Snowy toys to limited edition models – Tintin fans will love this shop.

4 Victoria Embankment Gardens
MAP M4 ▪ WC2

During the summer, outdoor concerts are held in these attractive gardens by the river.

5 Savoy Hotel
MAP M3 ▪ Strand WC2

Enjoy a traditional afternoon tea in the Thames Foyer of this grand old London hotel *(see p64)*.

Victoria Embankment Gardens

6 London Coliseum

Opened in 1904, the home of the English National Opera has retained its Edwardian flavour, with gilded cherubs in the foyer *(see p70)*.

7 River Cruises
MAP M4 ▪ Embankment WC2

Embankment Pier is the boarding point for a range of trips, from sight-seeing and dining cruises to the striking Tate Boat linking both branches of the Tate Gallery *(see pp28–31)*.

8 Oasis Sports Centre
MAP M2 ▪ 32 Endell Street WC2 ▪ Adm

Famous for its heated outdoor pool, there is also an indoor pool, squash courts, gym, sauna and sun terrace.

9 Benjamin Franklin House
MAP E4 ▪ 36 Craven Street WC2

In the only remaining home of this founding father of the US, his scientific discoveries during his 16 years in London are explored in a Medical History Room, a Discovery Room and a Demonstration Room *(see p66)*.

10 Cleopatra's Needle
MAP F4 ▪ Victoria Embankment WC2

Much older than London itself, this granite obelisk was originally erected in Heliopolis around 1450 BC and transported to London in 1878. Its inscriptions and hieroglyphics document the achievements of the pharaohs of ancient Egypt.

Riverboat cruising along the Thames

Shopping

1 **Floral Street**
MAP M3 ■ Floral Street WC2

This stylish street is home to British designer Paul Smith, Camper shoes, Mulberry bags and chic French designer agnès b.

2 **Shorts Gardens**
MAP M2 ■ Covent Garden WC2

A good place for streetwear, this street is home to G-Star Raw and TShirt Store, along with beauty shops and Neal's Yard Dairy.

3 **Neal's Yard Remedies**
MAP M3 ■ 15 Neal's Yard WC2H

Remedies, toiletries and make up, all made with purely natural ingredients, have been sold at this shop for more than 30 years.

4 **Stanfords**
MAP M3 ■ 12–14 Long Acre WC2

With an extensive range of travel guides, literature, maps and gifts, this shop is a traveller's paradise. There is a small coffee shop, too.

5 **St Martin's Courtyard**
MAP L3 ■ Long Acre WC2

London's latest shopping and dining destination is a stylish yet charming urban village enclave, with alfresco tables and top-name stores.

6 **Pylones**
MAP M2 ■ 54 Neal Street

This French store is home to a kooky collection of colourful, eye-catching accessories and household goods. Ideal for unusual gifts for children and adults alike.

7 **Penhaligon's**
MAP M3 ■ 41 Wellington Street WC2E

In business since the 1870s, this eccentric British perfumery has a glorious range of fragrances and accessories for both men and women. Their luxury candles make perfect elegant gifts.

Penhaligon's perfumery

8 **Benjamin Pollock's Toyshop**
MAP M3 ■ 44 The Market WC2E

The place to go for theatrical gifts, and traditional toys such as puppets and musical boxes (see p106).

9 **The Tea House**
MAP M2 ■ 15a Neal Street WC2

Over a hundred teas – from Moroccan Minty to Mango & Maracuja – are on sale at this speciality shop in Neal Street. There are also novelty teapots and books on how to master the very English art of tea-making.

10 **Thomas Neal Centre**
MAP L2 ■ 29–41 Earlham Street WC2

This upmarket shopping mall has a range of fashionable boutiques over two floors. On the lower floor there is a café and restaurant.

Benjamin Pollock's Toyshop

See map on pp104–5

Pubs and Cafés

1 Amphitheatre Bar at the Royal Opera House
MAP M2 ■ Covent Garden WC2

Head upstairs during the day for coffees, cakes and drinks.

2 Wild Food Café
MAP M2 ■ 14 Neal's Yard WC2

Long known as the Whole Food Café, this vegan and vegetarian eatery now focuses on organic, preferably wild, foods that have been cooked as little as possible.

3 Freud
MAP L2 ■ 198 Shaftesbury Avenue W1

This small basement attracts a designer crowd in the evenings. Huge choice of coffees (some with liqueurs), cocktails and bottled beers.

4 Canela
MAP L2 ■ 33 Earlham Street WC2 (within the Royal Opera House)

Portuguese treats await those who eat here. Try the black bean stew with pork, the chunky sandwiches filled with Serrano ham and the luscious lemon tarts.

5 The Lamb and Flag
MAP M3 ■ 33 Rose Street WC2

This traditional pub, serving cask bitter, is one of the oldest in the West End (see p77) and was frequented by Charles Dickens. Delicious roasts are served at Sunday lunchtimes.

6 Snog
MAP M3 ■ 5 Garrick Street WC2

If you want some low-calorie pampering then Snog's fat-free organic yogurts are well worth checking out. There are four flavours plus plenty of healthy and not-so-healthy things to dollop on top.

7 Gordon's Wine Bar
MAP M4 ■ 47 Villiers Street WC2

An ancient and atmospheric candle-lit cellar where wine, port and Madeira are served from the barrel in schooners or beakers.

8 Lowlander
MAP M2 ■ 36 Drury Lane WC2

Belgian beer and European cuisine served in a relaxed setting attract drinkers and diners alike to this popular spot.

9 Porterhouse
MAP M3 ■ 21–2 Maiden Lane WC2

There are excellent beers and a great atmosphere to be enjoyed in this pub, which boasts snugs and bars over 12 levels.

10 Monmouth Coffee Company
MAP L2 ■ 27 Monmouth Street WC2

The best place in London to buy and sample really good coffee, as well as a wonderful small café of great character that serves delicious French pastries (see also p92).

The cavernous interior of Gordon's Wine Bar

Restaurants

PRICE CATEGORIES
For a three-course meal for one with half a bottle of wine (or equivalent meal), taxes and extra charges.

£ under £25 ££ £25–50 £££ over £50

1 The Ivy
MAP L2 ▪ 1–5 West Street WC2
▪ 020 7836 4751 ▪ £££
Mere mortals need to book several months ahead to get a table in London's most star-struck restaurant, but it's worth waiting for the delicious brasserie-style food and lively atmosphere.

2 Abeno Too
MAP L3 ▪ 17–18 Great Newport Street WC2 ▪ 020 7379 1160 ▪ ££
Okonomi-yaki – Japanese comfort food, rather like a cross between an omelette and a savoury pancake – is cooked on a hot grill right in front of you in this specialist restaurant.

3 Mon Plaisir
MAP L2 ▪ 19–21 Monmouth Street WC2 ▪ 020 7836 7243 ▪ ££
One of the oldest French restaurants in London, with four rooms, each of a different size and feel. Daily specials keep the menu fresh. Set lunch and pre-theatre menus offer better value for money.

4 Rock and Sole Plaice
MAP M2 ▪ 47 Endell Street WC2 ▪ 020 7836 3785 ▪ £
This is simply the best place in central London to get traditional English fish and chips.

5 The Delaunay
MAP N2 ▪ 55 Aldwych WC2B ▪ 020 7499 8558 ▪ £–££
Open from breakfast until late, seven days a week. this elegant restaurant offers an extensive à la carte menu inspired by the grand cafés of Europe. Patrons can also enjoy breakfast or brunch, and even afternoon tea.

Great Queen Street restaurant

6 Souk Medina
MAP L2 ▪ 1A Shorts Gardens WC2 ▪ 020 7240 1796 ▪ ££
A taste of Marrakech, from the exotic ambience to the mint tea and *tagines*.

7 Orso
MAP M3 ▪ 27 Wellington Street WC2 ▪ 020 7240 5269 ▪ ££
Contemporary Italian cuisine is served in a stylish setting. Pre- and post-theatre menus are available.

8 L'Atelier de Joël Robuchon
MAP L2 ▪ 13–15 West Street WC2 ▪ 020 7010 8600 ▪ £££
Experience fine dining from the man who mentored such culinary luminaries as Gordon Ramsay. *(See p74.)*

9 Rules
MAP M3 ▪ 35 Maiden Lane WC2 ▪ 020 7836 5314 ▪ No disabled access ▪ £££
London's oldest restaurant has been famed since 1798 for its "porter, pies and oysters" *(see p74)*.

10 Great Queen Street
MAP M2 ▪ 32 Great Queen Street WC2 ▪ 020 7242 0622 ▪ ££
A sibling of the Anchor and Hope *(see p74)* pub with the same bustling atmosphere and unpretentious food.

See map on pp104–5

TOP 10 Bloomsbury and Fitzrovia

Charles Dickens

Literary, legal and scholarly, this is the brainy quarter of London. Dominated by two towering institutions, the British Museum and University College London, and bolstered by the Inns of Court, it could hardly be otherwise. It is an area of elegant squares and Georgian façades, of libraries, bookshops and publishing houses. Most famously, the Bloomsbury Group, known for novelist Virginia Woolf *(see p52)*, lived here during the early decades of the 20th century. Fitzrovia's reputation as a raffish place was enhanced by the characters who drank at the Fitzroy Tavern, such as Welsh poet Dylan Thomas (1914–53) and the painter Augustus John (1878–1961).

AREA MAP OF BLOOMSBURY AND FITZROVIA

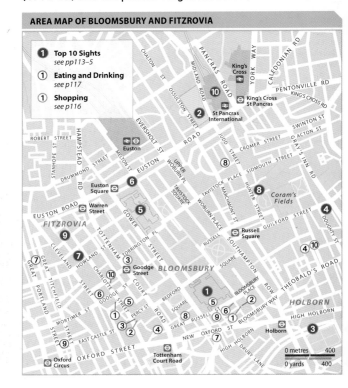

1 Top 10 Sights
see pp113–5

1 Eating and Drinking
see p117

1 Shopping
see p116

The red brick exterior of the British Library

British Museum
See pp12–15.

British Library
**MAP L1 ■ 96 Euston Road NW1
■ Open 9:30am–6pm Mon & Fri,
9:30am–8pm Tue–Thu, 9:30am– 5pm
Sat, 11am–5pm Sun & public hols
■ Permanent exhibitions are free
■ www.bl.uk**

The British Library holds copies of everything published in the UK and Ireland, as well as many historical publications from around the world. "Readers" have free access to these, while everyone else can enjoy the space and the regular exhibitions. A permanent display in the Sir John Ritblat Treasures Gallery includes the earliest map of Britain (1250), a Gutenberg Bible (1455), Shakespeare's first folio (1623), Handel's *Messiah* (1741) and many breathtaking illuminated manuscripts. The glass walls in the core of the building reveal the huge leather volumes from the King's Library, donated by George III. There are regular talks and events, a café and restaurant.

Sir John Soane's Museum
**MAP N1 ■ 13 Lincoln's Inn
Fields WC2 ■ Open 10am–5pm Tue–
Sat (closed public hols)
■ www.soane.org**

A particular pleasure of this unique museum is watching visitors' faces as they turn a corner and encounter yet another unexpected gem. Sir John Soane, one of Britain's leading 19th-century architects, crammed three adjoining houses with antiques and various other treasures, displayed in the most ingenious of ways. The basement crypt, which he designed to resemble a Roman catacomb, is particularly original. *The Rake's Progress* (1753), a series of eight paintings by Hogarth, is another highlight.

The houses are situated on the northern side of Lincoln's Inn Fields, the heart of legal London, where gowned and bewigged lawyers roam. Lincoln's Inn, located on the east side of the square, is one of the best-preserved Inns of Court in London, with part of it dating from the 15th century.

Sir John Soane's Museum

4 Charles Dickens Museum

MAP F2 ▪ 48 Doughty Street WC1
▪ Open 10am–5pm daily ▪ Adm
▪ www.dickensmuseum.com

Home to Charles Dickens from 1837 to 1839, during which time he completed some of his best work (including *The Pickwick Papers, Oliver Twist* and *Nicholas Nickleby*), this five-storey house offers a fascinating glimpse into the life and times of the great Victorian author and social reformer. The rooms are laid out just as they might have been in Dickens' time. Nearby Doughty Mews provides another step back to Victorian times.

5 University College London

MAP K1 ▪ Gower Street WC1 ▪ MAP E2 ▪ Bloomsbury ▪ 020 7679 2000 ▪ www.ucl.ac.uk/museums

Founded in 1836, UCL is one of the world's leading multidisciplinary universities and has many fascinating collections of international importance, including the Petrie Museum of Egyptian Archaeology, the Grant Museum of Zoology and the extensive UCL Art Museum. The university hosts public lectures, workshops and excellent exhibitions, as well as accomplished performances at its Bloomsbury Theatre in Gordon Street.

BLOOMSBURY CONNECTIONS

Many Bloomsbury streets and squares are named after members of the Russell family – the Dukes of Bedford. The first Duke features in Shakespeare's *Henry V*. In 1800, the 5th Duke (**below**) sold his mansion in Bedford Place and retired to the country. The current Duke has turned the family seat, Woburn Abbey, into a huge tourist attraction.

6 Wellcome Collection

MAP E2 ▪ 183 Euston Road NW1 ▪ Open 10am–6pm Tue, Wed, Fri & Sat, 10am–10pm Thu, 11am–6pm Sun ▪ www. wellcomecollection.org

The medical collection of businessman and philanthropist Sir Henry Wellcome (1853–1936), founder of one of the world's leading pharmaceutical companies, explores connections between medicine, life and art in the past, present and future, and has regular exhibitions.

St Pancras International Station

BT Tower
MAP D2

At 190 m (620 ft), this was the tallest building in London when it opened in 1965. It is now used as a media and telecommunications hub and is closed to the public. The Tower Tavern on Clipstone Street has a good large-scale diagram explaining the tower's constituent parts (as well as serving hand-pulled beer).

 Foundling Museum
MAP E2 ■ 40 Brunswick Square WC1 ■ Open 10am–5pm Tue–Sat, 11am–5pm Sun ■ Adm
■ www.foundlingmuseum.org.uk

Established in 1739 by Thomas Coram, the Foundling Hospital pro-vided a refuge for abandoned children until it closed in 1954. The original interiors from the hospital are on display at the museum, which also tells the stories of the thous-ands of children who were cared for here. Also on display are artworks donated by 18th- and 19th-century artists, including Gainsborough, Reynolds and Hogarth.

Fitzroy Square
MAP D2 ■ Fitzroy Square W1

Much of this square, completed in 1798, was designed by Scottish architect Robert Adam. Its many residents have included Victorian prime minister Lord Salisbury, who lived at No. 21, and the playwright George Bernard Shaw and the novelist Virginia Woolf occupied No. 29 at different times.

St Pancras International Station
MAP E1 ■ Euston Road NW1

One of the glories of Victorian Gothic architecture, this railway terminus, opened in 1868, was designed by Sir George Gilbert Scott. Most of the frontage is in fact the St Pancras Renaissance Hotel. Eurostar trains depart from here.

BT Tower

BLOOMSBURY AND FITZROVIA ON FOOT

 MORNING

Arrive at the **British Museum** (see pp12–15) at 10am (opening time) so that you can enjoy the Great Court in peace. View Norman Foster's glass dome while having coffee at the café here. Then wander the museum's extra-ordinary galleries. Don't miss the great Assyrian bas-reliefs on your way out.

Browse the antiquarian book and print shops, such as **Jarndyce** (see p116), along Great Russell and Museum streets. Turning left up Little Russell Street, noticing the fine Hawksmoor church of St George's. Loop around **Bloomsbury Square** and check out the list of Bloomsbury group literary figures posted here. Head west to Bedford Square with its Georgian houses. Cross Tottenham Court Road and carry on to Charlotte Street.

AFTERNOON

See the photos of literary figures such as Dylan Thomas in the basement bar of **Fitzroy Tavern** (see p117) at No.16 Charlotte Street, while enjoying a pre-lunch drink. If you fancy something more exotic than pub grub, try some barbecued Japanese food at **Roka** (see p117) a little further along Charlotte Street.

After lunch, amble up to the **Brunswick Centre** for some shopping, from food to fashion. This awesome concrete-and-glass megastructure was a 1960s housing and retail complex. Catch a cult flick at arthouse cinema **The Renoir**, or have a coffee at **Carluccio's** (One, The Brunswick).

See map on p112 ←

Shopping

① London Review Bookshop

MAP M1 ■ 14 Bury Place WC1

Opened by the literary magazine the *London Review of Books*, this shop by the British Museum is a favourite among readers for its informed staff and richly varied stock. It also regularly hosts readings by a wide range of authors.

② Hobgoblin Music

MAP K1 ■ 24 Rathbone Place WC1

If you're looking for a Chinese flute, mandolin, Irish drum or any other folk instrument, then this wonderful shop is the place to come, with an endlessly fascinating range from every part of the world.

③ Heals

MAP E2 ■ 196 Tottenham Court Road W1

London's leading furniture store is a showcase for the best of British design. There is also a good café.

④ Maggie Owen

MAP F2 ■ 13 Rugby Street WC1

This former dairy in the heart of Bloomsbury sells chic, contemporary costume jewellery and accessories from across Europe.

⑤ British Museum Shop

MAP L1 ■ 22 Great Russell Street WC1

Find a wide range of exquisite crafts and jewellery in this museum shop.

Everything from a pair of earrings modelled on those of ancient Egypt to a replica Roman bust to contemporary crafts can be found.

⑥ Contemporary Ceramics Centre

MAP L1 ■ 63 Great Russell Street WC1

An outstanding gallery that showcases the very best in contemporary studio ceramics, particularly work by British potters.

⑦ James Smith & Sons

MAP L1 ■ 53 New Oxford Street WC1

Established in 1830, James Smith & Sons is a beautiful shop that will meet all your umbrella, parasol, cane and walking stick needs.

⑧ L. Cornelissen & Son

MAP M1 ■ 105a Great Russell Street WC1

This specialist art supplies shop has wood panelling and rows of glass jars full of pigments.

⑨ Jarndyce

MAP L1 ■ 46 Great Russell Street WC1

This handsome antiquarian bookshop specializes in 18th- and 19th-century British literature.

⑩ Thornback & Peel

MAP F2 ■ 7 Rugby Street WC1

For quirky and quintessentially British screen-printed tea towels, coasters and cushions.

London Review Bookshop

Eating and Drinking

PRICE CATEGORIES

For a three-course meal for one with half a bottle of wine (or equivalent meal), taxes and extra charges.

£ under £25   **££** £25–50   **£££** over £50

1 Roka
MAP K1 ■ 37 Charlotte Street W1 ■ 020 7580 6464 ■ £££

Japanese robatayaki cuisine involves slow-cooking the food on skewers over a charcoal grill. At Roka, this is done at the centrally placed grill, in full view of the customers.

2 Truckles of Pied Bull Yard
MAP M1 ■ Off Bury Place WC1 ■ 020 7404 5338 ■ No disabled access ■ ££

This wine bar really comes to life in the summertime, when the outdoor terrace is filled with drinkers enjoying chilled rosé and Pimm's on comfortable sofas.

3 House of Ho
MAP K1 ■ 1 Percy Street W1 ■ 020 7323 9130 ■ ££

Set in a lovely four-storey Georgian townhouse and decorated with modern flair, this Vietnamese restaurant serves traditional meals with a contemporary twist. Enjoy a bowl of *pho*, Vietnamese noodle soup.

4 Hakkasan
MAP K1 ■ 8 Hanway Place W1 ■ 020 7927 7000 ■ £££

Its location may not be salubrious but this Michelin-starred Chinese restaurant and cocktail bar is classy.

5 Fitzroy Tavern
MAP K1 ■ 16 Charlotte Street W1

The pub that gave its name to the surrounding area (Fitzrovia) attracts a lively after-work crowd. Good Samuel Smith beer is reasonably priced. The Pear Shaped Comedy Club is held here every Wednesday.

Villandry Foodstore

6 Salt Yard
MAP K1 ■ 54 Goodge Street W1 ■ 020 7637 0657 ■ ££

Spanish and Italian tapas, including Old Spot pork belly with cannellini beans and fried courgette flowers.

7 Villandry Foodstore
MAP J1 ■ 170 Great Portland Street W1 ■ 020 7631 3131 ■ ££

Attached to an excellent food shop, the restaurant has a simple, modern-French-brasserie style menu. There is also a café and bar.

8 Norfolk Arms
MAP E2 ■ 28 Leigh Street WC1 ■ 020 7388 3937 ■ ££

This gastropub serves tapas-style portions of Mediterranean food. It's a local favourite.

9 Carluccio's
MAP J2 ■ 8 Market Place W1 ■ 020 7636 2228 ■ £

A touch of authentic Italy in this quiet square behind Oxford Street. Eat handmade pasta at pavement tables.

10 Gaucho
MAP K1 ■ 60A Charlotte St WC1 ■ 020 7580 6252 ■ £££

Hearty steaks are cooked on a genuine Argentinian *asado* barbecue at this stylish chain.

See map on p112

🔟 Mayfair and St James's

Guard at Buckingham Palace

This is where royalty shop and the rest of us go to gaze. Many of the wonderful shops around here were established to serve the royal court. Piccadilly – named after the fancy collars called "picadils" sold at a shop in the street in the 18th century – divides St James's to the south from Mayfair to the north, where top shops continue up Bond Street, Cork Street and Savile Row to Oxford Street. Home to the Royal Academy of Arts since 1868, Mayfair has long been one of the best addresses in town. Today most of London's top-flight art galleries are here.

AREA MAP OF MAYFAIR AND ST JAMES'S

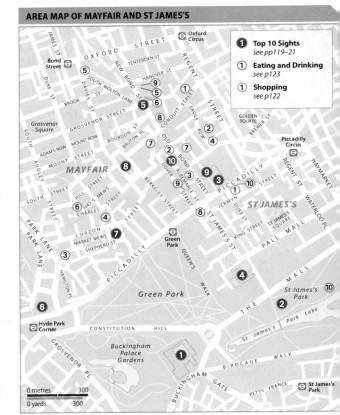

> 1 **Top 10 Sights**
> see pp119–21
>
> 1 **Eating and Drinking**
> see p123
>
> 1 **Shopping**
> see p122

1 Buckingham Palace
See pp24–5.

2 St James's Park
MAP K5–L5 ■ SW1 ■ Open
5am–midnight daily

This is undoubtedly London's most elegant park, with dazzling flower beds, exotic wildfowl on the lake, an excellent restaurant/café next to the lake *(Inn the Park, 020 7451 9999 to book)* and music on the bandstand in summer. The bridge over the lake has a good view to the west of Buckingham Palace and, to the east, of the former Colonial Office from where civil servants once governed the British Empire that covered one fifth of the world. *(See p56.)*

3 Royal Academy of Arts
MAP J4 ■ Burlington House, Piccadilly W1 ■ Open 10am–6pm daily (10pm Fri) ■ Free (admission charge for temporary exhibitions) ■ www.royalacademy.org.uk

Major visiting art exhibitions are staged at Burlington House, home of Britain's most prestigious fine arts institution. The building is one of Piccadilly's few surviving 17th-century mansions – you can see the former garden front on the way up to the Sackler Galleries. Near the entrance is Michelangelo's

The Royal Academy of Arts

Madonna and Child (1505) – part of the Royal Academy's permanent collection and one of only four Michelangelo sculptures in the world to be found outside Italy. In the Royal Academy's popular annual summer exhibition, new works by both established and unknown artists are displayed *(see p63)*.

4 St James's Palace
MAP K5 ■ The Mall SW1
■ Closed to public

Built by Henry VIII, on the site of the former Hospital of St James, the palace's redbrick Tudor gatehouse is a familiar landmark *(see p54)*.

Buckingham Palace as seen from St James's Park

5 Bond Street
MAP J3–J4

London's most exclusive shopping street, Bond Street (which is known as New Bond Street to the north and Old Bond Street to the south) has long been the place for high society to promenade: many of its establishments have been here for over 100 years. The street is home to top fashion houses, elegant galleries such as Halcyon and the Fine Art Society, Sotheby's auction rooms and jewellers such as Tiffany and Asprey. Where Old and New Bond Street meet, there is a delightful sculpture of wartime leaders Franklin D Roosevelt and Winston Churchill on a bench – well worth a photograph.

6 Apsley House
MAP D5 ▪ 149 Piccadilly, Hyde Park Corner W1 ▪ Open Apr–Oct: 11am–5pm Wed–Sun; Nov–Mar: 10am–4pm Sat & Sun ▪ Adm

Designed by Robert Adam in the 1770s as the home of the Duke of Wellington (see p51), Apsley House is given over to the paintings and memorabilia of the great military leader, and is still partly occupied by the family. The paintings include *The Waterseller of Seville* by Diego Velázquez. Antonio Canova's nude statue of Napoleon has special poignancy.

AMERICANS IN MAYFAIR

America's connection with Mayfair dates from World War II when Eisenhower stayed on Grosvenor Square. In 1960 the US Embassy **(below)** opened on land leased from the Grosvenor Estate, who it is said refused to sell the freehold unless their estate in Florida, confiscated after the War of Independence, was returned.

7 Shepherd Market
MAP D4

This square was named after Edward Shepherd who developed the area in around 1735. Today, this pedestrianized area in the heart of Mayfair, between Piccadilly and Curzon Street is a good place to visit on a summer evening for a drink or dinner. Ye Grapes, dating from 1882, is the principal pub, while local restaurants include L'Artiste Musclé, Le Boudin Blanc and The Market

The imposing façade of Apsley House

The Grapes in Shepherd Market

Brasserie. In the 17th century, an annual May Fair was held here, giving the wider area its name.

8 Berkeley Square
MAP D4

This pocket of green in the middle of Mayfair was planted in 1789 and its 30 huge plane trees may be the oldest in London. In 1774 Clive of India, hero of the British Empire, committed suicide at No. 45. Memorial benches in the square bear moving inscriptions, many from Americans billeted here during World War II. It was the London base of P G Wodehouse's Bertie Wooster and Jeeves.

9 Burlington Arcade
MAP J4 ▪ 51 Piccadilly W1
www.burlington-arcade.co.uk

This arcade of bijou shops was built in 1819 for Lord George Cavendish of Burlington House (see Royal Academy of Arts p119) to prevent people from throwing rubbish into his garden. The arcade of luxury stores is patrolled by uniformed beadles who control unseemly behaviour.

10 Royal Institution
MAP J3 ▪ 21 Albemarle Street W1 ▪ Museum open 9am–6pm Mon–Fri ▪ www.rigb.org

The Royal Institution was founded in 1799 to encourage the practical application of new scientific knowledge. Its most influential member was Michael Faraday (1791–1867), a pioneer of electro-technology. The three floors of the Faraday Museum explore science, the highlight being Faraday's 1850s magnetic laboratory.

EXPLORING ST JAMES'S

Cork Street
Royal Academy of Arts
Brown's
St James's Church
Burlington Arcade
Fortnum and Mason
St James's Palace
Inn The Park
Green Park
St James's Park
Buckingham Palace
St James's Park station

▶ MORNING

Starting from St James's Park Tube, walk up through Queen Anne's Gate, noting the lovely 18th-century houses. Pass through the alley in the corner into Birdcage Walk, then **St James's Park** (see p119). Get a coffee from Inn the Park and watch the pelicans before heading to **Buckingham Palace** (see pp24–5) for the Changing the Guard at 11:30am. Afterwards, head up The Mall past **St James's Palace** (see p119) into St James's Street. Turn into Jermyn Street, and check out such traditional shops as cheeseseller Paxton and Whitfield and perfumery Floris. Walk through St James's Church near the end of the street, leaving by the north exit onto Piccadilly, where a craft market is held Tue–Sat. Head west down Piccadilly to Fortnum & Mason.

AFTERNOON

Fortnum & Mason (see p78) is the perfect place to have lunch, in the Fountain restaurant, where the dieter's choice is caviar and half a bottle of champagne.

Cross Piccadilly to the **Royal Academy of Arts** (see p119) and enjoy their permanent collection, including Michelangelo's *Madonna and Child*. Window-shop along Burlington Arcade and the **Cork Street** galleries (see p122). Turn into Bond Street, heading for **Brown's Hotel** (see p176) to relax over a lavish English tea.

See map on p118 ←

Shopping

1 Fortnum & Mason
MAP J4 ▪ 181 Piccadilly W1

Famous for its food hall and restaurants, this elegant department store still has male staff who wear coat-tails *(see p78)*. Try the extravagant ice creams in the Parlour restaurant or enjoy their afternoon tea.

2 Asprey
MAP J3 ▪ 167 New Bond Street W1

The UK royal family have bought their jewels here for more than a century. Other luxury items to be found here include exquisite vases, handbags and silver gifts.

3 Charbonnel et Walker
MAP J4 ▪ 1 The Royal Arcade, 28 Old Bond Street W1

One of the best chocolate shops in town with a tempting array of hand-made goodies. Fill one of the pretty boxes, which come in a range of sizes, with your own choice of treats.

4 Gieves and Hawkes
MAP J3 ▪ 1 Savile Row W1

Purveyors of fine, handmade suits and shirts to the gentry since 1785, this shop is one of the best known in a street of expert tailors. Off-the-rack clothes are also available.

5 Browns
MAP D3 ▪ 24–7 South Molton Street W1

London's most famous designer clothing store stocks pieces by Lanvin, Balenciaga, Alexander McQueen and Stella McCartney among many others.

6 Mulberry
MAP J3 ▪ 50 New Bond Street W1

Come here for must-have leather handbags, purses and other luxurious accessories and shoes.

7 Cork Street Galleries
MAP J3

Cork Street is famous for its art galleries. You can buy works by the best artists here, from Picasso and Rothko to Damien Hirst and Tracey Emin or just window-shop.

8 Sotheby's
MAP J3 ▪ 34–5 New Bond Street W1

View everything from pop star memorabilia to Old Master paintings at this fine arts auction house founded in 1744.

9 Fenwick
MAP J3 ▪ 63 New Bond Street W1

A small, upmarket department store with designer labels, accessories and expensive lingerie.

10 Hatchards
MAP K4 ▪ 187 Piccadilly W1

Established in 1797, this well-respected bookshop is the oldest in the UK, and the official supplier of books to the Queen and other royals.

Fortnum & Mason, the iconic department store on Piccadilly

Eating and Drinking

PRICE CATEGORIES
For a three-course meal for one with half a bottle of wine (or equivalent meal), taxes and extra charges.

£ under £25   ££ £25–50   £££ over £50

Verandah seating at Inn the Park

1 Sketch

MAP J3 ▪ 9 Conduit Street
W1 ▪ 020 7659 4500 ▪ £££

The cooking here is some of the finest London has to offer. The Gallery is informal and features British artist David Shrigley's work. The pricier Lecture Room attracts the fashionable and famous.

2 Momo
MAP J3 ▪ 25 Heddon Street
W1 ▪ 020 7434 4040 ▪ £££

Brilliantly decorated in a kasbah style, this modern, North African restaurant serves *tajines* and couscous. The Mo Café next door serves tea and snacks.

3 Galvin at Windows

MAP D4 ▪ 22 Park Lane W1
▪ 020 7208 4021 ▪ £££

This restaurant at the top of the Hilton has fine London views, and superb French-influenced cuisine to match. Perfect for a special occasion.

4 Tamarind
MAP J4 ▪ 20 Queen Street W1
▪ 020 7629 3561 ▪ £££

This Indian restaurant doesn't disappoint. The food is original and seasonal. Great-value set menus.

5 Bond & Brook
MAP J3 ▪ Fenwick, 63 New
Bond Street W1 ▪ 020 7629 9161 ▪ £

Mix and match delicious small dishes at this restaurant and bar.

6 The Greenhouse
MAP D4 ▪ 27a Hay's Mews W1
▪ 020 7499 3331 ▪ £££

Exquisite two Michelin-starred modern European cuisine in a serene Mayfair location.

7 The Square
MAP J3 ▪ 6–10 Bruton Street
W1 ▪ 020 7495 7100 ▪ Disabled access ▪ £££

Wonderful French food is on offer at this sophisticated modern restaurant with two Michelin stars and four AA rosettes.

8 The Wolseley
MAP J4 ▪ 160 Piccadilly W1
▪ 020 7499 6996 ▪ ££

The Art Deco interior gives this famous brasserie an air of glamour *(see p75)*. You need to book well ahead for the formal restaurant.

9 Pescatori
MAP J4 ▪ 11 Dover Street W1
▪ 020 7493 2652 ▪ £££

This Mayfair restaurant serves fresh fish and seafood cooked with modern Italian flair.

10 Inn the Park
MAP L5 ▪ St James's Park SW1
▪ 020 7451 9999 ▪ ££

In the leafy surroundings of St James's Park you can enjoy excellent and reasonably priced food as you watch the world go by through the restaurant's large glass windows.

See map on p118 ←

🔟 Kensington and Knightsbridge

This is where London's gentry live. Harrods is the opulent heart of the area; the cultural highlights are the great museums of South Kensington. Princess Diana lived in Kensington Palace and shopped in Beauchamp Place.

Gate detail, Kensington Palace

Foreign royalty have homes here, too. Such mansions need the finest furnishings, and some of London's best antique shops are in Kensington Church Street and Portobello Road, one of the liveliest places to be on a Saturday.

AREA MAP OF KENSINGTON AND KNIGHTSBRIDGE

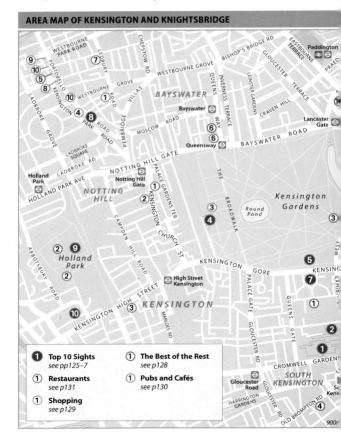

① **Top 10 Sights** see pp125–7	① **The Best of the Rest** see p128
① **Restaurants** see p131	① **Pubs and Cafés** see p130
① **Shopping** see p129	

900r

1 Natural History Museum
Explaining the world of animals and minerals *(see pp20–21)*.

2 Science Museum
This museum explores science and technology *(see pp22–3)*.

3 Victoria and Albert Museum
MAP B5–C5 ■ Cromwell Road SW7 ■ Open 10am–5:45pm daily (to 10pm every Fri) ■ www.vam.ac.uk

A cornucopia of treasures is housed in this enchanting museum named after the devoted royal couple and affectionately known as the V&A.

The elegant Kensington Palace

There are fine and applied arts from all over the world, from ancient China to contemporary Britain. Highlights include some extraordinary plaster copies of statues, and monuments and artifacts from the Italian Renaissance. Displays are arranged over seven floors of galleries. The stunning British Galleries display more than 3,000 objects illustrating the best of British art and design since 1500 *(see p60)*.

4 Kensington Palace
MAP A4 ■ Kensington Palace Gardens W8 ■ Open 10am–6pm (till 5pm Nov–Feb) daily ■ Adm ■ www.hrp.org.uk

This is a delightful royal residence on a domestic scale, which is still in use by members of the royal family: Diana, Princess of Wales lived here, as did Princess Margaret, the Queen's sister. A £12 million transformation of the palace was completed in 2012, giving the public access to more areas, including a new public garden. Tours and exhibits offer glimpses into both the public and the private lives of some of the palace's most illustrious former residents *(see p54)*.

5 Albert Memorial
MAP B4
■ Kensington Gardens SW7

This edifice to Queen Victoria's beloved consort, Prince Albert, is a fitting tribute to the man who played a large part in establishing the South Kensington museums. Located opposite the Royal Albert Hall, the memorial was designed by George Gilbert Scott and completed in 1876. At its four corners are statues representing the Empire, which was at its height during Victoria's reign.

6 Harrods

MAP C4 ▪ 87–135 Brompton Road SW1

No backpacks, no torn jeans – the doormen of Harrods ensure even the people in the store are in the best possible taste. This world-famous emporium began life in 1849 as a small, impeccable grocer's, and the present terracotta building was built in 1905. It is most striking at night, when it is illuminated by 11,500 lights. The store has more than 300 departments and on no account should you miss the wonderfully tiled and decorated food halls, which are great for picnic foods as much as for exotic specialities. Pick up a floor plan as you go in *(see p78 and p129)*.

7 Royal Albert Hall

MAP B5 ▪ Kensington Gore SW7 ▪ Open for performances and tours ▪ www.royalalberthall.com

When Queen Victoria laid the foundation stone for The Hall of Arts and Sciences, to everyone's astonishment she put the words "Royal Albert" before its name, and today it is usually just referred to as the Albert Hall. This huge, nearly circular building, modelled on Roman amphitheatres, seats 5,000. Circuses, film premieres and all manner of musical entertainments are held here, notably the Sir Henry Wood Promenade Concerts, familiarly known as the Proms *(see p71)*.

PRINCE ALBERT

Queen Victoria and her first cousin Prince Albert of Saxe-Coburg-Gotha (**below**) were both 20 when they married in 1840. A Victorian in every sense, his interest in the arts and sciences led to the founding of the great institutions of South Kensington. He died at the age of 41, and the queen mourned him for the rest of her life. They had nine children.

8 Portobello Road

MAP A3–A4

Running through the centre of the decidedly fashionable Notting Hill, Portobello Road, with its extensive selection of antique shops, is a great place to spend some time. The famous market starts just beyond Westbourne Grove, with antiques, fruit and vegetables, sausages, bread and cheeses, then music, clothes and bric-à-brac. Under the railway bridge there is a young designers' clothes market on Fridays and Saturdays. Take a seat by the window at GAIL's Artisan Bakery (No. 138)

The red brick and terracotta exterior of the Royal Albert Hall

 A formal garden in Holland Park

and enjoy coffee and cake or a sandwich while watching it all go by. Ethnic street food is otherwise what goes down best, and the Caribbean flavour spills over into the colourful clothes stalls (see p79).

9 Holland Park
MAP A4–A5 ■ Ilchester Place W8

There is a great deal of charm about Holland Park, where enclosed gardens are laid out like rooms in an open-air house. At its centre is Holland House, a beautiful Jacobean mansion, which was largely destroyed in a bombing raid in 1941. What remains is used as a youth hostel and the backdrop for summer concerts. Peacocks roam in the woods and in the gardens, including the Dutch Garden, where dahlias were first planted in England.

10 Leighton House Museum
MAP A5 ■ 12 Holland Park Road W14 ■ Open 10am–5:30pm Wed–Mon ■ Adm

All the themes of the Victorian Aesthetic movement can be found in the extraordinary Leighton House. It was designed by Lord Leighton (see p50) and his friend George Aitchison in the 1860s. Its high point is the fabulous Arab Hall, with a fountain and stained-glass cupola. Other friends contributed friezes and mosaics, but many features are original, notably the Islamic tiles, collected by Leighton and his friends on their travels.

KENSINGTON ON FOOT

▶ MORNING

Start at the South Kensington Tube station, and follow the signs to the **Victoria & Albert Museum,** (see p125). Spend a delightful hour wandering in the Medieval and Renaissance Galleries. Follow Old Brompton Road to the **Brompton Oratory** (see p59), where you should take a look at its sumptuous Italianate interior, with 12 marble Apostles. Cross the road for a coffee and a pastry at Patisserie Valerie.

Turn right into Beauchamp Place, where window shopping takes in creations by such English designers as Bruce Oldfield and Caroline Charles. Continue down into Pont Street, and turn left up Sloane Street. Check out Hermès, Chanel and Dolce e Gabbana before walking up towards Knightsbridge Tube, turning left into Brompton Road for Harrods.

Harrods has a choice of 30 bars and restaurants, including the Oyster Bar, and the Georgian Restaurant on the fourth floor.

AFTERNOON

Just five minutes north of Harrods, **Hyde Park** (see p56) offers a peaceful walk along the south bank of the Serpentine. Heading for **Kensington Palace** (see p125), you pass the famous statue of JM Barrie's *Peter Pan* and the Round Pond, where model-makers sail their boats. West of here, the palace's costume exhibit includes many of Princess Diana's dresses. Next door, **The Orangery** (see p130) provides a restorative cup of tea.

See map on pp124–5 ←

The Best of the Rest

① Royal College of Music
MAP B5 ▪ Prince Consort Road SW7 ▪ Open 10am–4pm Mon–Fri ▪ www.rcm.ac.uk

The UK's leading music college stages musical events throughout the year. The beautiful 1894 building, designed by Sir Arthur Blomfield, also houses a Museum of Music.

② Holland Park Opera
MAP A4–A5 ▪ Abbotsbury Road W14 ▪ Adm ▪ www.operahollandpark.com

An open-air theatre in Holland Park hosts an annual summer season of opera, while art exhibitions are held regularly in the Ice House and Orangery (see p127).

③ Serpentine Gallery
MAP B4 ▪ Kensington Gardens W2 ▪ Open 10am–6pm Tue–Sun

In the southeast corner of Kensington Gardens, this gallery houses temporary exhibitions of contemporary art (see p63).

④ Christie's
MAP B5 ▪ 85 Old Brompton Road SW7 ▪ Open 9am–5pm Mon–Fri (7:30pm Mon), 11am–5pm Sat & Sun

Visiting the salerooms here is like going to a small museum. Experts value items brought in by the public.

⑤ Electric Cinema
MAP A3 ▪ 191 Portobello Road W11 ▪ www.electriccinema.co.uk

London's oldest purpose-built movie theatre, this is also one of the

Royal College of Music

prettiest. It offers luxury seats and 3-D technology, and also has a bar and restaurant.

⑥ Queens Ice and Bowl
MAP A3 ▪ 17 Queensway W2 ▪ Bowling 10am–11pm daily (from 11am Sun); skating 10am–11pm daily ▪ Adm ▪ www.queensiceandbowl.co.uk

Enjoy ice-skating, ten-pin bowling and karaoke here – but try to avoid the after-school crowd.

⑦ Royal Court Theatre
MAP C5 ▪ Sloane Square SW1 ▪ www.royalcourttheatre.com

Since the 1960s this has been the pre-eminent theatre for new writing, producing work by both established and new playwrights.

⑧ Lido Café Bar
MAP C4 ▪ Hyde Park W2

Sit out on one of the lakeside tables. Jazz and poetry sessions take place on summer evenings.

⑨ Speakers' Corner
MAP C3 ▪ Hyde Park W2

This corner of Hyde Park attracts assorted public speakers, especially on Sundays.

⑩ Hyde Park Stables
MAP B3 ▪ 63 Bathurst Mews W2 ▪ 020 7723 2813

Ride around Hyde Park or take lessons – the best place for horse riding in London.

Electric Cinema, Portobello Road

Shopping

1 Harrods
MAP C5 ▪ 87–135 Brompton Road SW1
London's most famous store has over 300 departments full of the finest goods that money can buy. Specialities include food, fashion, china, glass and kitchenware (see p78 and p120).

2 Harvey Nichols
MAP C4 ▪ 109–125 Knightsbridge SW1
Another top London store. There are seven glorious floors of fashion, beauty and home collections alongside one floor dedicated to high-quality food (see p78).

3 Burberry
MAP C5 ▪ 2 Brompton Road SW1
Burberry sells its famous trenchcoats as well as checked clothing and distinctive luggage.

The Burberry store in Knightsbridge

4 Sloane Street
MAP C5
A dazzling concentration of luxury and designer shops extends along the street south of the vast Harvey Nichols department store.

5 Artisan du Chocolat
MAP C5 ▪ 89 Lower Sloane Street SW1
Combining artistry and craftsmanship, Gerard Coleman creates some of London's most innovative chocolates.

The iconic Harrods building

6 Rigby & Peller
2 Hans Road SW3 ▪ 020 7225 4760 ▪ Tube Knightsbridge
Famous for their high-quality lingerie, swimwear and corsetry, and their superb fitting service, this company has held the Royal Warrant since 1960. Make an appointment for service fit for a queen.

7 Designers Guild
MAP B6 ▪ 267–277 King's Road SW3
Designers Guild's fabrics and wallcoverings have a fresh, vibrant style all of their own and the variety on show is stunning.

8 Cutler and Gross
MAP C5 ▪ 16 Knightsbridge Green SW1
Treat yourself to the latest eyewear and browse the superb collection of retro classics.

9 John Sandoe Books
MAP C5 ▪ 10 Blacklands Terrace SW3
An unmissable experience for the discerning bibliophile, this bookshop is crammed to the rafters with a wonderful selection of volumes.

10 Ceramica Blue
10 Blenheim Crescent W11 ▪ Tube Ladbroke Grove
This delightful little Notting Hill shop stocks a unique, highly eclectic range of ceramics, glassware, fabrics and other household accessories.

See map on p124–5 ←

Pubs and Cafés

1 Beach Blanket Babylon
MAP A3 ■ 45 Ledbury Road W11

Famous for its wildly decadent interior, this bar serves lunch during the day, and becomes a swanky cocktail lounge in the evenings. A good place to mingle with the fashionable Notting Hill crowd.

2 Churchill Arms
MAP A4 ■ 119 Kensington Church Street W8

Filled with intriguing bric-à-brac and Churchill memorabilia, this is a large, friendly Victorian pub. Inexpensive Thai food is served in the conservatory at lunchtime and for dinner until 10pm.

3 The Orangery
MAP A4 ■ Kensington Palace W8

Open for breakfast, lunch and afternoon tea, this delightful café is located in an elegant conservatory with an outdoor terrace that overlooks Kensington Gardens. It was originally built for Queen Anne in 1704 (see p54).

4 Portobello Gold
MAP A3 ■ 95–97 Portobello Road W11

This trendy bar, used by local antique dealers, has a suitably alternative atmosphere and an upstairs Internet bar. There is also a conservatory restaurant.

5 Nag's Head
MAP C4 ■ 53 Kinnerton Street SW1

A short walk from Hyde Park is this little gem serving Adnams beer and quality pub food. The low ceilings and wood panelling add to the cosy, village-like atmosphere here.

6 Paxton's Head
MAP C4 ■ 153 Knightsbridge SW1

A popular watering hole for both locals and visitors, this old pub caters for all tastes, with cocktails and flavoured vodkas as well as real ales Traditional pub fare is also served.

7 Montreux Jazz Café
MAP C5 ■ 87–135 Brompton Road SW1

A trendy café on the third floor of Harrods (see p129). The decor and eclectic menu of light bites, hot drinks and cocktails, are inspired by Switzerland's Montreux Jazz Festival

8 Trailer Happiness
MAP A3 ■ 177 Portobello Road W11

The bar's kitsch but cosy decor is the perfect place to enjoy some of the liveliest cocktails in town.

Cosy interior of Trailer Happiness

9 The Castle
MAP A3 ■ 225 Portobello Road W11

This busy gastropub is a great spot for craft beer and people-watching.

10 Portobello Stalls
Portobello Road W11 ■ Tube Westbourne Park

Along the market there are stalls offering ethnic food of every kind. The area also has a good choice of cafés around Portobello Green.

Restaurants

PRICE CATEGORIES
For a three-course meal for one with half a bottle of wine (or equivalent meal), taxes and extra charges.

£ under £25   ££ £25–50   £££ over £50

1 Clarke's
MAP A5 ■ 124 Kensington Church Street W8 ■ 020 7221 9225 ■ £££

The menu consists of whatever chef Sally Clarke decides to cook for the evening meal. No matter what it is, it will be excellent.

2 Belvedere
MAP A4 ■ Holland Park W8 ■ 020 7602 1238 ■ ££

The restaurant's romantic setting in Holland Park is enhanced by its good European food. From the patio in summer, you may hear distant opera from the park's open-air theatre.

3 Kitchen W8
MAP A5 ■ 11–13 Abingdon Road W8 ■ 020 7937 0120 ■ £££

Haunch of venison with creamed chanterelles is typical of this chic but comfortable restaurant, perfect for a romantic dinner.

4 Amaya
MAP C5 ■ Halkin Arcade, Motcomb Street SW1 ■ 020 7823 1166 ■ Disabled access ■ £££

Amaya's dishes take modern Indian cuisine to a new level. Flash-grilled scallops, spinach and fig tikkis, and tandoori duck are served up in a rosewood-panelled dining room.

5 Dinner by Heston Blumenthal
MAP C4 ■ Mandarin Oriental Hyde Park, 66 Knightsbridge SW1 ■ 020 7201 3833 ■ £££

Chef Heston Blumenthal celebrates British cuisine at his two-Michelin-starred restaurant, with creative dishes based on historical recipes from the 14th to the 19th centuries.

6 Royal China
MAP A3 ■ 13 Queensway W2 ■ 020 7221 2535 ■ ££

A tempting variety of dim sum, including delicious *char siu* buns, are the main attraction here.

7 The Ledbury
MAP A3 ■ 127 Ledbury Road W11 ■ 020 7792 9090 ■ £££

Praise has been heaped on chef Brett Graham's food, which mixes global influences with *haute cuisine*.

Stained glass window, Bibendum

8 Bibendum
MAP C5 ■ 81 Fulham Road SW3 ■ 020 7581 5817 ■ £££

This former Michelin tyre factory, resplendent with colourful tiles and stained glass, is the fabulous setting for a restaurant and oyster bar.

9 Ognisko
MAP B5 ■ 55 Exhibition Road SW7 ■ 020 7589 0101 ■ ££

Fine, Polish cuisine in an elegant dining room. An alfresco terrace can be enjoyed on warmer nights.

10 Mr Chow
MAP C4 ■ 151 Knightsbridge SW1 ■ 020 7589 7347 ■ £££

You'll find authentic Chinese dishes such as drunken fish in this long-established, fashionable restaurant.

See map on p124–5

⭘10 Regent's Park and Marylebone

Once a medieval village surrounded by fields and a pleasure garden, Marylebone is now an elegant area. In the 19th century, the area's grand mansion blocks were used by doctors to see wealthy

Ceramic plate, Wallace Collection

clients. The medical connection continues today in the discreet Harley Street consulting rooms of private medical specialists. Encircled by John Nash's magnificent terraces is Regent's Park, where office workers, kids and dog walkers enjoy the inviting lawns and fabulous flowers.

AREA MAP OF REGENT'S PARK AND MARYLEBONE

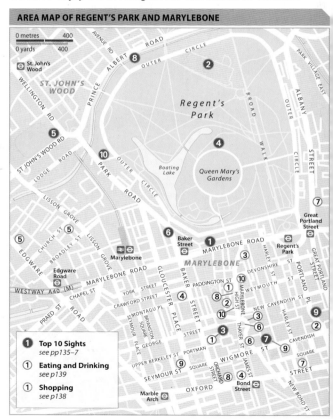

1 **Top 10 Sights**
see pp135–7

1 **Eating and Drinking**
see p139

1 **Shopping**
see p138

Previous pages An aerial view of central London

1 Madame Tussauds
MAP C2 ■ Marylebone Road NW1 ■ Open 9:30am–5:30pm, extended hours weekends and holidays ■ Adm ■ www.madametussauds.com

Madame Tussauds museum of waxwork models of the famous has long been one of London's major attractions. The interactive Scream prison has live, unhinged inmates jumping out of shadowy corners. Arrive early to avoid the queues or book a timed ticket (see p68).

2 London Zoo
MAP C1 ■ Regent's Park NW1 ■ Open 10am–5pm daily (till 3pm Nov–mid-Feb, 4pm mid-Feb–Mar, Sep & Oct ■ Adm ■ www.zsl.org

Lying on the northern side of Regent's Park, London Zoo is home to over 750 different animal species. The zoo is heavily into conservation and you can learn about the breeding programmes of endangered animals, such as the western lowland gorillas and Sumatran tigers. A map is provided and their booklet is full of fascinating animal lore (see p68).

3 Wallace Collection
MAP D3 ■ Manchester Square W1 ■ Open 10am–5pm daily ■ www.wallacecollection.org

"The finest private collection of art ever assembled by one family," is the claim of the Wallace Collection, and it is hard to disagree. Sir Richard Wallace, who left this collection to the nation in 1897, was not only outrageously rich but a man of great

Fountain in Regent's Park

taste. As well as many galleries of fine Sèvres porcelain and an unrivalled collection of armour and furniture, there are a number of old masters by English, French and Dutch artists, including Frans Hals' *The Laughing Cavalier* (see p62).

4 Regent's Park
MAP C1–D2 ■ NW1 ■ Open 5am–dusk daily

The best part of Regent's Park is the Inner Circle. Here are Queen Mary's Gardens, with beds of wonderfully fragrant roses, the Open Air Theatre with its summer Shakespeare plays, and the Garden Café, which is one of the best of the park's six cafés. Rowing boats, tennis courts and deck chairs can be rented and in summer musical performances take place on the bandstand (see p56).

Penguin swimming at the Penguin Beach exhibit, London Zoo

⑤ Marylebone Cricket Club Museum

MAP B2 ■ St John's Wood NW8
■ Open Mon–Fri (call 020 7616 8500 as hours vary on match days) ■ Adm
■ www.lords.org

Founded in 1787, the MCC is the governing body of the game, and its home ground, Lord's, is a venue for Test matches. The world's oldest sporting museum is included in a guided tour of the ground. Its star exhibit is the tiny trophy known as The Ashes.

⑥ Sherlock Holmes Museum

MAP C2 ■ 221b Baker Street NW1
■ Open 9:30am–6pm daily ■ Adm
■ www.sherlock-holmes.co.uk

Take a camera when you visit here so you can have your picture taken sitting by the fire in the great detective's front room, wearing a deerstalker hat and smoking a pipe. This museum is great fun, with some entertaining touches. A Victorian policeman stands guard outside, uniformed maids welcome you and, upstairs, wax dummies re-enact moments from Holmes's most famous cases *(see p50)*.

⑦ Wigmore Hall

MAP D3 ■ 36 Wigmore Street W1 ■ www.wigmore-hall.org.uk

One of the world's most renowned recital venues presents 450 events a year, featuring song, early music,

REGENCY LONDON

Regent's Park was named after the Prince Regent (the future George IV) who employed John Nash in 1812 to lay out the park on the royal estate of Marylebone Farm. Nash was given a free hand and the result is a delight. Encircling the park are sumptuous Neo-Classical terraces, including Cumberland Terrace (**below**), named after the Duke of Cumberland.

chamber music, including new commissions as well as a diverse education programme. This beautiful hall, built in 1901 in Renaissance style, is reputed to have one of the best concert acoustics in the world.

⑧ Regent's Canal

MAP C1

John Nash wanted the canal to go through the centre of his new Regent's Park, but objections from neighbours, who were concerned about smelly canal boats and foul-mouthed crews, resulted in it being sited on the northern side of the

Canal boats moored along Regent's Canal

BBC Broadcasting House

park. In 1874, a cargo of explosives demolished the Macclesfield Bridge beside London Zoo.

⑨ BBC Broadcasting House

MAP J1 ■ Portland Place W1
■ www.bbc.co.uk/showsandtours

Synonymous with the BBC, Broadcasting House has sailed majestically down Portland Place like a great liner since it was built in 1932. Redevelopment has now turned it into a state-of-the-art digital centre for BBC Radio, TV and BBC News and online services. Fans of "the Beeb" can take a 90-minute tour and learn a few tricks of the trade, or grab themselves audience-member tickets, available for a range of radio and TV shows.

⑩ London Central Mosque

MAP C2 ■ 146 Park Road NW8

Five times a day the muezzin calls the faithful to prayer from the minaret of the London Central Mosque. Built in 1978, with a distinctive copper dome, it acts as a community and cultural centre for followers of Islam. It is a hospitable place: step inside and see the sky-blue domed ceiling and its shimmering chandelier. Prayer mats cover the floor for the faithful who turn towards Mecca to pray.

EXPLORING MARYLEBONE

▶ MORNING

Before setting out for the day, reserve a ticket for **Madame Tussauds** *(see p68)* for the afternoon. Start at **Bond Street Tube**, exiting on Oxford Street. Opposite is **St Christopher's Place**, a narrow lane with charming shops, which opens into an attractive pedestrian square. Stop for a coffee break at one of Sofra's pavement tables.

Continue into **Marylebone Lane**, a pleasant side street of small shops, which leads to **Marylebone High Street** and its wide choice of designer shops. Stop awhile in the peaceful memorial garden of **St Marylebone Parish Church**, planted with various exotic trees. Methodist minister and hymn-writer Charles Wesley (1707–88) has a memorial here.

AFTERNOON

For lunch, buy some delicious fish and chips from the Golden Hind *(see p139)*. For a lighter snack, try Natural Kitchen at 77/78 Marylebone High Street.

After lunch, bypass the infamous lines of people outside **Madame Tussauds** and spend an hour and a half checking out the celebrity wax figures.

Cross Marylebone Road to Baker Street, for tea and a sandwich at **Reubens** *(see p139)*, before heading for the charming **Sherlock Holmes Museum** at No. 221b, a faithful reconstruction of the fictional detective's home.

See map on p134 ←

Shopping

1 Daunt Books
MAP D3 ■ 83–84 Marylebone High Street W1
All kinds of travel books and literature are arranged along oak galleries in this atmospheric Edwardian travel bookshop.

2 Marylebone Farmers' Market
MAP D3 ■ Cramer Street Car Park W1
With over 40 producers, this is London's biggest farmers' market. Held every Sunday 10am to 2pm.

3 The Conran Shop
MAP D3 ■ 55 Marylebone High Street W1
Set in an old stable building with a rooftop garden, Conran sells homeware and furniture in the best of both modern British and classic mainland European design, such as a Mies van der Rohe reclining chair.

4 Dr. Martens
MAP C3 ■ 368 Oxford Street W1C5
Home to the distinctive boots continually favoured by Britain's youth subcultures.

5 Alfie's Antiques Market
MAP C2 ■ 13–25 Church Street NW8
Vintage jewellery, fashion, art and furniture are all under one roof, plus there is a café for when you're all shopped out.

6 Marylebone Lane
MAP D3 ■ Off Marylebone High Street W1
This charming lane off Marylebone High Street still has plenty of quirky gems to tempt the shopper.

7 John Lewis
MAP D3 ■ 300 Oxford Street W1
This sophisticated department store prides itself on being "never knowingly undersold". If you can prove another shop sells the same item for less, you pay the lower price. It has a gifts department on the second floor, and the staff are both helpful and knowledgeable.

8 Selfridges & Co
MAP D3 ■ 400 Oxford Street W1
Opened in 1909, this store has a handsome Neo-Classical façade. A London institution, Selfridges is great for designer fashion for women. Its award-winning food hall is wonderful.

9 Margaret Howell
MAP D3 ■ 34 Wigmore St W1
Classic elegance for both men and women from one of Britain's top designers at her flagship store.

10 Le Labo
MAP D2 ■ 28A Devonshire Street W1
A luxury perfumery where the fragrances can be made to order with a personalized label.

Long oak galleries in the Edwardian interiors of Daunt Books

Eating and Drinking

PRICE CATEGORIES
For a three-course meal for one with half
a bottle of wine (or equivalent meal),
taxes and extra charges.

£ under £25   ££ £25–50   £££ over £50

1 The Wallace Restaurant
MAP D3 ■ Hertford House,
Manchester Square W1 ■ 020 7563
9505 ■ Disabled access ■ ££

Located in the courtyard of the
Wallace Collection (see p135), this
smart café serves delicious lunches,
including big salads. The menu
changes regularly.

2 Artesian
MAP J1 ■ 1C Portland Place
W1 ■ 020 7636 1000 ■ ££

Voted the World's Best Bar four
years in succession, Artesian exudes
style and sophistication with
cocktails to die for.

3 Caffè Caldesi
MAP D3 ■ 118 Marylebone
Lane W1 ■ 020 7487 0754 ■ ££

This light and airy Italian eaterie
offers classic dishes and a good
wine list. The upstairs restaurant
is slightly more formal.

4 Reubens
MAP C3 ■ 79 Baker Street W1
■ 020 7486 0035 ■ ££

One of the best kosher restaurants
in London, this offers such comfort
food as chopped liver and salt beef.

5 Mandalay
MAP B2 ■ 444 Edgware Road
W2 ■ 020 7258 3696 ■ £

A Burmese café where the food is
a pleasing mix of Thai, Chinese,
and Indian. Friendly, inexpensive
and unpretentious.

6 Golden Hind
MAP D3 ■ 73 Marylebone Lane
W1 ■ 020 7486 3644 ■ £

Started in 1914, this no-nonsense
little place is popular with locals and
offers customers fish cakes with
Greek salad as well as traditional
English fish and chips.

7 Queen's Head & Artichoke
MAP D2 ■ 30–32 Albany Street NW1
■ 020 7916 6206 ■ ££

A snug upstairs dining room and a
downstairs bustling, wood-panelled
bar offer a wide range of good food.

A range of cheeses at La Fromagerie

8 La Fromagerie
MAP D3 ■ 2–6 Moxon Street
W1 ■ 020 7935 0341 ■ ££

Sample the fine cheese and
charcuterie plates here, along with
delicious seasonal dishes.

9 Locanda Locatelli
MAP C3 ■ 8 Seymour Street W1
■ 020 7935 9088 ■ £££

Georgio Locatelli is one of the finest
Italian chefs in the UK. Dishes are
presented with great skill and care.

10 The Providores and Tapa Room
MAP D3 ■ 109 Marylebone High
Street W1 ■ 020 7935 6175 ■ ££–£££

On the ground floor, the Tapa Room
serves exciting fusion cuisine;
upstairs is a more sophisticated
foodie experience.

See map on p134

🔟 The City

The ancient square mile of London, defined roughly by the walls of the Roman city, is a curious mixture of streets and lanes with medieval names, state-of-the-art finance houses and no fewer than 38 churches, many of them, including St Paul's Cathedral, designed by Sir Christopher Wren. Don't miss the City's old markets: Smithfield still operates as a meat market, Leadenhall is in many ways more attractive than Covent Garden, while the former fish market of Billingsgate offers a great view of the once busy Pool of London.

Bust of William Shakespeare, Guildhall Art Gallery

AREA MAP OF THE CITY

1 Top 10 Sights
see pp141–3

1 Eating and Drinking
see p145

1 City Churches
see p144

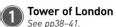

1 **Tower of London**
See pp38–41.

2 **St Paul's Cathedral**
See pp42–5.

3 **Tower Bridge**
MAP H4 ▪ 020 7403 3761
▪ Open Apr–Sep: 10am–5:30pm;
Oct–Mar: 9:30am– 5pm ▪ Adm
▪ www.towerbridge.org.uk

When the Pool of London (the stretch of the Thames between Limehouse and Tower Bridge) was the gateway to the city, this bridge (see p65) was constantly being raised and lowered for sail and steam ships bringing their cargoes from all corners of the Empire. Pedestrians who needed to cross the river when the bridge was open had to climb up the 200 steps

Tower Bridge in the sunlight

of the towers to the walkway overhead. Today, visitors on the 90-minute Tower Bridge Exhibition tour enjoy panoramic views from the 42-m (140-ft) high glass-floored walkways. The entrance is at the northwest tower. It ends with a hands-on experience in the massive engine room, and exits via a shop on the south bank of the river.

4 **Barbican Centre**
MAP R1 ▪ Silk Street EC2
▪ Box office: 020 7638 8891
▪ www.barbican.org.uk

Host to music, dance, theatre, film and art events with top visiting performers and artists (see p70). There is also an excellent library, cafés and restaurants. Opened in 1982, the centre is part of the Barbican Estate, which houses over 4,000 people and also contains the Guildhall School of Music. Access from the Barbican station is along a marked route and several stations are within walking distance. The centre looks across a lake to St Giles Cripplegate church.

The Brutalist-style Barbican Centre

5 Museum of London
MAP R1 ▪ 150 London Wall
EC2 ▪ Open 10am–6pm daily
▪ www.museumoflondon.org.uk

The world's largest urban history museum reveals insights into prehistoric, Roman and medieval London, and its social development up to the present day, through the fascinating "War, Plague and Fire" and "World City" galleries. Visitors can also experience a re-creation of a Victorian Street (see p60).

6 Guildhall
MAP G3 ▪ Guildhall Yard, Gresham Street EC2 ▪ Call to check opening times on 020 7332 1313
▪ www.guildhall.cityoflondon.gov.uk

For around 900 years the Guildhall has been the administrative centre of the City of London. City ceremonies are held in its magnificent 15th-century Great Hall, which is hung with banners of the main livery companies. In the Guildhall Library you will find rotating displays of historic manuscripts and a collection of watches and clocks, from the Worshipful Company of Clockmakers – some date from the 1600s.

7 St Katharine Docks
MAP H4 ▪ E1 ▪ skdocks.co.uk

Located near Tower Bridge and the Tower of London, this is the place to come and relax, to watch the rich on their yachts and the working sailors

St Katharine Docks

DICK WHITTINGTON

A stained-glass window in St Michael, Paternoster Royal, depicts Dick Whittington (and his cat) (**below**) – hero of a well-known London rags-to-riches fairy tale. In fact, Richard Whittington, who was Lord Mayor of London four times between 1397 and 1420, was a wealthy merchant and the City's first major benefactor. He pioneered public lavatories, building them to overhang the Thames.

on the Thames barges. There are several cafés, the Marble Quay and a number of popular bars and restaurants (see p65).

8 Guildhall Art Gallery and London's Roman Amphitheatre
MAP G3 ▪ Gresham Street EC2
▪ Call to check opening times on 020 7332 3700

On the east side of Guildhall Yard is the Guildhall Art Gallery, containing two floors of paintings that cover more than 400 years of art. Many works of art are associated with the City, and there are a number of romantic 19th-century paintings, including some pre-Raphaelite works. Combine the visit with a look at the remains of London's only Roman amphitheatre.

9 Bank of England Museum

MAP G3 ■ Bartholomew Lane EC2 ■ 020 7601 5545 ■ Open 10am–5pm Mon–Fri ■ www.bankofengland.co.uk

This fascinating museum, located within the impressive walls of the Bank of England, tells the history of the bank from its foundation in 1694 to the present day. Its unique collections of coins, banknotes and artefacts are supplemented by audio-visual and interactive displays. Visitors can even handle a real gold bar.

10 Monument

MAP H4 ■ Monument Street EC3 ■ Open 9:30am–5:30pm daily (to 6pm Apr–Sep) ■ Adm ■ www.themonument.info

Standing at 61 m (202 ft), this monument by Sir Christopher Wren offers panoramic views of the City of London. The height of this free-standing stone column is equal to its distance from the baker's shop in Pudding Lane where the Great Fire of London began in 1666 – the event that it marks. Inside, 311 stairs spiral up to a viewing platform; when you return to the entrance, you will receive a certificate to say that you have made the climb.

The Monument, completed in 1677

THE CITY ON FOOT

▶ MORNING

Start with a brisk trot up the 311 steps of the Monument and see how the surrounding narrow streets all slope down towards the Thames. Descend and carry on down Fish Street Hill and across Lower Thames Street to the historic church of **St Magnus the Martyr** *(see p144)*, where a model of the former London Bridge shows the city's great landmark as it was until the 18th century.

Return up Fish Street Hill and Philpot Lane to Lime Street to see the Lloyd's of London building and the affectionately named "Gherkin", 30 St Mary Axe. Enter the ornate, 1881 Leadenhall Market building for trendy shops, restaurants and bars, and a delicious lunch at Luc's Brasserie in the market.

AFTERNOON

After lunch, see the City's historic financial buildings along Cornhill. Notice the Royal Exchange's grand Corinthian portico, behind which is a high-end shopping centre. Opposite is the Mansion House, official residence of London's Lord Mayor. To the north, across Threadneedle Street, is the Bank of England. Continue into Lothbury and along Gresham Street to Guildhall to admire the medieval Great Hall.

Head up Wood Street to the **Barbican Centre** *(see p141)* for coffee or the pre-theatre menu at the Lounge by the lake. Check the programme for the day's events and take in a performance.

See map on pp140–41

City Churches

1 **St Paul's Cathedral**
See pp42–5.

2 **St Bartholomew-the-Great**
MAP R1 ▪ West Smithfield EC1
▪ Open 8:30am–5pm (4pm in winter)
Mon–Fri, 10:30am–4pm Sat,
8:30am–8pm Sun ▪ Adm
This is one of London's oldest
churches, built in the 12th century.
Some Norman architectural details
may be seen *(see p59)*.

3 **St Katharine Cree**
MAP H3 ▪ Leadenhall Street
EC3 ▪ Call 020 7488 4318 for
opening times
One of eight churches to survive the
Great Fire of London in 1666, this
dates from about 1630. Purcell and
Handel both played on its organ.

4 **St Sepulchre-without-Newgate**
MAP Q1 ▪ Holborn Viaduct EC1
▪ Open 11am–3pm Mon–Fri & Sun
The largest church in the City after
St Paul's, St Sepulchre is
famous for its peal of 12
bells. Recitals are held
throughout the week.

5 **St Mary-le-Bow**
MAP G3 ▪
Cheapside EC2 ▪ Open
7:30am–6pm Mon–
Wed, to 6:30pm Thu,
to 4pm Fri
St Mary-le-Bow was
rebuilt by Christopher
Wren after its
destruction in the
1666 Great Fire
of London.

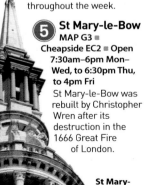

St Mary-le-Bow

6 **St Magnus the Martyr**
MAP H4 ▪ Lower Thames Street
EC3 ▪ Open 10am–4pm Tue–Fri
Designed by Wren in the 1670s, the
splendid church retains its elegant
pulpit. Celebrated choral recitals
take place throughout the year.

7 **All Hallows by the Tower**
MAP H3 ▪ Byward Street EC3 ▪
Open 8am–6pm Mon–Fri, 10am–5pm
Sat and Sun, except during services
Take a guided tour of the church,
which dates from Saxon times.

The dome of St Stephen Walbrook

8 **St Stephen Walbrook**
MAP G3 ▪ 39 Walbrook EC4
▪ Open 10am–4pm Mon–Tue & Thu,
11am–3pm Wed, 10am–3:30pm Fri
Christopher Wren's parish church is
considered to be one of his finest.

9 **St Mary Woolnoth**
MAP G3 ▪ Lombard Street EC3
▪ Open 7:15am–5:15pm Mon–Fri
One of Nicolas Hawksmoor's six
surviving London churches, this was
built in his typically bold Baroque
style and completed in 1727.

10 **St Lawrence Jewry**
MAP R2 ▪ Guildhall EC2
▪ Open 8am–5pm Mon–Fri
Beautiful stained-glass windows of
historic figures are the highlight here

Eating and Drinking

1 St John
MAP F2 ■ 26 St John Street EC1 ■ 020 7251 0848 ■ Disabled access to bar but not to restaurant or toilets ■ ££

A delightful British restaurant famous for "nose-to-tail" dining with bold flavours and a focus on offal. Delicious light bar meals available (see also St John Bread & Wine, p163).

2 Viaduct Tavern
MAP Q1 ■ 126 Newgate Street EC1 ■ 020 7600 1863 ■ £

Built on the site of a former jail, this former Victorian gin palace has a unique period atmosphere thanks to its ornate wall paintings and other original fittings. Sandwiches and snacks are served all week, but not at weekends when the pub is closed.

3 Hawksmoor
MAP G3 ■ 10 Basinghall Street EC2 ■ 020 7397 8120 ■ ££

Huge and bustling, Hawksmoor has revived the old London tradition of the steakhouse, with a variety of cuts, all cooked perfectly to order. Carnivore heaven.

4 Sweetings
MAP R2 ■ 39 Queen Victoria Street EC4 ■ Open 11:30am–3pm Mon–Fri ■ No reservations ■ ££

This is a weekday lunchtime haven for fish lovers. Starters such as potted shrimp are followed by plaice and Dover sole.

5 Vertigo 42
MAP H3 ■ Tower 42, 25 Old Broad Street EC2 ■ 020 7877 7842 ■ Reservations required ■ ££

Ostentatious, sky-scraping champagne bar on the 42nd floor.

Sauterelle in the Royal Exchange

6 Sauterelle
MAP H3 ■ Royal Exchange EC3 ■ 020 7618 2480 ■ £££

Sophisticated French dining in the mezzanine-level gallery of the City's Royal Exchange.

7 City Càphê
MAP G3 ■ 17 Ironmonger Lane EC2 ■ Lunch only ■ £

Small and very popular Vietnamese café in the heart of the City with the classic pork banh mi a speciality. It gets pretty busy so you may need to queue, but it's well worth the wait.

8 1 Lombard Street
MAP G3 ■ 1 Lombard Street EC3 ■ 020 7929 6611 ■ £££

Modern European fare served in a former banking hall. This is one of the city's most striking dining locations. Open Mon–Fri only.

9 Café Below
MAP G3 ■ Cheapside EC2 ■ 020 7329 0789 ■ ££

Café in the crypt of St Mary-le-Bow church. Serves breakfast and lunch (Mon–Fri), and dinner (Wed–Fri).

10 Shaw's Booksellers
MAP Q2 ■ 31–34 St Andrew's Hill EC4 ■ 020 7489 7999 ■ ££

Quirky pub and bar with a splendid array of beers and wines. Mon–Fri.

See map on p140–41

TOP 10 North London

Beyond Regent's Park, London drifts up into areas that were once distant villages where the rich built their country mansions. Parts of their extensive grounds now make up the wild and lofty expanse of Hampstead Heath. Some of the "villages", such as

Karl Marx's tombstone Highgate Cemetery

Hampstead and Highgate, are still distinct from the urban sprawl that surrounds them, with attractive streets full of well-preserved architecture. Other parts of north London have different flavours – from bustling Camden, with its canalside market and lively pubs, to fashionable Islington, with its clothes and antique shops and smart bars.

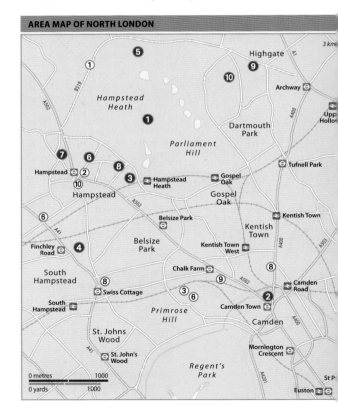

AREA MAP OF NORTH LONDON

1 Hampstead Heath and Parliament Hill

Heath Information Centre, Staff Yard, Highgate Road NW5 ■ Tube Hampstead ■ 020 7482 7073

A welcome retreat from the city, this large, open area is one of the best places in London for walking. Covering 3 sq km (1.5 sq miles) of countryside, it contains ancient woodlands and ponds for swimming and fishing. The top of Parliament Hill has great city views and is a popular place for kite-flying.

2 Camden Markets

Camden High Street and Chalk Farm Road NW1 ■ Tube Camden Town

The most exciting north London markets are open daily from

The 19th-century Keats House

10am–6pm, and linked by the busy and colourful Camden High Street. Camden Market, near the Tube station, has stalls selling clothes, shoes and jewellery. Further up the road, by the canal, both Camden Lock Market and the stalls of Stables Market sell arts and crafts, and ethnic and vintage goods. There are plenty of bars and cafés, plus stalls selling street food (see p79).

3 Keats House

10 Keats Grove NW3 ■ Train to Hampstead Heath, Tube Hampstead or Belsize Park ■ 020 7332 3868 ■ Open Nov–Feb: 11am–5pm Fri–Sun (Mar–Oct: check website) ■ Adm ■ www.cityoflondon.gov.uk

Keats Grove, off Downshire Hill, is one of the loveliest areas of Hampstead. The house where the poet John Keats wrote much of his work contains facsimiles of his fragile manuscripts and letters, and personal possessions (see p50). Hosts poetry readings and talks.

4 Freud Museum

20 Maresfield Gardens NW3 ■ Tube Finchley Road ■ 020 7435 2002 ■ Open noon–5pm Wed–Sun ■ Adm ■ www.freud.org.uk

Sigmund Freud, the founder of psychoanalysis, came to live here when his family fled Nazi-occupied Vienna. The house contains Freud's collection of antiques, his library, including first editions of his own works, and the famous couch on which his patients related their dreams (see p50).

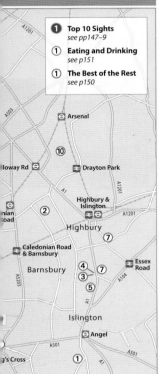

Arsenal

⑩

loway Rd

Drayton Park

Highbury & Islington

② A1201

Highbury

⑦

Caledonian Road & Barnsbury

Barnsbury

④ ⑦

③ Essex Road

⑤

Islington

Angel

's Cross

①

Eighteenth-century Kenwood House, Hampstead Heath

(5) Kenwood House

Hampstead Lane NW3 ■ Tube Golders Green or Archway then bus 210 ■ 020 8348 1286 ■ Open 10am–5pm daily ■ Tours available ■ Free ■ www.english-heritage.org.uk

This magnificent mansion, filled with Old Masters, is set in an idyllic lakeside estate on the edge of Hampstead Heath. Vermeer's *The Guitar Player* and a self-portrait by Rembrandt are among the star attractions. Concerts are held in the summer – audiences picnic in the grassy bowl – and there is a shop and café *(see p63)*.

(6) Burgh House

New End Square NW3 ■ Tube Hampstead ■ 020 7431 0144 ■ Open noon–5pm Wed–Fri, Sun ■ Free

Built in 1704 and housing Hampstead Museum, it has a good selection of local books and a map of the famous people who have lived in the area. The panelled music room is used for concerts and meetings, the Peggy Jay Gallery has contemporary art exhibitions, and the café has a terrace and a cosy indoor space.

(7) Fenton House

Hampstead Grove NW3 ■ Tube Hampstead ■ 020 7435 3471 ■ Open Mar–Nov: 11am–5pm Wed–Sun ■ Adm ■ www.nationaltrust.org.uk/fenton-house

This splendid 17th-century mansion is the oldest in Hampstead. Its exceptionally fine collection of

HAMPSTEAD WELLS

Hampstead's heyday began in the early 18th century, when a spring in Well Walk (**below**) was recognized as having medicinal properties. This brought Londoners flocking to take the waters in the Pump Room within the Great Room in Well Walk, which also housed an Assembly Room for dances and concerts. The spa gradually fell into disrepute, but Hampstead retained its fashionable status.

Oriental and European porcelain, furniture and needlework was bequeathed to the National Trust with the house in 1952. A formal walled garden contains an orchard.

(8) 2 Willow Road

2 Willow Road NW3 ■ Train to Hampstead Heath ■ 020 7435 6166 ■ Open Mar–Oct: 11am–5pm Wed–Sun ■ Adm ■ www.nationaltrust.org.uk/2-willow-road

Designed in 1939 by the architect Ernö Goldfinger for himself and his wife, artist Ursula Blackwell, this is one of the most interesting examples

of modern architecture in the UK.
Goldfinger designed all the furniture
and collected works by Henry Moore,
Max Ernst and Marcel Duchamp.
Admission from 11am–2pm is strictly
limited to hourly tours.

9 Lauderdale House

**Highgate Hill, Waterlow Park
N6 ▪ Tube Archway ▪ 020 8348 8716
▪ Open 11am–4pm Wed–Fri, 1:30–
5pm Sat, 10am–5pm Sun**

Dating from the late 16th century,
Lauderdale House was once
associated with Charles II and his
mistress Nell Gwynne. It now houses
a popular arts and cultural centre,
with regular concerts and exhibitions.

10 Highgate Cemetery

**Swain's Lane N6 ▪ Tube
Archway ▪ 020 8340 1834 ▪ East
Cemetery: open 10am–4pm Mon–Fri,
11am–4pm Sat–Sun, last adm 30 min
prior to closing ▪ Closed for funerals
(phone to check) ▪ West Cemetery:
booked guided tours only, 1:45pm
Mon–Fri, 11am–3pm Sat–Sun ▪ Adm
for both ▪ www.highgate-cemetery.org**

Across the heath from Hampstead,
Highgate developed as a healthy,
countrified place for nobility who
built large mansions here. Many
famous people who lived in the area
are buried in Highgate Cemetery.
Opened in 1839, its Victorian
architecture and fine views soon
made it a very popular outing for
Londoners. Karl Marx and novelist
George Eliot are buried in the less
glamorous East Cemetery.

Highgate Cemetery

EXPLORING NORTH LONDON

▶ MORNING

Starting at Hampstead Tube
station, head left down pretty
Flask Walk (the Flask pub once
sold spa water) to the local
museum in **Burgh House** for
some background on the area.
Then spend some time exploring
the many attractive back streets,
most of which are lined with
expensive Georgian houses and
mansions. Visit Well Walk,
fashionable in the days of the
Hampstead spa (a fountain in
Well Passage on the left still
remains).

Stop for a coffee at one of the
many cafés along Hampstead
High Street and then make your
way to **Keats House** *(see p147)*,
spending half an hour looking
around. Afterwards, a stroll across
Hampstead Heath to **Kenwood
House** will prepare you for lunch.

AFTERNOON

The Brew House at Kenwood
serves excellent light meals and
has a fine position beside the
house, overlooking the lake. After
lunch, visit the house itself.

Leave the Heath by the nearby
East Lodge and catch a No. 210
bus back towards Hampstead.
The bus passes the **Spaniards Inn**
(see p63) and Whitestone Pond,
the Heath's highest point. Alight
at the pond and walk to the Tube
station, taking a train to Camden
Town. Spend the rest of the afternoon in lively **Camden Lock
Market** *(see p147)*, ending the day
on the **Lock Tavern** roof terrace.

See map on pp146–7

The Best of the Rest

(1) Sadler's Wells
MAP F2 ▪ Rosebery Avenue EC1 ▪ 020 7863 8000 ▪ www.sadlerswells.com
London's premier venue for dance attracts internationally renowned artists and companies from around the world (see p71).

(2) Freightliners Farm
Sheringham Road N7 ▪ Tube Highbury & Islington, Caledonian Road ▪ 020 7609 0467 ▪ www.freightlinersfarm.org.uk
A little bit of the countryside in the city with animals, produce, gardens and a vegetarian café.

(3) Almeida Theatre
Almeida Street N1 ▪ Tube Angel or Highbury & Islington ▪ 020 7359 4404 ▪ www.almeida.co.uk
This famous local theatre attracts top actors and directors from the UK and the US.

(4) Alexandra Palace
Alexandra Palace Way N22 ▪ Tube Wood Green ▪ 020 8365 2121
Set in the 196 acres of Alexandra Park, this reconstructed 1873 exhibition centre offers a range of amusements, including regular antique fairs and an ice-skating rink.

(5) King's Head Theatre Pub
MAP F1 ▪ 115 Upper Street N1 ▪ 020 7226 8561 ▪ www.kingsheadtheatre.com
A busy, delightful Victorian pub with a 110-seat theatre hosting opera performances and new plays at the back. A wide selection of wines and real ale.

Alexandra Palace

(6) Camden Arts Centre
Arkwright Road NW3 ▪ Train or tube to Finchley Road ▪ 020 7472 5500 ▪ www.camdenartscentre.org
Known for its fascinating contemporary art exhibitions and excellent art book shop.

(7) Estorick Collection
39A Canonbury Square N1 ▪ Tube Highbury and Islington ▪ 020 7704 9522 ▪ www.estorickcollection.com
Elegant Georgian house with a superb collection of 20th-century Italian art, including works by Amedeo Modigliani and Emilio Greco.

(8) Hampstead Theatre
Eton Avenue NW3 ▪ Tube Swiss Cottage (exit 2) ▪ 020 7722 9301 ▪ www.hampsteadtheatre.com
This important fringe theatre is a venue for ambitious new writing, and has produced plays by innovative English writers such as Harold Pinter, Michael Frayn and Mike Leigh.

(9) Roundhouse
Chalk Farm Road NW1 ▪ Tube Chalk Farm ▪ 0300 678 9222 ▪ www.roundhouse.org.uk
This former Victorian railway shed is now an exciting venue for both theatre and music.

(10) Emirates Stadium Tours
Hornsey Road, Highbury N7 ▪ Tube Arsenal ▪ 020 7619 5000
The tour of the stadium – home to Arsenal Football Club – takes in the directors' box, home changing room, players' tunnel and the Arsenal Museum.

Eating and Drinking

PRICE CATEGORIES
For a three-course meal for one with half a bottle of wine (or equivalent meal), taxes and extra charges.

£ under £25 ■ ££ £25–50 ■ £££ over £50

1 Spaniards Inn
Spaniards Road NW3 ■ 020 3731 8406 ■ Tube Hampstead or East Finchley ■ ££

One of London's most famous old pubs, this offers traditional English pub food and gourmet burgers.

2 The Flask
14 Flask Walk NW3 ■ Tube Hampstead ■ 020 7435 4580 ■ ££

Dating from 1700, this pub has a country atmosphere and good cask beer and home-made pub food.

3 Manna
4 Erskine Road, Primrose Hill NW3 ■ Tube Chalk Farm ■ 020 7722 8028 ■ ££

Global vegetarian and vegan cuisine is served with style in this modern restaurant with a friendly ambience.

4 Antepliler
MAP G1 ■ 139 Upper Street N1 ■ 020 7226 5441 ■ ££

Antepliler celebrates Turkish cuisine, with irresistable aromatic meats, melt-in-the-mouth aubergines and silky, creamy yoghurt.

5 Camino
MAP E1 ■ 3 Varnisher's Yard N1 ■ 020 7841 7330 ■ ££

Offering tapas and great cocktails as well as Spanish wines, sherries and traditional cider, Camino has a relaxed atmosphere and lively bar.

6 Lemonia
89 Regent's Park Road NW1 ■ Tube Chalk Farm ■ 020 7586 7454 ■ ££

Traditional and modern Greek dishes served in a brasserie-style setting. There is an attractive conservatory.

Spaniards Inn, Hampstead Heath

7 Ottolenghi
MAP G1 ■ 287 Upper Street N1 ■ 020 7288 1454 ■ ££

Yotam Ottolenghi has revitalized London's approach to Middle Eastern food with his flavourful dishes based on the finest – and sometimes unusual – ingredients.

8 Arancini Brothers
115A Kentish Town Road NW1 ■ Tube Camden Town ■ 020 3583 2242 ■ £

A characterful café whose speciality is arancini, risotto rice balls stuffed with a mix of vegetables and mozzarella, coated with flour and fried. There are plenty of options, all made on the premises and all delicious.

9 Rotunda
MAP E1 ■ 90 York Way N1 ■ 020 7014 2840 ■ ££

A classy restaurant with fine views of the Battlebridge Basin. The menu changes regularly and uses seasonal ingredients; the meat is sourced from their own farm.

10 Louis Patisserie
32 Heath Street NW3 ■ Tube Hampstead ■ 020 7435 9908 ■ £ (cash only)

This wonderful old tea room is part of Hampstead folklore. Sink into a comfortable sofa and sample some of the tempting cakes on offer.

See map on pp146–7

TOP10 South and West London

The palaces that once graced London's river to the south and west of the city centre were built in places that remain popular today, from Hampton Court and Richmond in the west, downriver to Greenwich. There, on a deep meander in the Thames, a vast Tudor palace was the dramatic first sight of the city for anyone arriving by ship. It has been replaced by Wren's handsome Old Royal Naval College, a stunning building that is the high point of this UNESCO World Heritage Site and the start of the many delights of Greenwich, home of Greenwich Mean Time and *Cutty Sark*, the world's last surviving tea clipper.

Shepherd Gate Clock, Greenwich

Richmond's palace has also disappeared, but opposite the Park lies Kew Palace in the grounds of the incomparable Royal Botanic Gardens. Chiswick House, Ham House and Syon House are the best of a number of palatial mansions near Richmond, while culture is catered for in the Dulwich Picture Gallery and the Horniman Museum.

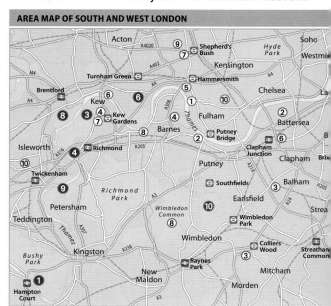

AREA MAP OF SOUTH AND WEST LONDON

Hampton Court

East Molesey, Surrey KT8 ■
Train Hampton Court ■ **0844 482
7777** ■ **Open Apr–Oct: 10am–6pm
daily; Nov–Mar: 10am–4:30pm daily
(last adm 1 hour before closing)** ■
Adm ■ **www.hrp.org.uk**

Originally leased and substantially
enlarged by Cardinal Wolsey in 1514,
Hampton Court was handed over to
Henry VIII in 1528. Visiting this historic Tudor palace and its extensive
grounds is a popular day out from
London. As well as family trails and
special exhibitions, audio tours are
available and costumed interpreters
bring the Tudor world to life. Events
held through the year include a
week-long music festival in June,
which regularly attracts big-name
performers. In July, the grounds are
filled by the world's largest flower
show, organized by the Royal
Horticultural Society. Trains from
Waterloo take about half an hour but
for a delightfully leisurely trip, catch
a boat from Westminster Pier, which
takes about four hours (see p54).

Greenhouses, Royal Botanic Gardens

Greenwich

Greenwich SE10 ■ **Train to
Greenwich; DLR Cutty Sark,
Greenwich** ■ **Royal Observatory
Greenwich: Open 10am–5pm daily**
■ **Adm** ■ **www.visitgreenwich.org.uk**
■ **www.rmg.co.uk**

The World Heritage Site of
Greenwich includes Sir Christopher
Wren's Old Royal Naval College,
Greenwich Park (see p57), the
Planetarium and the Royal
Observatory Greenwich where the
Prime Meridian, longitude 0°, was
established. Bordering the park are
the Queen's House (see p55) and
National Maritime Museum (see p60).
Greenwich has some excellent
restaurants and shops as well as
historic Greenwich Market. The
nearby restored tea clipper, Cutty
Sark (see p65), is a must-see.

Royal Botanic
Gardens, Kew

Kew TW9 ■ **Train & Tube Kew Gardens**
■ **020 8332 5655** ■ **Open 9:30am daily
(10am May–Oct); closing times vary
between 4:15–5:30pm in winter and
6–7:30pm in summer. Call for info** ■
Adm ■ **www.kew.org**

This former royal garden holds the
world's largest plant collection of
around 30,000 specimens. Kew
Palace and Queen Charlotte's
Cottage (see p54) were used as
residences by George III, whose
parents, Prince Frederick and
Princess Augusta, laid the first
garden here. Take a Kew Explorer
Land train tour of the gardens – you
can get on and off it any time.

ondon
ridge
wark
Rotherhithe
Canary
Wharf ⑤
Thames
A13
Isle of
Dogs
3 km
⑨
alworth
A200
Deptford
Greenwich ②
berwell
A202
A2
Lewisham
Peckham
A2
Dulwich
⑤
Forest
Hill ⑦
A205 Catford
A205
Hither
Green
/est
wich
0 kilometres 3
0 miles 3
per
vood

Georgian buildings lining the bank of the Thames, Richmond

4 Richmond

Train to Richmond ■ Museum of Richmond: open 11am–5pm Tue–Fri, 10am–4pm Sat ■ www.museumofrichmond.com

This attractive, wealthy riverside suburb, with its quaint shops and pubs and pretty lanes, is particularly worth a visit for its delightful riverside walks and its vast royal park which is home to red and fallow deer (see p57). There is also a spacious Green, where cricket is played in summer, which is overlooked by the lovely restored Richmond Theatre and the early 18th-century Maids of Honour Row, which stands next to the last vestiges of an enormous Tudor palace. For some history visit the local Museum, in the Old Town Hall, where the visitor information centre is based.

5 Dulwich Picture Gallery

Gallery Road SE21 ■ Train to North or West Dulwich ■ 020 8693 5254 ■ Open 10am–5pm Tue–Sun ■ Adm

The oldest purpose-built public art space in England, this gallery (see p62) is located opposite the main entrance to Dulwich Park and is well worth the journey from central London. Apart from the stunning collection, there are regular exhibitions, lectures and other events, as well as over 12,000 sq m (130,000 sq ft) of lawns on which to relax.

6 Chiswick House

Burlington Lane, Chiswick W4 ■ Tube Turnham Green ■ 020 8995 0508 ■ Open Mar–Sep: 10am–6pm Sun–Wed; Oct: 10am–5pm Sun–Wed ■ Adm (house) ■ www.chgt.org.uk

This piece of Italy in London is a high spot of English 18th-century architecture. The villa, with its dome, portico and beautifully painted interiors, was built for Lord Burlington by architect William Kent. Temples, statues and a lake complete the Italianate gardens.

7 Horniman Museum

100 London Road SE23 ■ Train to Forest Hill ■ 020 8699 1872 ■ Open 10:30am–5:30pm daily ■ www.horniman.ac.uk

Built in 1901 by Frederick Horniman, this distinctive museum appeals to both adults and children. It has a superb anthropological collection, along with galleries on natural

GREENWICH PALACE

The ruins of this enormous royal riverside palace lie beneath the Old Royal Naval College. Many of the Tudor monarchs lived here, including Henry VII and Henry VIII – who was born here. Abandoned under the Commonwealth in 1652, it was eventually demolished for Wren's present buildings.

history. There is also a state-of-the-art aquarium (admission charge) and a café overlooking the gardens.

⑧ Syon House and Park

Brentford, Middlesex ▪ Train to Kew Bridge ▪ 020 8560 0882 ▪ Open mid-Mar–Oct: 11am–5pm Wed, Thu & Sun (gardens: 10:30am–5pm daily) ▪ Adm ▪ www.syonpark.co.uk

This sumptuous Neo-Classical villa is home to the Duke of Northumberland. It has fine Robert Adam interiors and a 0.4-sq-km (0.2-sq-mile) garden landscaped by Capability Brown and dominated by a splendid conservatory.

⑨ Ham House and Garden

Ham Street, Richmond, Surrey ▪ Train to Richmond ▪ 020 8940 1950 ▪ Check website for opening hours ▪ Adm ▪ www.nationaltrust.org.uk/ham-house-and-garden

This outstanding 17th-century house and garden was at the centre of court intrigue during Charles II's reign. Its interiors are richly furnished and there is a fine picture collection. The Orangery serves dishes made from its garden produce.

The front of Ham House

⑩ Wimbledon Lawn Tennis Museum

Church Road, Wimbledon SW19 ▪ Tube Southfields ▪ 020 8946 6131 ▪ Open 10am–5pm daily ▪ Adm ▪ www.wimbledon.com

With a view of the famous Centre Court, the museum tells the story of tennis, from its gentle, amateur beginnings to its professional status today. The first tennis championships were held in Wimbledon in 1877.

A DAY EXPLORING MARITIME GREENWICH

▶ MORNING

Start the day from Westminster Pier, because the best way to arrive at **Greenwich** (see p153) is by boat. The journey takes 50–60 minutes and there are terrific river sights on the way (see pp64–5). Visit the historic tea clipper **Cutty Sark** (see p165) which reopened in 2012 after extensive restoration.

Behind is Greenwich Market, liveliest on weekends. Grab a coffee here, and then explore the surrounding streets, full of antique and other charming shops. Turn into Wren's Old Royal Naval College, visit the magnificent Painted Hall and admire its murals, then walk around the Grand Square and down to the river. Stop for some lunch and a pint at the old Trafalgar Tavern on the far side of the Naval College overlooking the river.

AFTERNOON

After lunch, make your way to the **National Maritime Museum** (see p60), Queen's House and the **Royal Observatory Greenwich** (see p153), which is on the hill behind. Explore the fascinating museum, the largest of its kind in the world, then make your way to the observatory. This is the home of world time, and stands on the 0° longitude Prime Meridian. You can be photographed with one foot in the eastern hemisphere and one in the west. Return to Central London by boat, Emirates Air Line (see p156), DLR or rail from Greenwich.

See map on pp152–3

The Best of the Rest

1 Brixton Market
Electric Avenue to Brixton Station Road SW9 ■ Tube Brixton ■ brixtonmarket.net

This lively market lies at the heart of London's Caribbean community. Shop for secondhand vinyl, fresh produce and bargain fabrics, and enjoy a range of street food in nearby Brixton Village and Market Row.

2 Battersea Park
Entertainments in this large park include a boating lake, a children's zoo, sports facilities, and a gallery. There is also a woodland walk, the riverside Peace Pagoda, and sculptures by Henry Moore and Barbara Hepworth (see p69).

3 Merton Abbey Mills
Watermill Way SW19 ■ Tube Colliers Wood ■ www.mertonabbeymills.org.uk

An arts and crafts village on the River Wandle, with a working Victorian watermill, a children's theatre and weekend craft market.

4 WWT London Wetland Centre
Queen Elizabeth Walk SW13 ■ Train to Barnes ■ Open 9:30am–6pm daily (winter: 9:30am–5pm) ■ Adm ■ www.wwt.org.uk

Managed by the Wildfowl & Wetlands Trust, this haven for wild birds and animals is one of the best urban wildlife sites in Europe.

5 Emirates Air Line
27 Western Gateway Royal Docks E16 and Greenwich Peninsula SE10 ■ Open Apr–Sep 7am–9pm Mon–Fri (from 8am Sat, 9am Sun), Oct–Mar closes 8pm ■ Adm ■ www.emiratesairline.co.uk

This cable car links Docklands with Greenwich Peninsula, offering great views of the city and river.

6 Battersea Arts Centre (BAC)
Lavender Hill SW11 ■ Train to Clapham Junction ■ 020 7223 2223 ■ www.bac.org.uk

One of the main fringe theatre venues in the capital, with a huge programme of activities.

7 Bush Theatre
7 Uxbridge Road W12 ■ Tube Shepherd's Bush ■ 020 8743 5050 ■ www.bushtheatre.co.uk

This off-West End theatre is one of London's premier showcases for new writers.

8 Wimbledon Common
Wimbledon Common SW19 ■ Train to Wimbledon ■ www.wpcc.org.uk

Visit the windmill then enjoy a walk. Head for southside pubs the Crooked Billet and the Hand in Hand.

9 Firepower
Royal Arsenal, Woolwich SE18 ■ Train to Woolwich Arsenal ■ Open 10am–5pm Tue–Sat ■ Adm ■ www.firepower.org.uk

An exciting museum at the historic home of the Royal Artillery. Includes a spectacular multimedia display.

10 World Rugby Museum
Rugby Road ■ Train to Twickenham ■ 020 8892 8877 ■ Call or check website for open hours ■ Adm ■ www.englandrugby.com/twickenham/world-rugby-museum

At Twickenham Stadium, the national home of rugby. A visit includes a tour of the impressive stadium.

The Emirates Air Line cable car

Eating and Drinking

PRICE CATEGORIES

For a three-course meal for one with half a bottle of wine (or equivalent meal), taxes and extra charges.

£ under £25   ££ £25–50   £££ over £50

The City Barge pub at Chiswick

1 The River Café
Thames Wharf, Rainville Road W6 ■ Tube Hammersmith ■ 020 7386 4200 ■ £££

The "best Italian restaurant outside Italy" is the long-standing reputation of this imaginative Hammersmith restaurant, housed in a converted warehouse with a river terrace.

2 Thai Square Putney Bridge
2–4 Lower Richmond Road SW15 ■ Tube Putney Bridge ■ 020 8780 1811 ■ ££

A brilliant view of the river from this smart, innovative glass restaurant makes it a good spot year-round, and the Thai menu is excellent.

3 Chez Bruce
2 Bellevue Road SW17 ■ Train to Wandsworth Common ■ 020 8672 0114 ■ £££

Stylish yet relaxed, Michelin-starred Chez Bruce serves excellent modern European food next to leafy Wandsworth Common. Service is impeccable and booking is essential.

4 The Glasshouse
14 Station Parade, Kew, TW9 ■ Tube Kew Gardens ■ 020 8940 6777 ■ No disabled access ■ £££

The food is exciting, modern European at this relaxed restaurant.

5 The Gate
51 Queen Caroline Street W6 ■ Tube Hammersmith ■ 020 8748 6932 ■ No disabled access ■ ££

Probably the best vegetarian restaurant in London, The Gate is worth hunting out. The gourmet menu changes regularly, and the meals are hearty and inventive.

6 The City Barge
27 Strand-on-the-Green W6 ■ Train to Kew Bridge ■ 020 8994 2148 ■ ££

Set in a delightful enclave of 18th-century Thames-side London, this appealing pub serves hearty food.

7 Inn at Kew Gardens
Kew Gardens Hotel, 292 Sandycombe Road, Kew TW9 ■ Tube Kew Gardens ■ 020 8940 2220 ■ ££

Perfectly located beside Kew Gardens, this lovely hostelry has great ales and moreish gastro food.

8 The Brown Dog
28 Cross Street SW13 ■ Train Barnes Bridge ■ 020 8392 2200 ■ ££

With its warm atmosphere, this gastropub feels like a real discovery. Beer is sourced locally and in the summer you can eat in the garden.

9 Esarn Kheaw
314 Uxbridge Road W12 ■ Tube Shepherd's Bush ■ 020 8743 8930 ■ £

Authentic Thai food, with all the usual favourites as well as more unusual dishes such as mud fish sweet and sour soup.

10 The Harwood Arms
Walham Grove SW6 ■ Tube Fulham Broadway ■ 020 7386 1847 ■ £££

The first gastropub to be awarded a Michelin star, the Harwood Arms offers delicious bar snacks and an inventive British menu.

See map on pp152–3

ᴛᴏᴘ10 East London

Always a vibrant, working-class area, the East End has also prided itself on providing a refuge for successive generations of immigrants, from French silk weavers to Jewish and Bangladeshi garment workers. Today, the media and finance worlds occupy stylish developments in the Docklands, galleries and restaurants have sprouted in Hoxton and trendy markets draw visitors who marvel at the area's unspoiled 18th- and 19th-century architecture.

Rugs, Spitalfields Market

AREA MAP OF EAST LONDON

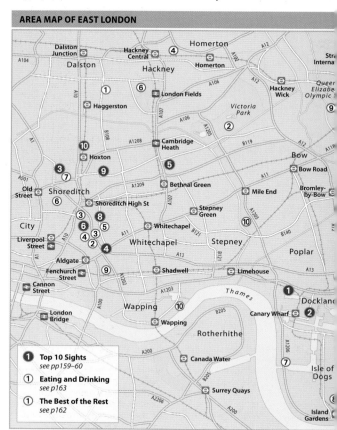

1 **Top 10 Sights**
see pp159–60

1 **Eating and Drinking**
see p163

1 **The Best of the Rest**
see p162

① Museum of London Docklands

West India Quay E14 ▪ Tube & DLR Canary Wharf, DLR West India Quay, Thames Clippers Canary Wharf Pier ▪ 020 7001 9844 ▪ Open 10am–6pm daily ▪ www.museumoflondon.org.uk

Set in a historic warehouse, this museum explores the history of London's river, port and people. A wealth of objects is on display. Don't miss Mudlarks, an interactive area for kids; Sailortown, an atmospheric re-creation of 19th-century riverside Wapping; and London, Sugar & Slavery, which reveals the city's involvement in the slave trade.

The iconic towers of Canary Wharf

② Canary Wharf

Tube & DLR Canary Wharf

The centrepiece of the Docklands development is Canary Wharf and the 240-m (800-ft) One Canada Square designed by the US architect Cesar Pelli. The tower is not open to the public but parts of the complex are, including the mall, with shops, restaurants and bars. The star of the area's exciting architecture is the stunning Canary Wharf station, designed by Norman Foster.

③ Hoxton

Tube Old Street or train Hoxton

Once renowned as a hub for British contemporary art (thanks in large part to the now-closed White Cube art gallery on Hoxton Square), this trendy area is now home to a growing tech community around the junction of Old Street and City Road, dubbed 'Silicon Roundabout'. Lively at night, pubs and restaurants here include The Three Crowns, The Fox and 8 Hoxton Square *(see p162)*.

④ Whitechapel Gallery

MAP H3 ▪ 77–82 Whitechapel High Street E1 ▪ 020 7522 7888 ▪ Open 11am–6pm Tue–Sun (Thu 9pm) ▪ www.whitechapelgallery.org

This excellent gallery has a reputation for showing cutting-edge contemporary art from around the world. The gallery has launched the careers of David Hockney, Gilbert and George and Anthony Caro. Behind the distinctive 1901 Arts and Crafts façade there is a bookshop, café and restaurant.

Maryland
Forest Gate
Forest Gate A118
Stratford
① Stratford
A118
A112
West Ham Park
B165
West Ham
A114
Upton Park
Plaistow
A124
West Ham
A1011
Plaistow
A124
A112
A13
Canning Town
Canning Town
Pontoon Dock
A1020
Silvertown
Thames Barrier Park
Thames
North Greenwich
⑦
A102
A2052

0 kilometres   1
0 miles   1

5 V&A Museum of Childhood

Cambridge Heath Road E2 ▪ Tube Bethnal Green ▪ 020 8983 5200 ▪ Open 10am–5:45pm daily ▪ www. vam.ac.uk/moc

Everyone will find something to delight them here: from dolls and teddy bears to train sets and games through the ages. There are activities for children of all ages every day, plus special events at weekends and in school holidays, some linked to current exhibitions.

6 Spitalfields

MAP H2 ▪ Commercial Street E1 ▪ Main market Thu–Sun

Streets such as Fournier Street, lined with 18th-century Huguenot silk weavers' houses, are a reminder that this area, just east of the City, has provided a refuge for immigrant populations for centuries. London's oldest market, Old Spitalfields Market still has stalls selling food, with cafés and a large shopping complex around its edge. On Sundays the market draws hundreds of browsers and shoppers, eager to find a bargain among the fashion, vintage clothing, and crafts stalls here. There are also free events such as lunchtime concerts. Opposite is one of Europe's great Baroque churches. Christ Church, built between 1714 and 1729, was designed by Nicholas Hawksmoor.

THE HUGUENOTS IN LONDON

Driven from France in 1685, the Huguenots were Protestants fleeing religious persecution by Catholics. They were mostly silk weavers, whose masters and merchants settled in Spitalfields and built the beautiful Georgian houses around Fournier (**below**), Princelet and Elder streets. Spitalfields silk was famous for its fine quality, but by the mid-19th century the industry had declined.

7 Thames Barrier

Information Centre ▪ 1 Unity Way SE18 ▪ Train to Charlton, Tube North Greenwich ▪ 020 8305 4188 ▪ Open 10:30am–5pm Thu–Sun ▪ Adm

With its 10 curved gates rising like shark fins from the river, this impressive piece of engineering is a magnificent sight *(see p65)*.

8 Brick Lane

Brick Lane E1 ▪ Tube Aldgate East

Once the centre of London's Jewish population, this street is now the

The silver fins of the Thames Barrier

Brick Lane

heart of London's Bangladeshi community. Some of the city's best bagels are available from the 24-hour Brick Lane Beigel Bake, a famous dawn haunt for late-night revellers. There are inexpensive restaurants, vintage and designer shops and, on Sundays, a lively flea market.

⑨ **Columbia Road Market**
Columbia Road E2 ▪ Tube Old Street ▪ Petticoat Lane E1 ▪ Tube Aldgate East

Londoners head east on Sunday mornings for the bustling street markets. In addition to Petticoat Lane in Middlesex Street, with its bargain clothes and household items, and Brick Lane's bric-à-brac, there is the teeming plant and flower market in Columbia Road. A ten-minute walk from the north end of Brick Lane, Columbia Road is a delightful cornucopia of all things horticultural at bargain prices.

⑩ **The Geffrye**
MAP H2 ▪ 136 Kingsland Road E2 ▪ Train to Hoxton ▪ 020 7739 9893 ▪ Open 10am–5pm Tue–Sun

Set in a beautiful 18th-century almshouse, this fascinating museum explores the evolution of the home and home life from 1600 to the present day. A series of rooms and gardens are decorated in distinct period style, reflecting changes in society, behaviour, style and taste: wander through an oak-panelled 17th-century drawing room, a 1930s flat or a contemporary loft apartment. Period gardens are open from April to October.

A DAY AROUND THE EAST END

Elder Street · Old Spitalfields Market · Princelet Street · Fournier Street · Brick Lane · Whitechapel Gallery · Canary Wharf (4km) · DLR · Tower Gateway Station

▶ **MORNING**

Start at **Old Spitalfields Market** where a mixture of stalls hold sway during the week, and many more, selling clothes, food and collectibles, fill the floor on Sundays. Have a delicious breakfast at St John Bread & Wine opposite the market at 96 Commercial Street (see p163).

Walk around the corner into Fournier Street, where the gallery at No. 5 retains the panelling of the 18th-century silk weavers' houses. Stroll along Princelet and Elder streets, just off Fournier, for a taste of historic London.

Head into **Brick Lane** to browse among the sari and Bangladeshi gift shops and then stop for lunch at one of the many curry houses.

AFTERNOON

After lunch head to Whitechapel Road. Notice the Arts and Crafts façade of the **Whitechapel Gallery** (see p159). Pop into the gallery's stunning two-floor exhibition space dedicated to contemporary and modern art.

Finally, take a ride on the driverless Docklands Light Railway (from Tower Gateway), for some of the best views of East London. Emerge at Canary Wharf to see some impressive architecture around Cabot Square, and end the day with a drink at The Gun (see p163) on Cold Harbour.

Canary Wharf clock

The Best of the Rest

1 Theatre Royal Stratford East
Gerry Raffles Square E15 ▪ Train, Tube & DLR Stratford ▪ 020 8534 0310
This local theatre with an international reputation was established by the director Joan Littlewood in 1953.

2 Victoria Park
Bow E9 ▪ Tube Bethnal Green
One of East London's largest and most pleasant parks. There is a boating lake and ornamental garden.

3 Dennis Severs' House
MAP H2 ▪ 18 Folgate Street E1 ▪ 020 7247 4013 ▪ Call to check opening times ▪ Adm ▪ www.dennissevershouse.co.uk
This 18th-century silk-weaver's home (see p160) is kept in period and was created by artist Dennis Severs. Each room appears as if the inhabitants have only just left it – dinner is half-eaten and cooking smells emanate from the kitchen.

4 Sutton House
2–4 Homerton High Street E9 ▪ Train Hackney Central ▪ 020 8986 2264 ▪ Open noon–5pm Wed–Sun, daily in Aug ▪ Adm ▪ www. nationaltrust.org.uk/sutton-house
This Tudor merchant's house dates from 1535 and is one of the oldest in the East End.

5 House Mill
Three Mill Lane E3 ▪ Tube Bromley-by-Bow ▪ 020 8980 4626 ▪ Open May–Oct: 11am–4pm Sun ▪ Adm ▪ housemill.org.uk
Built in 1776, this tidal mill was once the country's largest. Today it is a working museum. Guided tours only.

6 London Fields Lido
London Fields Westside E8 ▪ Train Hackney Central ▪ 020 7254 9038 ▪ Adm
Amidst the greenery of London Fields is an Olympic-sized, Art Deco heated outdoor swimming pool.

7 Docklands Sailing & Watersports Centre
Millwall Dock, 235a Westferry Road E14 ▪ DLR Crossharbour ▪ 020 7537 2626 ▪ www.dswc.org
Enjoy sailing, kayaking and windsurfing facilities here.

8 Mudchute Farm
Pier Street E14 ▪ Open 8am–4pm daily ▪ DLR Mudchute ▪ 020 7515 5901
Britain's largest city farm has livestock and a riding school.

ArcelorMittal Orbit

9 ArcelorMittal Orbit
3 Thornton Street E20 ▪ Train, Tube & DLR Stratford ▪ Adm ▪ www.arcelormittalorbit.com
Designed by Anish Kapoor and Cecil Balmond for the 2012 London Olympics, this tower overlooks the Queen Elizabeth Olympic Park.

10 Mile End Park
Mile End Road E3 ▪ Tube Mile End ▪ 020 7364 0902
For skateboarders and would-be mountain climbers. There is also a go-kart track and an Ecology Park.

Eating and Drinking

PRICE CATEGORIES
For a three-course meal for one with half a bottle of wine (or equivalent meal), taxes and extra charges.

£ under £25   ££ £25–50   £££ over £50

1 The Richmond
316 Queensbridge Road E8
■ 020 7241 1638 ■ ££
This fashionable bar and restaurant is home to east London's first and only raw seafood bar.

2 Adiva
MAP H2 ■ 43A Commerical Street E1 ■ 020 7247 7181 ■ ££
Lebanese and Turkish fusion. Bring your own bottle, with small corkage fees. Belly dancing on Friday and Saturday evenings.

3 St John Bread & Wine
MAP H2 ■ 94–96 Commercial Street E1 ■ 020 7251 0848 ■ ££
This sister restaurant of St John (p145) is a much-loved local haunt. It has a great wine list, and the bakery sells amazing bread and cakes to go.

4 Canteen
MAP H2 ■ 2 Crispin Place, off Brushfield Street E1 ■ 0845 686 1122 ■ ££
Located in the complex next to Old Spitalfields Market, Canteen serves traditional British food all day.

5 Sheba
MAP H3 ■ 136 Brick Lane E1 ■ 0207 247 7824 ■ ££
There's plenty of competition to be found in Brick Lane, but Sheba has

St John Bread & Wine

8 Hoxton Square

maintained an impressively consistent record when it comes to producing classy curries.

6 The Fox
MAP H2 ■ 28 Paul Street EC2 ■ 020 7729 5708 ■ £££
Good food can be had upstairs in this lovely refurbished pub, which is frequented by City types looking for decent ales and wines.

7 8 Hoxton Square
MAP H2 ■ 8 Hoxton Square N1 ■ Train Hoxton ■ 020 7729 4232 ■ ££
This hip restaurant serves modern British cuisine and an imaginative weekend breakfast menu.

8 The Gun
27 Cold Harbour E14 ■ DLR South Quay/Blackwell ■ 020 7515 5222 ■ ££
This swish Docklands operation overlooking the Thames serves up quality gastropub food.

9 Café Spice Namaste
16 Prescot Street E1 ■ Tube Tower Hill & Aldgate ■ 020 7488 9242 ■ ££
One of the best Indian restaurants in London, serving pan-Indian food with Asian and European influences. Closed Sundays.

10 Prospect of Whitby
57 Wapping Wall E1 ■ Tube Wapping ■ 020 7481 1095 ■ ££
East London's oldest riverside pub dates to 1520, and has old beams, a pewter bar and great river views.

See map on pp158–9

Streetsmart

The light and spacious interior of
St Pancras International Station

Getting To and Around London

Arriving by Air

Five airports serve London: Heathrow, Gatwick, Stansted, Luton and City.

Heathrow, London's main airport, is 24 km (15 miles) west of central London. The **Heathrow Express** to Paddington is the quickest (and priciest) way into the centre, taking 20 minutes. Trains run from 5am until 11:30pm daily. The **Heathrow Connect**, which departs every 30 minutes is cheaper but slower. Cheaper still is the Tube, which takes 50 minutes to central London. Alternatively, **National Express** runs a coach service from Heathrow's bus station to **Victoria Coach Station**.

London's second airport, **Gatwick**, is 45 km (28 miles) south of London. The **Gatwick Express** train leaves the South Terminal every 15 minutes for Victoria railway station, taking 30 minutes. The National Express coach takes an hour longer, leaving for Victoria every 1.5–2 hours.

Stansted, London's third busiest airport, is 56 km (35 miles) northeast of London. The **Stansted Express** train to Liverpool Street takes 45 minutes and runs every 15 minutes. National Express provides 24-hour coaches to Victoria and Stratford, taking between 1 and 2 hours. From **Luton Airport**, 50 km (31 miles) north of the city, a shuttle bus takes passengers to Luton Airport Parkway station, from which trains go to St Pancras, taking 20 minutes. **Green Line** operates a 24-hour coach service to central London. **London City Airport** is 14 km (9 miles) from the centre. The airport is served by **Docklands Light Railway** (DLR) from Bank Tube station.

Arriving by Coach

Coaches from European and UK destinations arrive at Victoria Coach Station. The biggest operator in the UK is National Express, with **Eurolines** serving as its European arm.

Arriving by Rail

St Pancras International is the London terminus for **Eurostar**, the high-speed train linking the UK with the Continent. London's other main stations are Liverpool Street, King's Cross, Euston, Paddington, Waterloo, Charing Cross and Victoria.

Arriving by Sea and Channel Tunnel

Eurotunnel operates a drive-on-drive-off train service between Calais, in France, and Folkestone, in the south of England (35 minutes). Car ferries from Calais to Dover, the shortest Channel crossing, take around 90 minutes and the drive on to London takes around 1 hour and 50 minutes.

Passenger and car-ferry services also sail from other ports in northern France to the south of England, as well as from Bilbao and Santander in Spain to Portsmouth or Plymouth. Ferry services also run to other ports around the country from the Netherlands and the Republic of Ireland.

Travelling by Underground, DLR and Train

The **London Underground** or the "Tube" is the fastest and easiest way to get around the city, but trains are crowded during rush hour. The lines are colour-coded making it easy to follow with the map on the back cover of this book. Trains run daily (except 25 December) from around 5:15am to after midnight. Five lines run 24 hours a day on Fridays and Saturdays.

The DLR is an automated, driver-less light rail system connecting the City of London with the Docklands. **London Overground**'s rail network links the suburbs. The suburban boroughs are also served through **National Rail**.

Travelling by Bus

Slower but cheaper than the Tube, buses are also a good way of seeing the city as you travel. Routemaster heritage bus No 15 is particularly good for sight-seeing. To travel in the city between midnight and 6am, you will need a night bus which can be picked up at bus stops around Trafalgar Square and the West End. Bus routes are displayed on the **Transport for London** (TfL) website and on maps at bus stops. The destination is indicated on the front of the bus and the stops are announced onboard.

Tickets

TfL divides the city into six charging zones for Tube, DLR, London Overground and National Rail services. Zone 1 covers Central London. Tube and rail fares are expensive, especially individual tickets. The most economical tickets that can be used on all forms of transport in the city are Travelcards – daily, weekly or monthly paper tickets – and Visitor Oyster cards, which are "smartcards" that store credit to pay for journeys. Both types of tickets are available from the TfL website and Tube stations. Cash fares are not accepted on any central London buses.

By Taxi and Minicab

London's black cabs can be hailed anywhere; their "For Hire" sign is lit up when they're available. You can also find them at railway stations, airports and taxi ranks. A 10 per cent tip is customary. Black cabs can be ordered in advance from **Radio Taxis** and **Dial-a-Cab**. Only obtain a minicab by telephone, via the **Cabwise** service. Never pick one up on the street.

By Car

Expensive parking and congestion charging are designed to deter people from driving in Central London. Car rental is also not cheap. There are plenty of car-hire firms in London, including **Europcar** and **Thrifty**, which are likely to

offer deals. Drivers must show a valid licence and be aged 21 or even 25.

By Bicycle

You need a strong nerve to cycle in London's traffic, but it can be a great way to see the city. **Santander Cycles**, London's self-service cycle hire, has docking stations in central London. Bikes can also be rented from the **London Bicycle Tour Company**.

On Foot

Walking is a rewarding option in London. The centre is not large, and you will be surprised at how short the distance is between places that seem far apart on the Tube. Traffic drives on the left in the UK, so take care when crossing the road.

DIRECTORY

AIRPORTS

Gatwick
📞 0844 8920 322
🌐 gatwickairport.com

Heathrow
📞 0844 335 1801
🌐 heathrowairport.com

London City
📞 020 7646 0088
🌐 londoncityairport.com

Luton
📞 01582 405 100
🌐 london-luton.co.uk

Stansted
📞 0844 335 1803
🌐 stanstedairport.com

COACHES

Eurolines
🌐 eurolines.com

Green Line 757
🌐 greenline.co.uk/757

National Express
🌐 nationalexpress.com

Victoria Coach Station
MAP D5 ▪ 164
Buckingham Palace Rd
SW1
📞 0343 222 1234
🌐 tfl.gov.uk

TRAINS

Eurostar
🌐 eurostar.com

Gatwick Express
🌐 gatwickexpress.com

Heathrow Connect
🌐 heathrowconnect.com

Heathrow Express
🌐 heathrowexpress.com

National Rail Enquiries
📞 08457 484950
🌐 nationalrail.co.uk

Stansted Express
🌐 stanstedexpress.com

CHANNEL CROSSINGS

Eurotunnel
🌐 eurotunnel.com

UNDERGROUND/DLR/ BUSES/OVERGROUND

Transport for London
🌐 tfl.gov.uk

TAXIS AND MINICABS

Cabwise
🌐 tfl.gov.uk/cabwise

Dial-a-Cab
📞 020 7251 0581

Radio Taxis
📞 020 7272 0272

CAR HIRE

Europcar
🌐 europcar.co.uk

Thrifty
🌐 Thrifty.co.uk

BICYCLE HIRE

Santander Cycles
🌐 tfl.gov.uk

London Bicycle Tour Company
🌐 londonbicycle.com

Practical Information

Passports and Visas

Visitors from outside the European Economic Area (EEA) and Switzerland need a valid passport to enter the UK; EEA and Swiss nationals can use identity cards instead.

Those from the European Union (EU), the USA, Canada, Australia, New Zealand and Israel do not need a visa.

Visitors from other countries should check whether a visa is required at the **UK Visas and Immigration** website or with the UK Embassy in your country. Contact your London-based embassy if you lose your passport, need a visa or wish to extend your stay in the UK beyond six months.

Customs Regulations and Immigration

Visitors from EU states can bring unlimited quantities of most goods into the UK for personal use without paying duty. Exceptions include illegal drugs, offensive weapons, endangered species and some types of food and plants. For information about allowances from within and outside the EU, visit the UK government's website. If you need regular medicine, bring adequate supplies or a prescription with you.

Travel Safety

Visitors can get up-to-date travel safety information from the **Department of Foreign Affairs and Trade** in Australia, the **Foreign and Commonwealth Office** in the UK and the **State Department** in the US.

Travel Insurance

It's advisable to take out an insurance policy that covers cancellation or curtailment of your trip, theft or loss of money and baggage, and healthcare. Emergency treatment is usually free from the **National Health Service**, and there are reciprocal arrangements with other EEA countries, Australia, New Zealand and some others (check at www.nhs.uk/NHSEngland/health careabroad). But specialist care, drugs and repatriation are costly. Residents of EEA countries should carry a European Health Insurance Card (EHIC), which allows treatment for free or at reduced cost.

Health

No vaccinations are needed before visiting the UK. For emergency police, fire or ambulance services dial 999 or 112 – the operator will ask which service you require. If you need urgent medical help but the situation is not threatening, dial the 111 service instead. These numbers are free on any public phone.

There are a number of hospitals in central London with 24-hour emergency services. These include **St Mary's**, **St Thomas'** and **University College**. St Mary's, **Chelsea and Westminster** and **The Royal London** hospitals have specialist paediatric departments. St Mary's Hospital and St Thomas' have clinics for sexually transmitted diseases.

Pharmacies are open during business hours, some until late, and can give advice on minor ailments. **Boots** is a large chain with branches throughout London. The Piccadilly Circus store is open until midnight six days per week, from noon to 6pm on Sundays.

Many local dentists are listed in Yellow Pages and you can search for a nearby GP, dentist or pharmacy at www.nhs.uk/Service-Search.

Personal Security

Like all major cities, London has its share of bag-snatchers and pick-pockets. Wear a bag that closes effectively and conceal valuable items. Never leave items unattended on the Tube or in public spaces: they may cause a security alert.

Women travelling solo should stick to busy areas at night, avoid empty carriages on trains and use only licensed black cabs displaying an identification disc. Never hail a minicab on the street

Make sure possessions are insured, and if possible leave passports, tickets and travellers' cheques in the hotel safe. Report all thefts to the police, especially if you need to make an insurance claim. There is generally a police presence in busy areas, and there are several central police stations including **West End**

Central Station. In any emergency dial 999; for non-emergencies, call the police on 101.

Anything found on the Tube, buses, trains or black cabs is sent to the **Transport for London Lost Property Office**. Allow three to five days for items to get there; property is held for three months.

Disabled Travellers

The Tube has many stations with step-free access, but it remains difficult for the disabled to travel. The city's bus fleet is wheelchair-accessible. Braille maps, audio guides and advice are available from TfL. Most large hotels and attractions have wheelchair access and disabled toilets, but check before booking. **Disability Rights UK** publishes an annual guide listing recommended accommodation and runs the National Key Scheme for adapted toilets.

Recorded audio tours can often be hired at museums and galleries, which are useful to those with impaired vision. Call theatres and cinemas in advance to ask about disabled seating – **Artsline** has information on accessibility in arts venues. Many theatres have a sign-language interpreter at some performances.

Even if a restaurant has wheelchair access, the dining area may be on a different floor to the toilet, so check when booking.

Can Be Done specialises in holidays and tailor-made packages for the disabled. All the accommodation is wheelchair-adapted, while transfers and private sightseeing tours can be arranged in wheelchair-adapted vehicles.

Action on Hearing Loss and **The Royal National Institute for the Blind** can offer useful information and advice.

DIRECTORY

PASSPORTS AND VISAS

UK Visas and Immigration
w gov.uk/visas-immigration

EMBASSIES AND CONSULATES

Australia
MAP N2 ▪ Strand WC2
w uk.embassy.gov.au

Canada
MAP L4 ▪ 1 Trafalgar Square SW1
w unitedkingdom.gc.ca

US
MAP D3 ▪ 24 Grosvenor Square W1
w usembassy.org.uk

TRAVEL SAFETY

Australia
Department of Foreign Affairs and Trade
w dfat.gov.au/smartraveller.gov.au/

United Kingdom
Foreign and Commonwealth Office
w gov.uk/foreign-travel-advice

US
US Department of State
w travel.state.gov/

CUSTOMS REGULATIONS
w gov.uk/duty-free-goods

EMERGENCY SERVICES

Police, Fire, Ambulance
c 999 or 112

HEALTH SERVICES

Boots
MAP K3 ▪ 44–6 Regent Street, Piccadilly Circus W1
c 020 7734 6126

Chelsea and Westminster Hospital
MAP B6 ▪ 369 Fulham Road SW10

National Health Service
w nhs.uk

The Royal London Hospital
Whitechapel Road E1

St Mary's Hospital
MAP B3 ▪ Praed Street W2

St Thomas' Hospital
MAP N6 ▪ Westminster Bridge Road SE1

University College Hospital
MAP E2 ▪ 235 Euston Road NW1

PERSONAL SECURITY

West End Central Police Station
MAP J3 ▪ 27 Savile Row W1

TfL Lost Property Office
MAP C2 ▪ 200 Baker Street NW1
c 0343 222 1234

DISABLED TRAVELLERS

Transport for London accessibility
w tfl.gov.uk/transport-accessibility/

Disability Rights UK
w disabilityrightsuk.org

Artsline
w artsline.org.uk

Can Be Done
w canbedone.co.uk

Action on Hearing Loss
c 0808 808 0123/9000 (textphone)
w actionhearingloss.org.uk

The Royal National Institute for the Blind
c 0303 123 9999
w rnib.org.uk

Currency and Banking

The UK's currency is the pound sterling. One pound sterling (£1) is divided into 100 pence (100p). Paper notes are in denominations of £5, £10, £20 and £50. Coins are £2, £1, 50p, 20p, 10p, 5p, 2p, 1p. There's no limit on the amount of cash you can bring into the UK, but a pre-paid cash passport, used like a debit card, is more secure.

Opening hours for banks are generally 9:30am–4:30pm Monday to Friday; some branches also open on Saturday mornings. Most have ATMs (cash machines) in an outside wall or lobby – these can be accessed by card at any time of day or night. Beware of ATM crime, and always shield your pin from view.

Bureaux de Change are regulated, and their rates are displayed along with commission charges: either a flat fee or percentage charge. Many offer exchange without a commission fee, but their rates may be less favourable. **Chequepoint** at Gloucester Road, Kensington, is open 24 hours a day. High street banks and post offices change travellers' cheques and money, usually at better rates.

Most London establishments accept major credit cards such as Visa and MasterCard. American Express and Diners Club are less widely accepted. Credit cards are useful in hotels and restaurants, for shopping, car rental and reserving theatre or cinema tickets by phone.

They can also be used with a PIN number to obtain cash from an ATM.

Postal Services

Standard post in the UK is handled by the **Royal Mail**. There are post offices and sub-post offices throughout London, generally open from 9am–5:30pm Monday to Friday and until 12:30pm on Saturday. You can also buy stamps in shops, hotels and other outlets. The **Trafalgar Square Post Office** is the main one in the West End. Mail sent *Poste Restante* to this address can be stored for up to three months. Items posted in the UK will be kept for two weeks and for up to one month for mail posted overseas. **American Express** also provides a *Poste Restante* service for its customers.

Telephone and Internet

Most phoneboxes take coins (60p minimum) and credit cards. You will need at least £2 to make an international call. If you have difficulty contacting a number, call the Operator (100) or International Operator (155).

The code for London is 020: omit this when dialling from a landline within the city. When calling from abroad, dial the access code (+44) followed by 20, omitting the initial 0. To call abroad from London, dial 00 followed by the country code (61 for Australia; 1 for USA and Canada). To find a number, call a directory service such as 118 500; international directory

enquiries is on 118 505. Check before leaving home whether your mobile phone will work in the UK. To save money, consider buying a UK SIM card, or use a VoIP service, such as Skype (www.skype.com).

Internet access is very easy to find in London. Wi-Fi is available in most hotels, often for free, and in many public places. Both O2 (www.o2.co.uk/connectivity) and Virgin Media (on the Underground; www.my.virginmedia.com/wifi) offer Wi-Fi across central London, though you will need to register and pay for a daily or weekly pass to access their hotspots.

TV, Radio and Newspapers

Television channels have proliferated in recent years: BBC 1, BBC 2, BBC 3 and BBC 4 remain in public owner-ship. Check BBC News or Sky News for news and weather updates. Radio stations such as BBC London (94.9 FM), Capital FM (95.8 FM) and LBC (97.3 FM) carry constant news and travel updates for the capital.

For current events and all manner of happenings in London, consult the *Metro* or the *Evening Standard* (London's free morning and evening papers) and *Time Out*, the city's weekly listings magazine. A range of international newspapers and magazines, including *USA Today*, *International Herald Tribune* and major European papers, is on sale at many newsstands and newsagents around central London.

Opening Hours

Shops generally open from about 9am–6pm Monday to Saturday, with late-night shopping until at least 8pm on Thursdays. Sunday has limited trading hours: these vary but many stores open from 10am–4pm.

Major banks are open from 9am–5pm weekdays, and some also open until noon on Saturdays. Museum and gallery times vary widely: check before starting out. Last admission to many attractions is 30 minutes before closing.

Time Difference

London operates on Greenwich Mean Time, which is one hour behind continental European time and five hours ahead of US Eastern Seaboard time. The clock advances one hour during "British Summer Time", spanning the last Sunday in March until the last Sunday in October. At anytime of year you can check the correct time by dialling 123 on a BT landline to contact the 24-hour automated Speaking Clock service (note there is a charge for this service).

Electrical Appliances

The electricity supply is 240 volts AC. Plugs are of three-square-pin type. Most hotels have shaver sockets in the bathrooms.

Driving

EEA citizens can drive in the UK, so long as they carry their full and valid licence, registration and insurance documents. Other foreign nationals can drive a car or motor-cycle for 12 months, on the same terms. Inform your insurer before travelling.

Weather

London's weather is very unpredictable: an umbrella and raincoat are advisable all year round. To check ahead, visit the **Met Office** website, which carries detailed forecasts for the next five days. There are also regular weather forecasts on the radio and TV.

Tourist Information

Visit London is the official tourist organization for London; its services include a what's on guide and a useful accommodation booking scheme. It also has a list of all the Tourist Information Centres across London. Major visitor centres include the **City Information Centre** (open 9.30am–5.30pm Mon–Sat, 10am–4pm Sun) and **Discover Greenwich Visitor Centre** (open 10am–5pm), which offer advice on places to stay, guided tours, day trips and much more. Visitor Centres are also located in major transport hubs such as Piccadilly Circus and Victoria and Kings Cross St Pancras stations. The Visit London website has maps, events calendars and offers on theatre tickets.

Switchboard LGBT+ helpline provides information, support and a referral service for the lesbian, gay, bisexual and transgender community.

DIRECTORY

BUREAUX DE CHANGE

Chequepoint
MAP B5 ■ 71
Gloucester Road SW7
☎ 020 7341 9091
W chequepoint.com

POSTAL SERVICES

Trafalgar Square Post Office
MAP L4 ■ 24/28
William IV Street WC2

Royal Mail
☎ 0345 774 0740
W royalmail.com

NEWSPAPERS AND MAGAZINES

Metro
W metro.co.uk

Evening Standard
W standard.co.uk

Time Out
W timeout.com

WEATHER INFORMATION

Met Office
W metoffice.gov.uk

TOURIST INFORMATION

City Information Centre
MAP R2 ■ St Paul's Churchyard EC4
☎ 020 7606 3030

Discover Greenwich Visitor Centre
2 Cutty Sark Gardens SE10
☎ 020 8269 4799

Switchboard LGBT+ helpline
☎ 0300 330 0630
W switchboard.lgbt

Visit London
W visitlondon.com

Shopping

London is one of the world's great shopping cities and some of the best shopping areas have been picked out in this guidebook. There are several hundred shops on Oxford Street alone. Designer labels and expensive jewels are found in Bond Street, Knightsbridge and Sloane Street, while bespoke menswear is in Savile Row and St James's. Carnaby Street is good for mid-range clothes; while London's markets are the place to find street fashion, especially Camden, Petticoat Lane and Old Spitalfields.

Covent Garden is great for gifts, and the big West End stores (**Selfridges**, **John Lewis**, **Liberty**, **Harvey Nichols**, **Harrods**) are happy hunting grounds too. The main museums, galleries and tourist sites all have gift stores.

Art and antiques dealers gather around Mayfair and St James's, while the major commercial galleries are in the West End, especially in Bond Street and Cork Street. **Sotheby's** auction house is there, too. All kinds of antiques can be sought out in Portobello Road, Kensington Church Street and Chelsea's King's Road.

There are several huge out-of-town shopping malls, including **Westfield** in Shepherd's Bush and Stratford. Back in town, **One New Change** has around 40 outlets spread over three floors, and is just across the road from St Paul's Cathedral.

Large stores usually stage end-of-season sales in January and July. Most shops in London accept leading credit cards.

VAT (Value Added Tax) is charged at 20 per cent and almost always included in the marked price. Stores offering tax-free shopping display a distinctive sign and (for non-EU residents) will provide you with a VAT 407 form to validate when you leave the country.

Dining

The choice is vast, offering cuisines from across the globe. Italian, Indian and Chinese are perennial favourites with Londoners, and generally offer good value; Chinatown, in the West End, has several streets lined with restaurants – seek out those where the city's own Chinese community are eating. Other options include Thai, Greek, Turkish, Indonesian and Lebanese, while eateries offering Central and South American street food are especially in vogue of late.

Londoners generally have dinner between 7 and 9pm and lunch between 12.30 and 2pm, when pubs, cafés and fast-food restaurants fill up and sandwich bars have queues. This can be a good time to frequent smarter restaurants, which seek to attract lunchtime crowds by offering cheap menus. Also look out for set menus and pre-theatre deals, which can represent good value. A range of restaurant review sites offer both unbiased professional appraisals and local diners' reviews. The most popular are **London Eating** and **Open Table**, both of which include reliable online reservation services.

Trips and Tours

A ride on an open-top sightseeing bus is a great way of getting to know London; the best allow you to hop on and hop off at leisure. There are several operators including **The Original London Sightseeing Tour** and **Big Bus Tours**, with pick-up points dotted around the city. Some companies include a cruise along the Thames.

There's a plethora of boat services on the Thames, from commuter services to pleasure tours but they are run by different operators and tickets are not inter-changeable. Westminster and Embankment are the principal central London piers; boats from here go upriver to Hampton Court and downriver to Greenwich. It's safest to buy tickets at the piers, but all the options are listed on the **TfL** website.

Regent's Canal is a lovely backwater for idle cruising between Camden Lock and Little Venice. Catch a **London Waterbus Company** narrowboat at either end and stop off at London Zoo on the way.

Guided walking tours abound, with themes including Jack the Ripper, ghosts and hauntings and Shakespeare's London. The longest established operator, **London Walks**, offers a wide choice. For a healthy and eco-friendly sightseeing tour, join a guided jogging tour such as **City Jogging**, which run daily and cater or individuals and groups of all abilities.

Most of London's historic theatres offer backstage tours, including the **Royal Opera House** and the **Theatre Royal Drury Lane** – enquire about their costumed versions.

Where to Stay

London hotels can be pricey, but with so much choice, it pays to shop around, especially online. As well as hotels for every budget, there are B&Bs, hostels, self-catering apartments and private homes for rent. Budget hotel chains include **Novotel** and **Premier Inn**,

which frequently offer double rooms for under £100 per night. The **Bed & Breakfast and Homestay Association** can help with listings of privately owned properties, while home-swaps are available through **HomeLink** and **Intervac**. **Citadines**, **BridgeStreet** and others specialize in serviced apartments, particularly attractive for families.

Rates and Booking

London hotels usually quote room rates rather than prices per person and include VAT in their published rates, but not always breakfast. Look for

special offer deals: prices can be lower if you book a minimum of two nights, for example. The best deals at budget hotel chains are to be had online and well in advance. But do consider calling to request the best last-minute deals, too.

Visit London offers booking services through **Late Rooms** and **SuperBreak**. You can also reserve rooms in person at information res at Victoria and Liverpool Street rail stations, and at Heathrow Airport. Websites such as **Expedia** and **Travelocity** offer city breaks as well as accommodation.

DIRECTORY

SHOPPING

Harrods
MAP C5 ▪ 87–135
Brompton Road SW1
🔤 harrods.com

Harvey Nichols
MAP C4 ▪ 109–25
Knightsbridge SW1
🔤 harveynichols.com

John Lewis
MAP J2 ▪ 300 Oxford Street W1C
🔤 johnlewis.com

Liberty
MAP J2 ▪ Regent Street W1
🔤 liberty.co.uk

One New Change
MAP R2 ▪ 1 New Change EC4
🔤 onenewchange.com

Selfridges
MAP D3 ▪ 400 Oxford Street W1
🔤 selfridges.com

Sotheby's
MAP J3 ▪ 34–5 New Bond Street W1
🔤 sothebys.com

Westfield
🔤 uk.westfield.com

DINING

London Eating
🔤 london-eating.co.uk

Open Table
🔤 opentable.co.uk

WHERE TO STAY

Bed & Breakfast and Homestay Association
🔤 bbha.org.uk

BridgeStreet
🔤 bridgestreet.com

Citadines
🔤 citadines.com

Expedia
🔤 expedia.co.uk

Home Link
🔤 homelink.org

Intervac
🔤 gb.intervac-homeexchange.com

Late Rooms
🔤 laterooms.com

Novotel
🔤 novotel.com

Premier Inn
🔤 premierinn.com

SuperBreak
🔤 superbreak.com

Travelocity
🔤 travelocity.com

Visit London
🔤 visitlondonoffers.com

TRIPS AND TOURS

Big Bus Tours
📞 020 7808 6753
🔤 bigbustours.com

City Jogging
🔤 cityjoggingtours.co.uk

London Walks
📞 020 7624 3978
🔤 walks.com

London Waterbus Company
📞 020 7482 2660
🔤 londonwaterbus.com

The Original Tour
📞 020 8877 1722
🔤 theoriginaltour.com

Royal Opera House
🔤 roh.org.uk/visit/tours

TfL River Transport
🔤 tfl.gov.uk/modes/river/

Theatre Royal Drury Lane
🔤 theatreroyaldrurylane.co.uk

Places to Stay

PRICE CATEGORIES
For a standard, double room per night (with breakfast if included), taxes and extra charges.

£ under £100   ££ £100–200   £££ over £200

Character Hotels

Pavilion Hotel
MAP C3 ▪ 34–36 Sussex Gardens W2 ▪ 020 7262 0905 ▪ www.pavilion hoteluk.com ▪ ££
This "rock 'n' roll" hotel offers decadently glamorous themed rooms bearing names like Casablanca Nights and Enter The Dragon. You may find yourself staying next door to a celebrity.

Portobello Hotel
MAP A4 ▪ 22 Stanley Gardens W11 ▪ 020 7727 2777 ▪ www.portobello hotel.com ▪ ££
Brimming with character, each of the 21 rooms in this boutique hotel is individually decorated – some with wall-to-wall murals – and tastefully furnished. This is exactly the kind of hotel you would hope to find near London's great antiques market. A light snack menu accompanies, an honesty bar, which stocks wine, beer and spirits.

Blakes Hotel
MAP B6 ▪ 33 Roland Gardens SW7 ▪ 020 7370 6701 ▪ www.blakeshotels. com ▪ £££
This hotel is a Victorian delight, filled with sumptuous cushions and drapes, bamboo and bird cages. Each room is individually styled with exotica from all over the world. The Chinese Room bar and restaurant in the basement, designed by Anouska Hempel, continues the theme.

The Chesterfield
MAP D4 ▪ 35 Charles Street W1 ▪ 020 7491 2622 ▪ www.chesterfield mayfair.com ▪ £££
Set in the heart of Mayfair, just off Berkeley Square, this 4-star luxury hotel is full of British old-world charm. The honey at breakfast comes from the owners' bees. The fine dining restaurant serves excellent British food.

Durrants Hotel
MAP D3 ▪ George Street W1 ▪ 020 7935 8131 ▪ www.durrantshotel. co.uk ▪ £££
This Georgian hotel, located close to Marylebone High Street and Bond Street, has been in business since 1790. It has a comfortable, old-fashioned style, with antique furniture, light prints and modern bathrooms.

The Gore
MAP B5 ▪ 190 Queen's Gate SW7 ▪ 020 7584 6601 ▪ www.gorehotel. com ▪ £££
Originally opened in 1892, this hotel retains a relaxed, fin-de-siècle feel. Its Persian rugs, potted palms and paintings are in keeping with the elegance of the building, and rooms are furnished with antiques. The restaurant, 190 Queen's Gate, is also recommended.

Hazlitt's
MAP L2 ▪ 6 Frith Street W1 ▪ 020 7434 1771 ▪ www. hazlittshotel.com ▪ £££
A literary event as much as a hotel, Hazlitt's is located in the former townhouse of the essayist William Hazlitt (1778–1830). The hotel's literary feel is enhanced by its library of books signed by the many authors who have stayed as guests at the hotel.

The Rookery
MAP Q1 ▪ 12 Peter's Lane Cowcross Street EC1 ▪ 020 7336 0931 ▪ www. rookeryhotel.com ▪ £££
A warren of rooms has been linked together to create a brilliant hotel that evokes Victorian London, with a touch of the Gothic. The hotel takes its name from the gang of thieves who once haunted this area near Smithfield market.

York and Albany
MAP D1 ▪ 127–29 Parkway, NW1 ▪ 020 7382 5700 ▪ www.gordonram sayrestaurants.com/york-and-albany ▪ £££
Situated between Regent's Park and Camden, this is the Gordon Ramsay organization's version of a gastropub, with deliciously inventive cuisine. Above it is the surprisingly secluded townhouse, with nine beautiful, luxurious rooms and suites combining period fittings and cutting-edge electronics.

Designer Hotels

Hoxton Hotel
MAP H2 ■ 81 Great Eastern Street EC2 ■ 020 7550 1000 ■ www.thehoxton.com ■ ££
Set in the trendy area of Shoreditch, and now with a branch in Holborn too (199–206 High Holborn), the Hoxton offers small but cool individual rooms at reasonable prices. An "urban breakfast bag" is delivered to your room each morning.

Charlotte Street Hotel
MAP K1 ■ 15–17 Charlotte Street W1 ■ 020 7806 2000 ■ www.firmdalehotels.com ■ £££
Tasteful and comfortable, with padded armchairs and antiques, plus works by Bloomsbury artists. Log fires burn in the drawing room and library. The bustling Oscar bar and restaurant serves seasonal cuisine and tasty cocktails.

Eccleston Square Hotel
MAP D5 ■ 37 Eccleston Square SW1 ■ 020 3503 0750 ■ www.ecclestonsquarehotel.com ■ £££
Overlooking the lush gardens of Eccleston Square, this luxury boutique hotel is aimed at the ultra-sophisticated (no children under 13 are permitted) and comes complete with cutting-edge high-tech facilities.

Halkin
MAP D4 ■ Halkin Street SW1 ■ 020 7333 1000 ■ www.comohotels.com/thehalkin ■ £££
A startlingly beautiful hotel in a Georgian townhouse, which has been given a thoroughly modern overhaul with marble, glass, dark wood and oriental details. The Michelin-starred Basque restaurant overlooks the quiet garden and the rooms are equipped for modern communication.

Metropolitan
MAP D4 ■ Old Park Lane W1 ■ 020 7447 1000 ■ www.comohotels.com/metropolitanlondon ■ £££
Contemporary and stylish, this was one of the first of the classy modern hotels in London, with black-clad staff, cool interiors and bright, airy bedrooms. Go celebrity-spotting in the Met Bar or in Nobu, the hotel's fashionable Japanese-Peruvian restaurant.

No. 5 Maddox Street
MAP J3 ■ 5 Maddox Street W1 ■ 020 7647 0200 ■ www.living-rooms.co.uk/hotel/no-5-maddox-st ■ £££
Glass, steel and bamboo feature in the decor of these high-quality Japanese-style serviced apartments, with a restaurant delivery service, complimentary Artisan du Chocolat goodies, yoga mats, in-room spa treatments and full internet facilities.

Sanderson
MAP K1 ■ 50 Berners Street W1 ■ 020 7300 1400 ■ www.morganshotelgroup.com ■ £££
Designed by Phillipe Starck, this is London's most stylish hotel. Behind a 1950s office-block exterior, its plain decor is enlivened by Dalí-lips and Louis XV sofas, while wafting curtains and oil paintings decorate the ceilings of the sparse bedrooms. Facilities include a gym, a spa and complimentary use of bicycles. Make sure to book the Mad Hatter's afternoon tea.

St Martins Lane
MAP L3 ■ 45 St Martin's Lane WC2 ■ 020 7300 5500 ■ www.morganshotelgroup.com ■ £££
In the heart of the West End, the Sanderson's sister hotel has a lobby of theatrical proportions. The rooms have floor-to-ceiling windows and even the bathrooms (all of which have big tubs) are 50 per cent glass.

W London
MAP L3 ■ 10 Wardour St, Leicester Square W1 ■ 020 7758 1000 ■ www.wlondon.co.uk ■ £££
This glamorous West End hotel will have you feeling like the star of the show. The luxurious rooms feature designer beds and spa products. Cocktail-lovers will enjoy the bar, while the restaurant creates delicious Southeast Asian cuisine. There's also an on-site fitness centre and a spa with relaxing treatments.

Zetter
MAP F2 ■ 86–88 Clerkenwell Road EC1 ■ 020 7324 4444 ■ www.thezetter.com ■ £££
Modern and fun, this laid-back option offers luxuries like the latest in-room entertainment, walk-in rain showers and free espresso machines. Its Bistrot Bruno Loubet restaurant is a must.

Luxury Hotels

Brown's Hotel
MAP J4 ▪ Albemarle Street W1 ▪ 020 7493 6020 ▪ www.rocco-fortehotels.com ▪ £££
This Mayfair hotel was founded in 1837 by James Brown, valet to Lord Byron, to accommodate country society staying in London. Comprising 11 Georgian townhouses, it is decorated with contemporary as well as antique art, while retaining its intimacy and charm. It is renowned for its afternoon teas in the English Tea Room.

Claridge's
MAP D3 ▪ 49 Brook Street W1 ▪ 020 7629 8860 ▪ www.claridges.co.uk ▪ £££
This historic hotel established a reputation for glamour and style following its Art Deco makeover in 1929 and has maintained it ever since. Favoured by A-list celebrities, a stay here is guaranteed to make you feel pampered.

The Connaught
MAP D3 ▪ 1 Carlos Place W1 ▪ 020 7499 7070 ▪ www.the-connaught. co.uk ▪ £££
More discreet than London's other grand hotels, tucked away in a quiet corner of Mayfair, the Connaught has one of the finest hotel restaurants, with two Michelin stars.

The Dorchester
MAP D4 ▪ 53 Park Lane, W1 ▪ 020 7629 8888 ▪ www. thedorchestercollection. com ▪ £££
Part of the fabric of London, this classic hotel opened in 1931 and has been the pinnacle of glamorous London life ever since. Alain Ducasse at The Dorchester offers contemporary French fine dining and three Michelin stars. Book a "deluxe" room for a view over Hyde Park.

The Lanesborough
MAP D4 ▪ 1 Hyde Park Corner SW1 ▪ 020 7259 5599 ▪ www.lanesbor ough.com ▪ £££
In this luxurious hotel, the Regency decoration reaches a peak in Aspleys, a Heinz Beck restaurant, while all the rooms, with deep pile carpets and gleaming mahogany, are fitted with the latest entertainment and communications technology. There is also a spa and fitness centre.

ME London
MAP N3 ▪ 336–37 The Strand WC2 ▪ 020 7395 3400 ▪ www.melia.com ▪ £££
With its stunning pyramid-shaped reception atrium and shiny black-and-white decor, a visit to ME London is like stepping into a sci-fi film. The futuristic feel continues with the two ground-floor restaurants and the Radio Rooftop Bar, which has panoramic views across the city skyline.

The Ritz
MAP K3 ▪ 150 Piccadilly W1 ▪ 020 7493 8181 ▪ www. theritzlondon.com ▪ £££
One of London's most glamorous hotels, the Ritz is decorated in Louis XVI style, with shades of blue, yellow, pink and peach, gold and silk trimmings, chandeliers and period furniture. Afternoon tea in the Palm Court is popular and the opulent restaurant has a garden terrace.

The Savoy
MAP M4 ▪ Strand WC2 ▪ 020 7836 4343 ▪ www. fairmont.com/savoy ▪ £££
Fortunate in its riverside setting, the Savoy is London's top traditional hotel and has been restored to its original Art Deco splendour. Leisure facilities include a private pool and gym.

Shangri-La at The Shard
MAP H4 ▪ 31 St Thomas Street SE1 ▪ 020 7234 80 00 ▪ www.shangri-la.com/ london/shangrila ▪ £££
One of Asia's top hotel chains has opened a luxury hotel in London, occupying floors 34 to 52 of the city's highest skyscraper, the Shard. The rooms are spacious and the service attentive but it is the views that will make your stay such a memorable experience.

The Waldorf Hilton
MAP N3 ▪ Aldwych WC2 ▪ 020 7836 2400 ▪ www. waldorfhilton.co.uk ▪ £££
This is one of London's great Edwardian hotels, located a stone's throw from theatres and shopping. The leisure facilities are excellent.

Mid-Priced Hotels

Apex City of London Hotel
MAP H3 ▪ 1 Seething Lane EC3 ▪ 020 7702 2020 ▪ www.apexhotels. co.uk ▪ ££
The 4-star Apex has comfortable rooms with

state-of-the-art facilities and a smart restaurant. Great special offers are often available. There are two more Apex hotels in the city, one on Fleet Street and one on Copthall Avenue.

DoubleTree by Hilton London West End
MAP M1 ▪ 92 Southampton Row WC1 ▪ 020 7242 2828 ▪ www. crimsonhotels.com ▪ ££
Behind the Edwardian façade of this veteran Bloomsbury hotel are smart rooms with state-of-the-art facilities as well as duplex apartments with dining areas, kitchenettes and balconies. There's also a very good restaurant.

Grange Langham Court Hotel
MAP J1 ▪ 31–5 Langham Street W1 ▪ 020 7436 6622 ▪ www.grange hotels.com ▪ ££
Located in a quiet side street close to Oxford Circus, this enticing hotel, with its attractive façade, is as friendly inside as its exterior promises. There is a good restaurant, which serves mainly French cuisine..

Hotel La Place
MAP D2 ▪ 17 Nottingham Place W1 ▪ 020 7486 2323 ▪ www.hotellaplace. com ▪ ££
This charming townhouse in Marylebone offers a quirky individuality. Decor in the 20 rooms and cosy Le Jardin wine bar is often plushly ornate, and the hotel is always full of fresh flowers. A full English breakfast is included in the room rate. The owners take great

care of their guests, and have many who return again and again.

Malmaison
MAP G2 ▪ 18–21 Charterhouse Square EC1 ▪ 020 7012 3700 ▪ www. malmaison.com ▪ ££
Located in a lovely part of Smithfield, this boutique chain hotel is both charming and reasonably priced. As well as the comfortable rooms, it offers a gym, a beautifully chic brasserie and a stylish bar.

Meliá White House
MAP D2 ▪ Albany Street NW1 ▪ 020 7391 3000 ▪ www.melia-whitehouse. com ▪ ££
Close to Regent's Park, this classic 4-star hotel was originally built as a block of model apartments in 1936. Now refurbished as a comfortable 581-room hotel, it has spacious rooms, two restaurants (one serving Spanish cuisine) and a bar with a terrace open in summer.

Mercure London Bridge
MAP R4 ▪ 71–9 Southwark Street SE1 ▪ 020 7660 0683 ▪ www. mercure.com ▪ ££
Situated close to Tate Modern, this hotel boasts a smart contemporary design plus a high level of facilities, including a stylish bar and brasserie.

The Nadler Kensington
MAP A5 ▪ 25 Courtfield Gardens SW5 ▪ 020 7244 2255 ▪ www.thenadler. com ▪ ££
This "luxury budget" hotel offers free Wi-Fi, Gilchrist

& Soames toiletries and mini-kitchens with complimentary Fairtrade tea and coffee in every room. Its 65 rooms, each of which is decorated in contemporary style, range from singles and luxury bunks to family rooms and adjoining suites.

Park Lane Mews Hotel
MAP D4 ▪ 2 Stanhope Row, Park Lane W1 ▪ 020 7493 7222 ▪ www.park-lanemewshotel.net ▪ ££
Located in the heart of Mayfair, this 4-star hotel is just minutes away from Harrods, Oxford Street, Buckingham Palace and Hyde Park. Throughout, the decor is smart and traditional. The restaurant and lounge are perfect for relaxing in after a busy day of shopping.

myhotel Bloomsbury
MAP L1 ▪ 11–13 Bayley Street WC1 ▪ 020 3004 6000 ▪ www.myhotels. com ▪ £££
Just off Tottenham Court Road, this hotel is an oasis of calm, with a mystical, Oriental style and attentive staff. The rooms are light and feng-shui assured, with white orchids, fish tanks and candles for decoration.

The Royal Trafalgar
MAP L4 ▪ Whitcomb Street WC2 ▪ 0871 376 9037 ▪ www.thistle.com ▪ £££
The Thistle Group has nine hotels in London, many in prime locations. This one is next door to the National Gallery, close to Leicester Square, so staying here will save on transport costs. Rooms are stylishly furnished with all modcons.

For a key to hotel price categories see p174

Inexpensive Hotels

easyHotel Victoria
MAP D5 ■ 34–40 Belgrave Road SW1 ■ www.easy hotel.com ■ £
The company behind easyJet has entered the budget hotel market with bright, functional rooms. For the low price, expect no frills (TV and Wi-Fi cost extra) but they are the cheapest en suite double rooms in town. There are four more easyHotels in central London (two in Kensington and one each in Paddington and Old Street) and also at Heathrow, Luton and Croydon.

Lancaster Court Hotel
MAP B3 ■ 202–4 Sussex Gardens W2 ■ 020 7402 8438 ■ www.lancaster-court-hotel.co.uk ■ £
Between Paddington station and Hyde Park, Sussex Gardens is a quiet, pleasant street lined with inexpensive hotels. Lancaster Court offers basic, tidy rooms; note that Wi-Fi costs extra.

Arran House Hotel
MAP E2 ■ 77–9 Gower Street WC1 ■ 020 7636 2186 ■ www.arranhotel-london.com ■ ££
This child-friendly family-run hotel is located in a Georgian townhouse with soundproofed windows, a cosy lounge, and either shared or en suite bath-rooms. There is also a walled rose garden.

Bedford Hotel
MAP M1 ■ 83–95 South-ampton Row WC1 ■ 020 7636 7822 ■ www.imperialhotels.co.uk/bedford ■ ££
One of six large, good-value Bloomsbury hotels run by Imperial London Hotels, the Bedford's advantages are a good restaurant and a sunny lounge and garden. Simple yet comfortable rooms, some of which overlook the garden.

Brompton Hotel
MAP C5 ■ 30 Old Brompton Road SW7 ■ 020 7584 4517 ■ www.bromhotel.com ■ ££
Situated just by South Kensington Tube station and handy for visiting the Natural History, Victoria and Albert and Science Museums, this typical West London hotel has comfortable en suite rooms. Reception is on the first floor. On the ground floor is an American-style bar (not owned by the hotel) run by New Yorker Janet Evans, which serves fantastic cocktails.

Church Street Hotel
29–33 Camberwell Church Street SE5 ■ Tube Elephant and Castle, then 171 bus ■ 020 7703 5984 ■ www.churchstreet hotel.com ■ ££
Enjoy a vibrant slice of Latin America in this cheerful Hispanic-themed establishment in South London. The Colonial-style cocktail bar and Angels & Gypsies restaurant add extra spice. Although there is no Tube station nearby, Central London is only 20 minutes away by bus.

Columbia Hotel
MAP B3 ■ 95–9 Lancaster Gate W2 ■ 020 7402 0021 ■ www.columbiahotel.co.uk ■ ££
The Columbia is family-run and has a delightful leafy setting overlooking Hyde Park and Kensington Gardens. Originally townhouses, one of which was used as an American Red Cross Hospital during World War I, the hotel offers interconnected and 4-bed rooms for families.

Fielding Hotel
MAP M2 ■ 4 Broad Court, Bow St WC2 ■ 020 7836 8305 ■ www.thefielding hotel.co.uk ■ ££
Ideally situated for Covent Garden, this quaint room-only hotel is a warren of oddly shaped rooms, with showers and basins tucked in corners. Outside there is all of Covent Garden to breakfast in.

Morgan Hotel
MAP L1 ■ 24 Bloomsbury Street WC1 ■ 020 7636 3735 ■ www.morgan hotel.co.uk ■ ££
This cheerful family-run hotel is long established. Several rooms overlook the British Museum and all have air conditioning. The cosy breakfast area has framed London memorabilia on the walls.

Business Hotels

Holiday Inn Express London City
MAP H2 ■ 275 Old Street EC1 ■ 020 7300 4300 ■ www.hiexpress.com ■ £
One of a chain of value-for-money London hotels the Holiday Inn Express London City is not actually in the City, but backs onto fashionable Hoxton Square (see p159), an area known more for art than for business. There are several other branches across London.

Andaz Liverpool Street
MAP H3 ▪ 40 Liverpool Street EC2 ▪ 020 7961 1234 ▪ www.london.liverpoolstreet.andaz.hyatt.com ▪ £££
Built in 1884 as the railway hotel serving Liverpool Street station, Andaz (meaning "personal style" in Hindi) is friendly yet luxurious. It fuses a 5-star hotel with boutique design flair. Set in a redbrick building with stylish, minimalist rooms, it has seven restaurants and bars offering a great range of eating and drinking options.

The Bloomsbury Hotel
MAP L1 ▪ 16–22 Great Russell Street WC1 ▪ 020 7347 1000 ▪ www.doylecollection.com ▪ £££
This beautiful Neo-Georgian building was designed by Edwin Lutyens for the YWCA in the 1930s. The Queen Mary Hall is now a conference centre and the former chapel provides a quiet meeting room. The rooms have been designed for a mainly business clientele, with internet facilities and work desks.

Four Seasons at Canary Wharf
46 Westferry Circus E14 ▪ DLR Westferry ▪ 020 7510 1999 ▪ www.fourseasons.com/canarywharf ▪ £££
As smart and stylish as you would expect from a Canary Wharf hotel, the Four Seasons has a sleek, contemporary design. Rooms are all well equipped for business needs and also have window seats for enjoying the views. The restaurant opens onto a terrace during the summer.

London Bridge Hotel
MAP H4 ▪ 8–18 London Bridge Street SE1 ▪ 020 7855 2200 ▪ www.londonbridgehotel.com ▪ £££
Situated just over the river from the City, this handsome, modern, independently owned hotel is well equipped for business guests, with modern conference facilities. The Londinium restaurant serves modern British food.

Marble Arch Marriott
MAP D3 ▪ 134 George Street W1 ▪ 020 7723 1277 ▪ www.marriott.co.uk ▪ £££
A modern hotel near the western end of Oxford Street. Facilities include a bar and restaurant, gym, health club and swimming pool. There are also full business facilities in the executive lounge.

The Park Tower Knightsbridge
MAP C4 ▪ 101 Knightsbridge SW1 ▪ 020 7235 8050 ▪ www.theparktowerknightsbridge.com ▪ £££
This circular hotel is a Knightsbridge landmark – the skyline views get better and more expensive the higher up you go. Business guests are well catered for.

St Pancras Renaissance Hotel
MAP E1 ▪ Euston Road NW1 ▪ 020 7841 3540 ▪ www.marriott.co.uk/St.Pancras ▪ £££
Fronting St Pancras International Station, home of the Eurostar, this is the perfect hotel for those who commute regularly from Europe. It also happens to be one of London's grandest and most palatial Victorian buildings, designed by Sir George Gilbert Scott.

The Tower Hotel
MAP H4 ▪ St Katharine's Way E1 ▪ 0871 376 9036 ▪ www.guoman.com/tower ▪ £££
Many of the 800-plus rooms in this vast modern block close to Tower Bridge and St Katharine Docks boast spectacular river views.

B&Bs and Hostels

Clink261
MAP F2 ▪ 261–5 Grays Inn Road WC1 ▪ 020 7833 9400 ▪ www.clinkhostels.com ▪ £
Clink hostels are superior to the average hostel. The staff are friendly and the decor is stylish in the double rooms, dorms, self-catering kitchen, TV lounge and internet rooms. Although there is a bar, Clink261 has a fairly mellow feel; the bar of nearby Clink78 is livelier. The buffet breakfast is included in the room rate.

The Dictionary Hostel
MAP H2 ▪ 10–20 Kingsland Road, E2 ▪ 020 7613 2784 ▪ www.thedictionaryhostel.com ▪ £
Facilities on offer at this quirky hostel in the hip, alternative district of Shoreditch include a laundrette and free Wi-Fi. There's also a bar with evening entertainment, table football and a roof terrace. Dormitory and double rooms available.

For a key to hotel price categories see p174

Dover Castle Hostel

MAP G4 ▪ 6a Great Dover Street SE1 ▪ 020 7403 7773 ▪ www.dovercastle hostel.com ▪ £

This privately run hostel offers great value-for-money accommodation for backpackers. There are 60 beds in total, which range from 4 to 12 per dormitory-style room. There's free Wi-Fi and lockers can be rented. The late-licensed bar has live music every night.

Generator Hostel London

MAP E2 ▪ 37 Tavistock Place WC1 ▪ 020 7388 7666 ▪ www.generator hostels.com/london ▪ £

With decor somewhere between sci-fi and industrial chic, this youth-orientated hostel provides budget solutions for impecunious travellers. Private rooms are available as well as dorms. There's a cinema, café and bar, and the hostel arranges tours and other regular events.

Hyde Park Rooms

MAP B3 ▪ 137 Sussex Gardens W2 ▪ 020 7723 0225 ▪ www.hydepark rooms.com ▪ £

The no-frills rooms (some do not have en suite bathrooms) in this family-run B&B are all kept admirably spick and span, and the breakfasts are generous.

Palmers Lodge Swiss Cottage

40 College Crescent NW3 ▪ Tube Swiss Cottage ▪ 020 7483 8470 ▪ www.palmerslodges. com ▪ £–££

A converted Victorian mansion is an unlikely setting for a hostel, but this is budget accommodation at its most luxurious, with 24-hour reception and security, free Wi-Fi and car parking, plus an on-site bar and restaurant. There is another branch of Palmers Lodge, called Hillspring, in Willesden.

Smart Hyde Park View

MAP B3 ▪ 16 Leinster Terrace W2 ▪ 020 7402 4101 ▪ www.smart-hostels.com ▪ £–££

Situated just off Hyde Park, this is a more comfortable variation on a hostel, offering double rooms with private bathrooms as well as traditional dormitories.

St Christopher's Village

MAP G4 ▪ 161–65 Borough High Street SE1 ▪ 020 7939 9710 ▪ www. st-christophers.co.uk ▪ £

This is the largest of three hostels on this street run by St Christopher's Inns, and it's a self-professed "party hostel". There are other branches in Camden, Greenwich, Shepherd's Bush and Hammersmith. Private rooms are available as well as dormitories. There is a café, bar and roof terrace. One of the other branches, The Oasis (161–5 Borough High Street), is female only.

YHA Earl's Court

MAP A6 ▪ 38 Bolton Gardens, Earl's Court SW5 ▪ 0845 371 9114 ▪ www. yha.org.uk ▪ £

Set in a Victorian building with a courtyard garden, the rooms in this backpackers' hostel are minimalist in decor. Guests have access to comfortable shared areas.

Arosfa Hotel

MAP E2 ▪ 83 Gower Street WC1 ▪ 020 7636 2115 ▪ www.arosfa london.com ▪ ££

In the heart of Bloomsbury, near the British Museum, this Georgian townhouse has been renovated as a comfortable B&B, with modern bathrooms in its small but cosy rooms. The owners are welcoming, and there's a pleasant guest lounge as well as a little garden at the back. Book your room well in advance.

B&B Belgravia

MAP D5 ▪ 64–66 Ebury Street SW1 ▪ 020 7529 8570 ▪ www.bb-belgravia.com ▪ ££

Set within three Grade II listed Georgian town-houses, this B&B offers 17 en suite rooms, as well as 8 studios with kitchenettes and a delivered continental breakfast. Guests have 24-hour access to a lounge with an open fire, a laptop, a TV, daily newspapers and a coffee machine. There's also a garden and a small sun terrace. Guests can borrow bikes for free.

New Inn

MAP C1 ▪ 2 Allitsen Road, St John's Wood, NW8 ▪ 020 7722 0726 ▪ www.newinnlondon. co.uk ▪ ££

There are five boutique rooms above this gastropub offering locally sourced meat and fish, craft beers and great breakfast dishes.

Russell's B&B
123 Chatsworth Road E5 ▪ Train Hackney Central, then 242 bus ▪ 0797 666 9906 ▪ www.russells ofclapton.com ▪ ££

An upmarket guesthouse in Hackney that succeeds in being both homely and chic. A mix of antique furniture and stylish modern pieces decorate each room. A great location if you want to explore London's East End, but also a mere 30 minutes from the centre of London.

Aster House
MAP B5 ▪ 3 Sumner Place, SW7 ▪ 020 7581 5888 ▪ www.asterhouse. com ▪ £££

This B&B in a Victorian townhouse near South Kensington Tube station is peaceful and has traditional furnishings. It is within walking distance of the Science, Natural History and Victoria and Albert Museums. The buffet breakfast is served in the orangery.

Hotels Out of Town

Hampstead Village Guesthouse
2 Kemplay Road NW3 ▪ Tube Hampstead ▪ 020 7435 8679 ▪ www. hampsteadguesthouse. com ▪ ££

This large double-fronted Victorian family house, located just off the bottom of Hampstead High Street (and still full of the family's memorabilia and toys) is now run as a guesthouse. There is a pleasant garden in which guests can eat their breakfast (not included in the room rates) during the summer.

Hilton London Stansted Airport
Stansted Airport ▪ 01279 680 800 ▪ www.hilton. co.uk/stansted ▪ ££

A modern hotel with standard facilities, this is just a 6-minute journey to the terminal at Stansted Airport via shuttle bus, making it an ideal choice for early flights.

Hotel 55
55 Hanger Lane W5 ▪ Tube North Ealing ▪ 020 8991 4450 ▪ www. hotel55-london.com ▪ ££

The decor of this hotel is bright and modern, with plenty of colour and character. Dine in the inhouse restaurant Momo and unwind in the landscaped garden.

The Lodge Hotel
52–4 Upper Richmond Road SW15 ▪ Tube East Putney ▪ 020 8874 1598 ▪ www.thelodge hotellondon.com ▪ ££

Leafy Putney isn't that far from the centre of London, but this hotel has a calm out-of-town feel to it. Two Victorian houses have been joined together to provide 77 bedrooms along with a bar, lounge, library and restaurant.

The Mitre
291 Greenwich High Road SE10 ▪ Train to Greenwich ▪ 020 8293 0037 ▪ www.themitre greenwich.co.uk ▪ ££

Originally an 18th-century coaching inn, this bustling pub with 24 en suite rooms, including three family suites, is close to Greenwich's sights and transport links. Popular with locals, the pub serves good food, including hearty Sunday roasts. There is a conservatory and a garden but no parking.

Renaissance London Heathrow
Bath Road, Hounslow ▪ Tube Hounslow West ▪ 020 8897 6363 ▪ www. marriott.com ▪ ££

With a 24-hour fitness centre and soundproofed rooms, this hotel with views of Heathrow's runways is handy for getting to the airport.

Sofitel London Gatwick
North Terminal, Gatwick Airport ▪ 012 9356 7070 ▪ www.sofitel.com ▪ ££

Walk directly from Gatwick's North Terminal to this elegant hotel, which has a full range of facilities. It is linked to London by the Gatwick Express train service.

The Wimbledon Hotel
78 Worple Road SW19 ▪ Train and Tube Wimbledon ▪ 020 8946 9265 ▪ www.wimbledon hotel.com ▪ ££

This small family-run hotel is close to the All England Lawn Tennis and Croquet Club, making it ideal if you are planning to attend the famous tennis championships held there every summer.

St Paul's Hotel
153 Hammersmith Road W14 ▪ Tube Hammersmith ▪ 020 8846 9119 ▪ www.stpaulhotel.co.uk ▪ £££

This handsome 1884 Victorian building is now a boutique hotel. The Eventim Apollo and Olympia London are just a short walk away.

For a key to hotel price categories see p174

General Index

Page numbers in **bold** refer to Top 10 Highlights.

Acknowledgments

Author

Roger Williams is a London-born journalist and long-time Soho inhabitant. He has written and edited several dozen travel guides, including Dorling Kindersley's Eyewitness guides to Provence and Barcelona.

Additional Contributors
Vinny Crump, Joe Staines

Publishing Director Georgina Dee

Publisher Vivien Antwi

Design Director Phil Ormerod

Editorial Ankita Awasthi-Tröger, Michelle Crane, Rebecca Flynn, Rachel Fox, Fíodhna Ní Ghríofa, Freddie Marriage, Sally Schafer, Christine Stroyan

Design Tessa Bindloss, Richard Czapnik, Sunita Gahir, Marisa Renzullo, Jaynan Spengler

Picture Research Phoebe Lowndes, Susie Peachey, Ellen Root, Oran Tarjan

Cartography Subhashree Bharti, Suresh Kumar, Casper Morris

DTP Jason Little, George Nimmo, Joanna Stenlake

Production Olivia Jeffries

Factchecker Kate Berens

Proofreader Anna Streiffert

Indexer Kathryn O'Donoghue

Illustrator Chris Orr & Associates

Commissioned Photography Susie Adams, Max Alexander, Demetrio Carrasco, Geoff Dann, Mike Dunning, Steve Gorton, Frank Greenaway, John Heseltine, Ed Ironside, Colin Keates, Laurie Noble, Stephen Oliver, Rough Guides/Victor Borg, Rough Guides/Suzanne Porter, Rough Guides/Natascha Sturny, Rough Guides/Mark Thomas

Revisions Maria Edwards, Sumita Khatwani, Rahul Kumar, Hayley Maher, Neil Simpson, Hollie Teague

…lerrett 147tr; JAI/Alan Copson 7tr; …awel Libera 154t, Yang Liu 102-3, Loop …mages / Dave Povey 104tr, Loop Images …Eric Nathan 77bl; Leo Mason 70tl, …1cr; Reuters 25br; Robert Harding …orld Imagery 96b; Napoleon Sarony …tl; Hendrik Schmidt 53tl; Splash News …8bl; Homer Sykes 112tr; Mark Sykes …44cr; The Gallery Collection 16ca, 16br, …2tl; Steven Vidler 61cr,142cr.

…aunt Books: 138b.

…ean and Chapter of Westminster: Jim …yson 34bl.

…orling Kindersley: Courtesy of the …riends of Highgate Cemetery, London/ …oug Traverso 149tl; courtesy of the …atural History Museum, London/John …ownes 10clb, /Frank Greenaway 20cr, / …olin Keates 20cl; courtesy of the Royal …estival Hall, and Park Lane Group Young …rtists' Concert 81tl; Courtesy of The …cience Museum/Geoff Dann 10crb, / …ive Streeter 80b; Courtesy of the Wallace …ollection, London/Geoff Dann 134cr.

…reamstime.com: Acmanley 91tr; Tudor …ntonel Adrian 150b; Ajv123ajv 3tr, 164-5; …tezza 4clb, 87tr; Anizza 119tr, 156br; …rdazi 107tl; Anthony Baggett 79tl, …20cra; Baloncici 63cl, 125tr; …argotiphotography 135tr; Beataaldridge …t; Michal Bednarek 108tr; Mikhail …ajenov 6cl, Bombaert 161tl, Dan …reckwoldt 126b, 129tr, 136b, Anthony …rown 60t, Andrew Chambers 119b; …audiodivizia 143bl; Mike Clegg 161br, …2tr; Davidmartyn 135bl; Chris Dorney …t, 120b, 127tl, 142bl; Mark Eaton …5clb; Jorge Duarte Estevao 160b; …chael Foley 36cla, 114b, Haircutting …2cl; Jodi Hanagan 158cla; Francesco …ccardo Iacomino 96cra; Imaengine 15b; …shka777 113t; Dragan Jovanovic 128tr; …niragaya 4cla, 95tr, 105br, 146tr, 153tr; …orgios Kollidas 114cra, 126cra, Slawek …szakiewicz 129clb, Jan Kranendonk …2b, Charlotte Leaper 118tl, 159tr; …werkase 10-1b, 26bl; Maisna 137tl; Ac …anley 115bc; Mark6138 87br; Masyaka …clb; Mikecphoto 106cra; Krzysztof …ahlik 94tl; Nhtg 55tr; Onefivenine 28-9;

Sampete 64tl; Pere Sanz 26cla; Sinoleo 141tr; Socrates 86cla; Stuart456 4cr; Thevirex 79bc; Alexandra Thompson 140cra; Travelwitness 64b; Tupungato 91clb; Paul Wishart 70cr, 98b.

Electric Cinema: 128bl.

Getty Images: AFP/Dan Kitwood 81cl; Baron 53br; Bloomberg Anna Branthwaite 75tr; DeAgostini 30-1; Furture Light 65clb; Heritage Images 40tr, 45b; ICP 4b; Ian Kington 83tr; Pawel Libera 4t, 27cl; Max Mumby 38cla; Robert Harding World Imagery/Amanda Hall 38-9; Lizzie Shepherd 6tr.

Gordon's Wine Bar: 110b.

Great Queen Street: Patricia Niven 111tr.

By permission of IWM (Imperial War Museums): Richard Ash 61tl.

Inn the Park/Peyton and Byrne: 123tr.

J Sheekey: 101br.

La Fromagerie: 139cr.

London Review Bookshop: 116b.

National Portrait Gallery, London: 10cla, 18cr, 18bl, 19tr, 19c.

The National Trust Photo Library ©NTPL: Andrew Butler 76bl.

Natural History Museum, London: Kevin Webb 21tr.

OXO Tower Restaurant/Harvey Nichols: Jonathan Reid 93tr.

Penhaligon's: 109tr.

Philip Way Photography: 44tr, 45cl.

Robert Harding Picture Library: R. Richardson 36-7.

Royal National Theatre: Philip Vile 70br.

The Royal Collection Trust © Her Majesty Queen Elizabeth II 2015: Crown © HMSO 41cl; Derry Moore 25tl; Peter Packer 27br.

Rules Restaurant: 74t.

Sauterelle: 145tr.

Science Museum: 23crb, Greg Kinch 23tr

Courtesy of the Trustees of Sir John Soane's Museum/Caro Communications: Derry Moore 113br.

St John Group: Stefan Johnson 163bl.

St Paul's Cathedral: 42-3.

© Tate, London 2013: Norham Castle, Sunrise by Joseph Mallord William Turner 30cla; Carnation, Lily, Lily, Rose John Singer Sargent 31tr; ©ADAGP, Paris and DACS, London 2016 Fish Constantin Brancusi 29tr; Three Studies for Figures at the Base of a Crucifixion Francis Bacon 31crb; DACS, London 2016 /Whaam! (1963) Roy Lichetenstein 28b; /Three Dancers (1925) Pablo Picasso 28cra.

The City Barge Pub: 157tr.

Trailer of Happiness: 130crb.

Victoria and Albert Museum: 60bl.

Villandry Great Portland Street: 117tr.

Jacket

Front – **Getty Images:** Pawel Libera.
Spine – **Getty Images:** Pawel Libera.
Back – **Dorling Kindersley:** Rough Guides / Natascha Sturny.

Pull out map cover

Getty Images: Pawel Libera.

All other images are: © Dorling Kindersley. For further information see www.dkimages.com.

Penguin
Random
House

Printed and bound in China

First published in the UK in 2002
by Dorling Kindersley Limited
80 Strand, London WC2R 0RL

Copyright 2002, 2016 © Dorling
Kindersley Limited

A Penguin Random House Company

16 17 18 19 10 9 8 7 6 5 4 3 2 1

**Reprinted with revisions 2004, 2005, 2006
2007, 2008, 2009, 2010, 2012, 2013, 2014,
2015, 2016 (twice)**

A CIP catalogue record is available from the British Library.

ISBN 978 0 2412 0922 6

MIX
Paper from
responsible sources
FSC™ C018179

As a guide to abbreviations in visitor information blocks: **Adm** *= admission charge.*